Praise for *The Innovation Crisis*

The Innovation Crisis is an urgent call to take a hard look at why our faith communities are increasingly irrelevant. Ted presents an unvarnished look at why we're in crisis and offers proven solutions to not only overcome our malaise but actually set the pace for the future. This is more than a book; it's an invitation to participate in high-stakes change.

STEPHAN BAUMAN, former President/CEO of World Relief; author of *Seeking Refuge: On the Shores of the Global Refugee Crisis*

Many churches and faith-based nonprofits struggle to adapt to the rapidly changing technological landscape. In *The Innovation Crisis*, Ted Esler brings clarity to the extent of this challenge and paints a sobering picture of what continued failure will mean for the church's ability to engage with present and future generations. He also offers a roadmap for how church leaders and their communities can rethink the issues, identify the obstacles, and develop solutions. Every church and missions leader would benefit from reading this book.

JOHN CHESNUT, President/CEO, Wycliffe Bible Translators USA

A distinctive aspect and characteristic of Ted Esler's DNA is his ability to research, analyze, and comprehend a subject matter for the sole purpose of bringing about solutions. Effectively done, he addresses the topic of innovation in ministry today. This book highlights the problem and suggests solutions. My observation of Ted is that he is a fixer, which gives testimony to the accuracy of my endorsement of this book as an excellent read for inquiring minds on the subject of innovation in ministry.

RON E. NELSON, cofounder and CEO, Sowing Seeds of Joy

As a missionary leader, I expect innovation. But what many leaders find difficult to handle is disruption. It's messy. Ted's book provides insight into externally and internally induced disruption that—if approached with humility and discernment—can lead to a positive and fruitful future. It's a good read.

GREG MUNDIS, Executive Director, Assemblies of God World Mission

Ted is that voice in the crowd everyone stops to listen to. From innovating on the mission field to leading large organizations, Ted's wisdom comes from rich experience. His challenge to do more than maintain the status quo is God's necessary and timely word to all leaders and their teams that are asking God to give them the next step. Here in your hands is that next step.

TERRY SANDERSON, Lead Pastor, Calvary Church, St. Peters, MO

God's children are both designed and redeemed to innovate, but perhaps our vision has been blurred by "business as usual"? This book is a call to reclaim our identity as courageous and creative engagers of need and potential, and to watch for it in others—in men and women both. What do I see that others perhaps yet do not, and what might God be requiring of me to move toward it? Ted provides both solid inspiration and practical advice to release needed innovation in the body of Christ that would robustly enhance our mission to serve the world!

WENDY WILSON, Executive Director, Women's Development Track

Uber and Airbnb are examples of innovative companies that leveraged already existing products to service the world in new ways. These are just two examples of the kind of innovative culture in which we live. My friend Ted Esler understands there is an innovative crisis in the church and that if the church is going to reach this culture, one of the ways it will do so is through creative and imaginative innovation. I pray you will find this book encouraging and challenging as the church seeks to share and show the gospel in innovative ways contextual to our time.

ED STETZER, Executive Director, Wheaton College Billy Graham Center

The Innovation Crisis is disruptive in the best possible way, calling leaders to reawaken the creative fire that has grown cold. It is an invitation to creative possibilities, bold risks, and taking the first steps. Read this book and ignite your imagination.

PETER GREER, President & CEO, HOPE International; coauthor of *Mission Drift*

The Innovation Crisis speaks in plain language of the realities of today. Readers will see themselves and their ministries at various stages throughout the book. Frankly, it soon becomes personal and convicting. At the same time, Ted gives the picture of hope and courage to risk innovation backed by models of the past and imagination of the future. A clarion call to follow our Creator God in leading through innovation.

JO ANNE LYON, General Superintendent Emerita, The Wesleyan Church

Ted Esler's book, *The Innovation Crisis*, couldn't be more timely. Drawing on his knowledge of technology developments and as president of Missio Nexus—a worldwide association of ministry agencies and churches—Dr. Esler raises a fresh challenge for ministries in the post-pandemic, twenty-first century world. Instead of investing time and energy to reinstate ministry practices of the past, he challenges readers to seize the post-pandemic world as an opportunity for creative innovation. In this rapidly changing world, we always have more to learn, new generations to reach, and better tools than were available in previous ministry eras. This book is packed with new ideas to challenge your thinking, eye-opening examples of ministries that looked backward and failed and of others that employed new ideas and tools to charge forward. This book has found its moment. Read and be inspired.

CAROLYN CUSTIS JAMES, author of *Half the Church: Recapturing God's Global Vision for Women* and *Malestrom: Manhood Swept into the Currents of a Changing World*

This book is a gold mine of challenging insights for you and your leadership team—equal parts conviction and inspiration!

STEVE RICHARDSON, President, Pioneers USA

There truly is an innovation crisis occurring today among well-meaning churches and Christian ministries. With a clear biblical focus, combined with insights gleaned from decades of frontline leadership, Ted not only identifies the deficits that have caused the innovation crisis we are experiencing, but also offers workable solutions that can reverse the trend. Drawing richly from history, while introducing unique concepts such as "Eccliosystem" and "The Shoemaker Rules," Ted leads the reader into a new realm where God-honoring innovation can become the new norm and produce long-lasting results. I have known Ted for over two decades and he is more than qualified to lead us out of the innovation crisis and into more fruitful ministry.

JAMIE RASMUSSEN, Senior Pastor, Scottsdale Bible Church and author of *How Joyful People Think*

the innovation crisis

Creating
Disruptive
Influence
in the
Ministry
You Lead

TED
ESLER

MOODY PUBLISHERS

CHICAGO

Edited by Amanda Cleary Eastep
Interior Design: Puckett Smartt
Cover Design: Derek Thornton / Notch Design

All websites and phone numbers listed herein are accurate at the time of publication but may change in the future or cease to exist. The listing of website references and resources does not imply publisher endorsement of the site's entire contents. Groups and organizations are listed for informational purposes, and listing does not imply publisher endorsement of their activities.

Library of Congress Cataloging-in-Publication Data

Names: Esler, Ted, author.
Title: The innovation crisis : creating disruptive influence in the
   ministry you lead / Ted Esler.
Description: Chicago : Moody Publishers, [2021] | Includes bibliographical
   references. | Summary: "In The Innovation Crisis, Ted Esler shows you
   how to innovate in ways that change the ministry landscape. You'll
   discover the four stages of organizational culture-disrupting,
   innovating, sustaining, and stagnating-and gain strategies for staying
   in the innovation sweet spot. Because if you aren't innovating,
   stagnation isn't far away"-- Provided by publisher.
Identifiers: LCCN 2021014623 (print) | LCCN 2021014624 (ebook) | ISBN
   9780802421807 (paperback) | ISBN 9780802499288 (ebook)
Subjects: LCSH: Church work. | Christian leadership. | Change--Religious
   aspects--Christianity. | BISAC: RELIGION / Christian Living / Leadership
   & Mentoring | RELIGION / Christian Church / General
Classification: LCC BV4400 .E85 2021 (print) | LCC BV4400 (ebook) | DDC
   253--dc23
LC record available at https://lccn.loc.gov/2021014623
LC ebook record available at https://lccn.loc.gov/2021014624

Originally delivered by fleets of horse-drawn wagons, the affordable paperbacks from D. L. Moody's publishing house resourced the church and served everyday people. Now, after more than 125 years of publishing and ministry, Moody Publishers' mission remains the same—even if our delivery systems have changed a bit. For more information on other books (and resources) created from a biblical perspective, go to www.moodypublishers.com or write to:

Moody Publishers
820 N. LaSalle Boulevard
Chicago, IL 60610

1 3 5 7 9 10 8 6 4 2

Printed in the United States of America

This book is dedicated to Jim Esler, my brother. Jim passed away in February of 2020 after a two-year battle with brain cancer. Since my earliest days, I remember Jim building little radios and other electronic gizmos. He went on to patent inventions in the cardiac pacemaker industry. He never stopped innovating. Even in his last months, as memory and words were failing him, he doggedly worked at developing software.

If there is any innovation in me,
it is because of Jim's influence on my life.

CONTENTS

FOREWORD

Sometimes I play a game when I read the Bible I call "Which side would I be on?"

I try to guess whether I'd side with the disciples who told people to go home or side with Jesus who invited people to stick around. I wonder whether I'd be one of the leaders who accuses Jesus of eating with scum and being a drunkard, or whether I'd be at the table with Jesus raising a glass with my hands unwashed. And then, as I read about the early church, I wonder whether I'd side with Peter who insisted everyone follow the Old Testament law or with Paul who said it really didn't matter and, hey, here's some bacon.

I don't like the results of that game.

The ministry of Jesus was so highly disruptive and innovative that it frightens me (if you actually read Scripture for what it says, that is).

Let's be honest, a lot of Christians struggle with *innovation*.

The fact that our current approach to ministry has been failing at almost every level for decades now doesn't seem to bother us nearly as much as it should.

One of the reasons is something sociologists call "sunk cost bias." You're good at church. You've got a lot invested in it. It's been good to you.

Which is exactly why I'm so glad that Ted Esler has written this book.

In it, you'll encounter some super sharp observations, innovative thinking, really tough questions, challenging ideas, and a call to innovate that will hopefully make you (and me) uncomfortable enough to do something risky that might not work.

And that's exactly the point.

You and I live in an age where you either disrupt yourself or you get disrupted.

It's time to disrupt ourselves before culture finishes the work for us.

CAREY NIEUWHOF
Bestselling author, podcaster, and founding pastor, Connexus Church

1

A CRISIS
OF INNOVATION

"Expect great things; attempt great things."[1]
WILLIAM CAREY, SHOEMAKER

*No one sews a piece of unshrunk cloth on an old garment. If he does, the patch
tears away from it, the new from the old, and a worse tear is made. And no one
puts new wine into old wineskins. If he does, the wine will burst the skins—and
the wine is destroyed, and so are the skins. But new wine is for fresh wineskins.*
MARK 2:21–22

WHERE ARE THE INNOVATORS?

"Ted, who in the church today do you feel is doing something uniquely innovative and effective?"

I was speaking with a major church leader. He should have been the one telling me who the innovators are. I paused, stuttered, and then honestly replied, "I will have to think about that and get back to you."

"That's what I thought," he replied. "I see so little innovation among church leaders that I wonder what our future holds."

Little did this leader know that in a few short months, the world would be turned upside down by something called COVID-19. The rapid and almost total change that many of us in ministry would face was unthinkable in January 2020. By March, one of the core activities of the church, gathering, was essentially outlawed. Pastors stared into cameras instead of faces as auditoriums remained empty for months. Even one-on-one meetings became something done over software. Fear rose about a future drop-off in giving (a fear that did not materialize for most ministries). A two-week lockdown turned into months of lockdown. Businesses were shuttered while others prospered. The whole world was different.

Innovating is touted as a means of creating a preferred future. During the COVID-19 pandemic, change occurred at such a fast rate that few could keep up with the present, let alone worry about the future. Innovation was the need of the hour. The vast riches of the Internet were viable resources for deeper teaching, story-telling, and relationship building. The best most churches could do was film the traditional service for online viewing. The pandemic highlighted a lack of imagination and creativity.

The pandemic highlighted in stark terms the groaning in the church today for innovators. There was a time not long ago when the muscular megachurch movement seemed poised to provide us with ideas that would propel us into a better future. Scandals, politics, and ambition appear to have put this hope to rest. Missionary agencies and Christian nonprofit organizations also suffer from a lack of innovation. They feel old, antiquated, and small in a world of massive technology-driven megacorporations. While the church struggles to innovate, we watch lithe and capable businesses start in garages as side gigs. They innovate, grow, and dominate our lives and the stock market. Meanwhile, we in ministry leadership struggle to find the funding, people, and ideas to drive discipleship deep into the hearts of people.

Innovation is the use of something new to create solutions. It can include invention, the creation of something new, or it can be a mixing of existing things to create something new. It might be technological, but it is not limited to technology. It is about products, services, processes, and ideas. Innovation is most often focused on problem-solving but, as we shall see, sows the seeds of its own destruction by introducing its own problems.

How we think about innovation itself has changed. Innovation was once discussed only by business wizards and engineers. Today, innovation is expected to change the very nature of an industry, product, or service. Entrepreneurs pitch "paradigm shifts" all the time, in every sector. Ministry leaders, bound by tradition and facing a most uncertain future, are questing for a new era of innovation. We feel the spirit of innovation all around us in industry yet struggle to see how it can be brought to bear in ministry.

If you think this is an exaggeration, discuss innovation and the church with a business leader. What you will find, after the pleasantries, is a harsh assessment about a lack of creativity and innovation by ministries of all kinds. I suppose one might argue that the application of good business management in the church is innovative. That sort of innovation is not the expectation any longer. Now we are looking for creative ideas that move ministries in far more meaningful ways. Thus, while innovation has lagged, expectations have grown.

The network that I lead, Missio Nexus, presents an award for innovation each year. Associations give awards because they highlight the values that they want to see embodied in the membership. Our board decided that we would give a Lifetime of Service Award, highlighting faithful, lifelong service in the Great Commission. The other award was for innovation. We appeal to our membership, some thirty-thousand mission leaders, church leaders, staff, and missionaries, to provide us with nominees for these two awards.

Giving away the Lifetime of Service Award is one of the highlights of my year. The recipients are well-known Christian leaders who have influenced a generation or more of Great Commission ministry. I tell them they have no more than three minutes to talk to the audience, and

I still must work to get them to "land the plane," as they thank us and offer advice. It is a joyous time.

The innovation award is another story. Some years we struggle to give it because *no ministry is nominated for being innovative.* I often email, then call, then berate our members for suggestions. Sometimes, we compromise and give it for "excellence in ministry"—a sure sign that innovation is lagging. When we do have a recipient, it is also a time for joy. Yet there is something unfortunate when it is easy to celebrate the heroes of a past generation while we struggle to find contemporary examples of innovative ministries.

The unmet expectations I see in the ministry I lead is a symptom of a larger disease in the broader church. The bigger proof that we lack innovation is the failure of the church to capture the imagination and heart of the culture. We must consider our lack of imagination in creating the post-Christian world that we are now experiencing. We have lost our voice in culture. What we offer is not attractive to a society that has moved past our paradigms. We might be wearing skinny jeans to church, but that sort of window dressing is part of the problem. The world is looking for something new and different. If we want to regain that voice, we must innovate.

Jesus the Innovator

Contrast this to the ministry of Jesus and the first century church. Innovation fills the pages of the New Testament. We have the *new* covenant because it ushers in the fulfillment of the old covenant while introducing the kingdom of God. Each time Jesus opened His mouth, it was as likely as not that some innovative new way of understanding the world was about to be revealed. You want to be first? Be last. Rich people? Much harder for them to get into heaven. You want to throw a stone? Sure, if you are pure in heart, go for it. Jesus inaugurated a kingdom unlike any before or since. It needed *new* wineskins because the old could not contain it. Jesus gives a *new* commandment in John 13 ("that you love one another: just as I have loved you"). His followers struggled to keep up.

At one point His disciples chided Him for saying things that were hard to hear (cf. John 6:60). Why were His teachings so hard? Because they revealed a new way of seeing truth that had not been considered before. The cross, though explained and foretold by Jesus and the prophets, took His followers by surprise. In Matthew16:21 we read, "From that time Jesus began to show his disciples that he must go to Jerusalem and suffer many things from the elders and chief priests and scribes, and be killed, and on the third day be raised." What could be clearer? Then, when it happens, they scatter, unable to remember that He was coming back to life. It was paradigm busting. To quote an old movie, the idea was so preposterous that they couldn't "handle the truth."[2] Even *after* Jesus' resurrection, the disciples were still asking about its fulfilment in a political sense, not the much more expansive realm of the heart (cf. Acts 1:6).

The early church was also highly innovative. The inclusion of Gentiles in the kingdom was almost a bridge too far for the primarily Jewish early church. Considering Jewish history and the contents of the Old Testament, it is understandable. Jews were instructed not to mix it up with Gentiles. How then, in a relatively short span of a few chapters in Acts, do we find the broad embrace of the Gentiles into the church? Like any innovation, detractors to this concept lasted for years (read Galatians for evidence of this). These are all jaw-dropping innovations embedded in the core of New Testament Christianity.

The history of the church is an innovation history. When a plague hit the Roman Empire in AD 165, under the reign of Marcus Aurelius, estimates are that between 25 to 30 percent of the Roman population died.[3] To put that on a contemporary scale, that would be like a novel coronavirus killing anywhere from a billion to one and a half billion of the world's population today. That dwarves the COVID-19 pandemic.

The best guess we have is that the plague was smallpox.

Infected people were pushed out into the street to die. Who was there to serve? Christians, who even though they were under heavy persecution, risked their lives for the gospel. At a time when anybody who could leave Rome did, Christians stayed and served the sick and dying. Do you doubt this was innovation? Imagine how the pagan priests looked on, in shocked dismay that the Christians were gaining the upper hand in the culture. Perhaps they later asked, *Why didn't we think of that?* as the Empire's hatred for Christ faded.

Think of the innovations that Christianity introduced to the world:

- Christianity had a major influence on ending child abandonment, infanticide, abortion, and the sale of children as slaves and prostitutes.

- Modern medicine owes its beginning to hospital systems launched by Christians. This stretches back to third and fourth century. I recently drove by South Florida Baptist Hospital, reminding me of a time when health care and Christianity were inextricably linked.[4]

- Contrary to popular belief, science was supported by Catholic church leaders and members. Scientists such as Galileo were funded by church leaders.

- Natural rights extended the Greek view of democracy, creating universal civil rights. This is a direct result of Christian innovation in understanding basic human identity.

- The modern university was born from Christian education.

Since the Reformation (itself an innovation), I can think of only one globally influential innovation project that Christians have founded. That would be the global missionary movement. Over the past few hundred years, most innovation has been in the domain of industry.

Where Is Our Innovation?

If innovation is so much at the heart of the New Testament narrative, why do we see so little of it today? Perhaps one reason is our view of doctrine. Foundational truths are immovable. The gospel message itself is not up for further innovation. The work of the cross has been completed. We cannot innovate more grace into the sacrifice that Jesus made on our behalf. We will never write additional books for the New Testament canon. Yet, there is great room for innovation in loving others, communicating the gospel, celebrating His glory, fulfilling the Great Commission, taking care of widows and orphans, and working for justice and just about every other goal ministry leaders might consider.

The church produces weekly services like a factory. Unfortunately, they are numbingly the same from week to week and church to church. At times it appears to me that we are no better than McDonald's at delivering the exact same thing everywhere. We even export our way of doing church globally when cultural difference invites diversity in form.

As the leader of a missionary association, I am sometimes asked why, after two thousand years, the Great Commission goes unfulfilled. From a human vantage point, I have concluded that a lack of creativity and risk-taking by God's people are at the core of this failure. We are besieged by a poverty of imagination.

> **We are besieged by a poverty of imagination.**

I understand the overwhelming pressure that leaders face to be creative risk-takers. The typical ministry leader feels the strong current of innovation and change all around them. Yet our churches and organizations are more like the rocks and trees in the river as the floodwaters rise. We cling to them, hoping not to be swept up in the direction this river of change is taking us. What if we could direct this current instead of simply being washed along with it? What if the people we lead could let go of the rocks and branches and freely swim in the river of innovation?

Not long ago, I corresponded with a leader about the need for innovation. A donor was asking how the ministry was innovating considering the challenges in the world today. This leader asked, "Whatever happened to faithful service? It doesn't seem like it's good enough anymore." This CEO, who leads a multimillion-dollar-a-year Christian ministry, is struggling under the pressure that comes when there is no innovation. He knows there is an expectation to innovate. Yet, it is about all he can do to simply keep the ministry he operates up and running. Leaders are being weighed in the balance of innovation expectation and find themselves lacking. I know this because I feel it myself.

We Need a Whole New System

One way that frustration about innovation is real involves the call for a "whole new system." Domestically, we are faced with stagnant and declining congregations. The largest Protestant denomination in the United States, the Southern Baptist Convention, continues to see annual declines in membership going back to 2006.[5] Pew Research reports that close to 25 percent of people identify as religiously unaffiliated, an increase of 10 percent since 2007.[6]

On the global front, things appear to be healthier. While the Western church has stagnated, the "majority world" church has exploded. Yet, even in this story there are calls for radical change. We stand some two thousand years since Jesus gave the command to disciple all the nations. Vast cultures continue to exist with no churches, a lack of Scripture in a heart language, and no contextually appropriate gospel witness. The Joshua Project, perhaps the most cited source of information on the spread of the gospel globally, states that 42.5 percent of the world's people groups are unreached. This represents 3.23 billion people.[7] Some missiologists that I speak with believe that the world is becoming less reached despite reports that we are winning the globe.

Many missionaries raise support for their work. In fact, it is a growing trend for domestic church planters to also raise support. Missions pastors grow weary of repeated funding requests. They are frustrated that agencies have not come up with a new way to fund themselves apart from this model. Some see the system as racist, favoring rich, white congregations and discriminating against poor, minority churches. The missions pastor of one of America's largest churches told me, "I am sick and tired of this antiquated system of fundraising. When are we going to move past this and empower the church to be more involved? *We need a whole new system.*"

Frustration is also a reason given for the "business as missions" (BAM) movement. They see the donor support system, in which churches and individuals pledge financially to give to missionaries, as unsustainable and antiquated. They view their solution, using business to fund cross-cultural workers, as a whole new system.

Consider book titles such as *When Helping Hurts* (a call for a new way to approach relief and development work), *The Scandal of the Evangelical Mind* (a plea for academic rigor and thinking in evangelicalism), *Changing the Mind of Missions, Where Have We Gone Wrong?* (a new way to do global missions). These are all helpful calls for innovation, renewal, and reset in the spheres they address.

Leaders of the house church movement regularly write and speak about the need for "a whole new system." They decry the rapid growth of the megachurch, multisite churches, and online churches as diminishing community within the church. They often call for a new church that emphasizes discipleship instead of teaching as its primary contribution.

Look at the celebrity pastor role. I have yet to hear somebody argue that celebrity pastors are a good thing for the church. This model opens our congregations up to untold leadership dangers, from moral failures to financial greed. Yet, celebrity pastors write most of the books we read, speak at most of our conferences, and set the agenda for the church in the United States, Canada, and beyond. Even though the average local church size hovers close to one hundred people in the US and Canada, we look to celebrity megachurch pastors for our leadership material. Innovation for these large churches will not translate to the environment in which most churches do ministry. Perhaps we do need a whole new system to select our influencers.

With the onslaught of COVID-19, I was hopeful that perhaps churches would birth new, innovative models of ministry. It was hard for me to watch the virtual church services that were rolled out. Most were mirror images of the in-person services that already feel stale. There were a couple of songs, some announcements and a prayer, another song, a sermon, and then a song. The same order of worship, delivery style, and teaching methods were employed. This is despite pastors now having the combined contributions of the Internet to bolster their messages, support their points, borrow from other teachers, map the biblical sites, and collaborate with online chat, video, and text. Yet, every virtual church gathering I watched reproduced the in-person sermon without any significant departure. I am certain that there were stellar examples contrary to this. I had hoped a *global* pandemic would create the sparks that would lead to an inferno of innovation.

If you are like me, you understand the yearning for something new. Something that adapts to emerging cultural realities, sometimes creating culture, while communicating the ancient truths of the Bible. In fact, this is part of the challenge before us. People are most attracted to new things when they resonate with their deeply held human desires, wants, and needs. Instead, we in the church are serving up leftovers. Much of our message and how we deliver that message was designed for modernity. We now live in a postmodern world.

We face a crisis of innovation.

Shoemaker

This book is an exploration of innovation that can be brought to bear on kingdom initiatives. I have decided to bring along an old friend on this journey, William Carey. Carey is somebody who has gone before us and shown us the way. His work kickstarted the global missionary movement. He is a prime example of an innovator.

Our world is so different than the one Carey lived in that it is difficult to grasp the extent of what he did. He was born into a stratified society where one rarely, if ever, switched vocations. He was apprenticed in England as a shoemaker at fourteen years old. For most English people of the day, that apprenticeship would mean a lifetime of being a shoemaker. But four years later, Carey would experience a new birth in Christ. He drew a map of the world and hung it above his work bench. Andrew Fuller described it as "a large homemade map of the whole world pasted together of several sheets with population, religion, and other facts about every country written on the map in Carey's own hand."[8] I can imagine him sitting there, cutting and stitching leather as he looked up at the map and prayed.

Carey borrowed a Greek grammar book and taught himself New Testament Greek. He married a woman of his own class, who was poor and illiterate. She gave birth to his first child, who died two years later (along the way, other children would die as well). All the while he preached the Word, although he was not known for being particularly eloquent. He was influenced by Jonathan Edwards' book, *An Account of the Life of the Late Rev. David Brainerd.* His mission zeal grew, and in 1786 during a meeting of his denomination's leadership, he pled with them to consider overseas missionary work as a priority. An old minister spoke up, saying, "Young man, sit down! You are an enthusiast. When God pleases to convert the heathen, he'll do it without consulting you or me."[9]

This sort of apathy about the Great Commission led Carey to write a booklet in 1792, *An Enquiry into the Obligations of Christians to Use*

Means for the Conversion of the Heathens. Was Carey the first to consider missions as a major paradigm for the church? Certainly not. His appeal, however, was innovative in its approach. He used statistics, a description of the world as it was in that day, and outrageously suggested that the Great Commission compelled Christians to act. He organized a missionary agency in this same year. Carey "understood the times" (cf. 1 Chron. 12:32) and instinctively knew that now was the time for Protestant missionary work to go forward.

British missionaries to India proceeded Carey by some one hundred years. But the conditions for travel, the growth of the pietist movement in England, the rise of new structures called missionary societies, and the publication of Carey's booklet galvanized a movement. He rode the wave that had been created for him while also introducing his own innovations along the way.

His most famous words were preached around this time in his life. In a sermon based on Isaiah 54:2–3, he said "Expect great things; attempt great things."[10] The forward-thinking visionary, a humble cobbler from England, would not simply preach these words. He would then live them. He left for India. Just the voyage was a riskier step than most of us are willing to take. More so because he did this in opposition to the East India Company's desire to keep missionaries out of India. Britain did not want their money-making and exploitation of India hindered by an enthusiast like Carey.

Space does not allow for a complete telling of the hardships Carey faced or of those faced by his family because of his decisions. Suffice it to say that India, in the 1790s, was not a comfortable place for a missionary to live. His ministry highlights adaptability, resilience, and creativity. He formed a team with other significant missionaries. The most notable are Joshua Marshman and William Ward. They had the first memorandum of understanding known in the missions world. Its principles continue to influence how modern missionaries conduct their work. This team had to disassociate itself from the British because of the East India Company's influence. Carey, like modern-day travelers, needed a visa and a resident's permit. Because of the hostility of his own government toward him, he arranged this through the Danish to continue his work. Today, we call this sort of missionary a "creative access worker."

He translated the Bible into Bengali, Oriya, Marathi, Hindi, Assamese, and Sanskrit and parts of it into other dialects and languages. These achievements, had nothing else been accomplished, place him in a small group of people in human history. Not content with just translating the Bible, Carey also sought to honor Indian culture. He translated classic Sanskrit into English, making it available to Indian scholars for the first time in centuries. This was radical.

Translations needed to be distributed to activate their gospel message. To make this possible, he founded a printing business and an indigo factory. He was doing business as mission before any of us attended a conference on how to do it. He started Sunday schools, originally created to teach literacy to the impoverished, for Indian children. His actions reveal the wide swath of projects he was willing to take on to meet his objectives.

He led the resistance to the practice of *sati,* widow-burning, earning additional ire form the British leaders but even more from Hindu leaders. Carey cataloged the number of women whose lives ended through this cruel practice. He publicized it and went so far as to accuse the British of being complicit in the crime. Sati was already against the law in the region where Carey worked, but lax enforcement meant that hundreds of women were killed each year. Today we might argue about the role of social justice in missionary endeavors. Carey had no qualms about facing down societal evil. In addition to opposing sati, he also critiqued the caste system to the ire of local authorities.

During all this activity, he evangelized, started schools, churches, and even a college to train young men to be Bible teachers. His first convert, Krishna Pal, came to faith after an injury to his arm led him to visit the Carey team. He learned not only about caring for his arm, but also the love of God and the effects of sin. Carey visited him in his home and invited him back to his. Despite the incredible workload, William Carey was directly involved in the lives of the Indians.

This ministry was filled with disruptive innovation. At a time when the British Empire was draining India of its resources, Carey did quite the opposite. He not only shared the gospel message, he lifted Indian culture and blessed them in ways their own scholars did not. He was a flawed human being and made mistakes along the way. Yet, his legacy in India is impressive.

In addition to his Indian ministry, Carey unleashed a movement back home that continues to this day. We call him the father of the Modern Missions Movement because the church in the West rediscovered the Great Commission in part because of William Carey, who began his work out of his humble, shoemaking beginnings. Because of his work, hundreds of thousands of missionaries have set out in obedience to the call of the Great Commission. Carey exemplifies for us an understanding of the times, creativity, and risk-taking. He was an innovator who launched a movement.

Success Breeds Failure

Carey was mostly a founder. He started new things. Founders have freedoms that successive leaders do not have. Because most of us are working within ministry environments that have expectations, people, programs, and budgets, we often feel more like stewards than pioneers. But stewards can also be risk-takers. The parable of the talents reminds us of this truth. Leaders today must work toward aligning their vision with the work of the people within their churches and organizations. Institutionalization, the creation of policies, and managerial processes and bureaucracy all conspire against us leaders.

In Chris Zook and James Allen's book, *The Founder's Mentality*, they describe the "predictable crises of growth." Most of us do not consider growth to be crisis-inducing, but it is. In movement studies, researchers say that the fastest way for a social movement to end is for that movement to be successful. For organizations, including churches and ministries, a similar concept is in play. Contrary to what we often hear, starting a new ministry may not be as hard as keeping an existing ministry from losing its primary mission and vision.

I have heard people say, "Success breeds success." But a more accurate statement is "Success breeds failure." Success often leads to poor choices by leaders (they take on more than they can handle). Success sometimes becomes an impediment to risk-taking (leaders want to protect the gains that have been made). Success might lead to stagnation (when the status quo is all the leader and ministry know). Yes, success has many advantages. It beats failure hands down. But it also brings with it a set of problems, which, over time, can cause leaders to grow averse to innovation.

> **Starting a new ministry may not be as hard as keeping an existing ministry from losing its primary mission and vision.**

Leaders I have observed who are struggling with a lack of innovation are often sensing that past success is creating future failure. The ministry built to handle the growth that comes from success is typically focused on maintaining momentum. When momentum falters, the easiest thing to do is try to work harder. More effort is expended chasing smaller gains. Leaders, at least good ones, tire of this treadmill. This contributes to the desire for a whole new system and begs us to be innovators.

We also tend to train our entire ministry on what works. When something new comes along, people must be reoriented around whatever has been introduced. There are systemic reasons why this is a challenge. Take the ministry I lead as an example.

We produce lots of great online content for our members to use in their ministry. There are leadership materials, management items, courses, infographics, and plenty of other materials. We have built a team around creating these resources. At a recent board meeting, our youngest board member listened to my report on how many times these resources were accessed. At the end of the presentation, she raised her hand and asked if she could comment. "Of course," I replied, "all input is welcome."

She noted that she is a member of the millennial generation and that they prefer to upload rather than download. "Huh?" I responded, the apparent misfire of our current strategy dawning on me. Millennials want to interact with the material and with others about the material. They want to be polled, asked about their view, discuss things, and be a part of the resource. Downloading it, without the social connection around it, is simply not something that Millennials are going to do.

That was great insight. It is why we have diverse viewpoints on the board. Once I got past outright rejection of her observation (the typical human response to opposition), I began to think about implementing it. Our staff is small and laser focused on producing content and programs that delight our members. Not one of them was hired to spend their time interacting online with our members. Our website has been designed around content curation and presentation. This is quite different than an interactive platform. We designed a beautiful one-way pipe. We had even turned off comments because it was a hassle to monitor them all the time. As I thought about it, our entire approach to social media had faltered. Why would we be successful in creating online engagement when the organization, the machine, was built to do something else? For us to change our paradigm, we would have to, well, *change our paradigm*. We are on that path, but it is a massive change for us and will take some time to fully implement.

Last year I spoke with a former CEO of a ministry that had created a form of media ministry that was highly influential across the African subcontinent for over eighty years. This ministry was so successful that it influenced the church in almost every African nation. It was low-cost, low-tech, and easy to reproduce. But digital media obliterated its usefulness in the early 2000s. Attempts were made to upgrade the content for CDs and SD cards. Again, technology advanced. Digital media distribution on phones ended the need for physical media. Even in some of the most remote villages of Africa I have watched Bible studies in which all participants used their phones to hear teaching, interact over the material, and grow as disciples.

This ministry was built for physical media. When the CEO announced his plan to sell off the building and warehouse space, liquidate the inventory by throwing it away, and go fully online, the membership voted against the plan. They could not wrap their minds around a future in which there was no need for their facility. Instead of letting their CEO make the move to a new era, they doubled down on the old model because *they were built for it.* A few months later, COVID-19 hit, and ministry office spaces were vacated anyway. The building is now gone, along with most of the staff as the remaining few team members scramble to do what the CEO had suggested earlier.

Looking back, this all seems obvious. It rarely is obvious when the change is happening around you. Today's successful ministry strategy has rewarded us so that when threats come, the first thing we gravitate to is a doubling down on that strategy. The multisite church model of today will someday be the reason why leaders will not want to make changes to a newer church form. If you have ever been in an old, musty church building of a former era, smell that smell and remember it. That will be your church someday.

These dynamics are present in any ministry. They impact who you hire, how you organize the people, the way you choose to communicate, how much information you share, the kind of training you provide, how much line authority you give to staff, and so many other facets of organizational

> **The better managed a ministry is, the less likely it will be able to innovate.**

life. Well-managed organizations create alignment around their prime objectives to deliver strong results. But this alignment becomes an impediment. There is an irony here. The better managed a ministry is, the less likely it will be able to innovate. There is an antidote, and we will get to that in chapter 7.

In the church, we tend to practice "success modeling." We copy the most successful churches, develop a lists of "best practices," and elevate to positions of authority those leaders whose ministry has had success. While there is inherent value in this, there is also a danger. Instead of creating new expressions of our ministries, we copy existing ministry practices. This results in homogenized approaches rather than rich and diverse expressions of faith. We will discuss "the stack" in chapter 3 and see that we can mix and match existing services, ideas, and approaches with experiments. This is not typical, though. We tend to be better at copying than creating.

Getting Off the Calf-Path

Ted Fletcher was the founder of Pioneers. Pioneers focused on starting churches where there are the fewest, if any, Christians. They have sent thousands of people on mission across the world. Ted used to call attention to our propensity to follow others by quoting a poem by Sam Walter Foss, "The Calf-Path." You can find it at the end of this chapter. The main point of the poem is that following others is our default setting. Ted was a highly successful *Wall Street Journal* businessman. On a trip to visit missionaries when his career was at its zenith, his heart broke over the many cultures where there was no gospel presence.

He began applying to missionary agencies and collected a stack of rejection letters. At forty, he was considered too old, with too many kids and not enough training or experience in ministry. Ted was overwhelmed by the lack of attention being paid to the "least reached" parts of the globe. He had to act. In 1979, he started a new missionary agency, one that could not reject him. Today that missionary agency has over three thousand workers globally. Ted did not "stay on the calf-path," but rejected rejection. The missionary sending world has never been the same. When he founded Pioneers (originally called World Evangelical Outreach), few short-term teams would go to closed countries. Pioneers changed that. They also adopted a leaner, faster, and riskier approach to the training and sending of missionaries. Their explosive growth came out of Ted's own experience being denied as a worthwhile candidate.

Founders are unique people. They are the ones most likely to step off the calf-path and try something new. They are not bound by tradition or best practices. Because they are trailblazers, they tend to be misunderstood. Ted once told me how, when he proposed starting a new missionary agency focused on the hardest to reach places, people told him that there was "no need for another missionary agency." Those voices were partially correct. There was no need for an organization that did what the organizations were already doing. But there was a great need for a new, innovative organization that was willing to do ministry in ways the existing organizations were neglecting.

I sometimes ask church leaders if we need more ministry organizations. "No!" they immediately respond, almost in disgust. "We have plenty of organizations. We don't need any more of them." This reaction no doubt comes in part from the fundraising aimed at these leaders. Then I ask the same question, but in a different way. "What if we could empower the dreams of an army of creative, ministry entrepreneurs?" Then I get a completely different response.

Successful founders are entrepreneurs who are compelled to find expression for their vision. If that vision is one that the world needs, many of them create new organizations, start new churches, or creatively spur movements. We must encourage ministry entrepreneurs but we often, without realizing it, discourage them.

How many new churches does the world need? I think we need many, many more. I hope they are not carbon-copies of the ones we have. These efforts are often where innovation thrives. I am not making the case that existing churches cannot innovate or be entrepreneurial. Far from it, as you shall read in the following pages. I am making the point that it is important to empower innovators.

We face problems scoped to our specific roles, teams, organizations and wider affiliations like schools and denominations. Beyond these challenges lie the giants. In the wake of the George Floyd killing the nation discussed *systemic* racism. Systems produce both problems and solutions. Consider issues like human trafficking, illiteracy, poverty and similar, large scale, intractable, historical problems. These are intractably difficult issues that are "the despair of tidy minds."[11] Solving them, or at least mitigating them substantially, would also change the world.

How many new and creative ministries are needed to reach the billions of people who do not know Christ? How can we as the church meet the challenges of feeding the hungry, healing the sick, and seeing a more just world come about? Who is addressing the lack of discipleship, sacrifice, biblical literacy, and other problems in the church itself? It is going to take millions of ministry entrepreneurs exercising creativity, innovation, and execution to influence the billions. We will have to step off the tried and true calf-paths to launch into this new territory.

The Eccliosystem

Biologists remind us that living organisms exist within larger systems they call ecosystems. Similarly, each of our ministries live within a broader "eccliosystem." I derive this from the Greek word for church, "ekklesia." The eccliosystem embodies not only the people who make up the kingdom of God, but also the various ways they have organized themselves. These diverse expressions of the church are today sharing with each other in ways they never have before. Seeing the whole, rather than just the part we play, is a key to conquering the big problems we face.

In writing this book, I struggled with the right way to frame the target audience. There is much sloppy ecclesiology around the word church. It is like the word "love," which can refer to everything from "how much I like this chocolate" to sex. Context is everything. Innovation principles are applicable to a local church, a missionary agency, a Christian nonprofit organization, a loose network, or a range of other structures. There are also foundations, educational institutions (like Bible colleges and seminaries), NGOs, relief and development operations, and Christian health care institutions. There are formal associations, like the one I lead, Missio Nexus. These parts need to work together to accomplish the task that Christ set out to accomplish some two thousand years ago. Each has its own unique set of innovation challenges. Each of these ministries are but one small piece of the eccliosystem.

> The eccliosystem is not disadvantaged in resources, people, money, or vision. The challenge of our day is that of creativity and imagination.

Added to that is the diversity of the local church itself. From large, expansive megachurches in world-class cities to small, home-led church networks in rural villages, there is little to generalize about who we are. Demographics, doctrine, and governing structures reveal distinctions so great it can only be the miracle of Christ that unifies us as the body of Christ.

The eccliosystem is not disadvantaged in resources, people, money, or vision. I believe the challenge of our day is that of creativity and imagination. What would it look like for this tapestry to be woven together with common goals and objectives? How could the diversity be unified as Christ called His followers to be?

The borders that hem in our creativity and imagination include the very structures that give form to the components of the eccliosystem. These structures are the people, rules, organizational culture, and other things that make up our organized ministry efforts. The stronger these structures are, the more defined we make their missions and core value statements. The more success they seem to have within their niche, the harder it is for us to think bigger than they are. Innovation often happens across these artificial borders. These categories exist in our hearts and minds; they are rarely imbued with sacral blessing. We must think in terms of the larger systems. Do not interpret this to mean that both theology and relationship are not important. The kingdom requires both, and they are wonderfully interwoven into the eccliosystem.

Carey devoted an entire section to prayer in his treatise that launched the Protestant missions movement.[12] He wrote, "The most glorious works of grace that have ever taken place have been in answer to prayer." In addition to the resources within the eccliosystem, we can avail ourselves of spiritual blessings we have in God. Our innovation can be so much more than applying the principles of design and development from the tech industry, the best managerial practices of industry, or the combined knowledge of humanity as stored on the Internet.

One of the wonderful attributes of God is infiniteness. His love is not a scarce commodity that we must divvy up carefully in case the well runs dry. The genesis of the Great Commission is found in Genesis. The promise to Abraham is our continuing purpose: we are blessed to bless others. Borderless sharing within the eccliosystem is a boon to all. Can we see past our small goals and ambitions to bless each other, thus reaping the reward and promise of blessing ourselves? The payoff in solutions, particularly when focused on the big problems, could be significant. We will unpack examples of this in Bible translation, student ministry, city-wide transformation, and other arenas.

Can It Be Done?

We are surrounded by massive change spurred on by innovation. We expect innovation out of businesses. We look for it among medical practitioners, educators, and the military. Even government is expected to innovate. A visit to the department of motor vehicles will most likely leave you asking, "Why can't they organize this better?" We expect more. There is an innovation expectation and ministry leaders are being judged on whether we can deliver on it. Can we rise to the occasion?

I believe we can, and in the pages of this book, you will find the major ways that innovation is being implemented today. You will learn about the tools and methods used from Silicon Valley to the Rift Valley that spur on innovation. You will be introduced to concepts like the stack, slicing, aggregating, design thinking, and wicked problems. In place of large-scale waterfall planning, you will be asked to consider the genius of incremental innovation. If we plan to create, innovate, and lead something *new*, it will require us to look past the best practices, successful models, and the type of "wins" we have already won. The new rules of innovation are not the same as the tried and true managerial leadership models we are well accustomed to implementing. Concepts like "change management" are helpful, but they are meant to help us manage, not innovate.

I am going to present to you five simple rules that innovative leaders utilize to solve problems. These are the Shoemaker Rules. They are simple, yet transformational. With William Carey, shoemaker and innovator as our inspiration, these five simple concepts can help you see how innovation in your ministry is possible. Each rule is stand-alone, but taken together, they form the basis for the ministry change that can drive a new generation of entrepreneurial ministry forward.

The Journey before Us

The first half of the book is focused on the problems and opportunities that we encounter as faith-filled innovators. The next five chapters are **The Shoemaker Rules:**

1. See a Problem Worth Solving

2. Ride the Wave of Existing Innovation

3. Be Biased to Action

4. Empathize, then Strategize

5. Think Big

In chapter 2, I'll cover the pitfalls of success and how it makes future innovation difficult. We will also take a dive into the Innovation Spectrum, and you can evaluate where your ministry might fall. Chapter 3 is about the new forms of innovation that are available to us in the twenty-first century. We will draw a distinction between invention and innovation. We will look at platforms, network effects, matchmaking, slicing and aggregating, and scale and crowdsourcing. Chapter 4 looks at the nature of innovation. There are myths and misunderstandings about who innovators are and where innovation tends to rise. In chapter 5, we will see how systems thinking, system design, and design thinking play a role in leveraging innovation. Ministry design thinking is laid out as a plausible way to take any problem and innovate solutions.

In the second half of the book, we will look at concrete "means" (to borrow Carey's word) by which we can put innovation into action. What can we innovate on, what does it mean to lead innovation, and what are the attributes of innovators? We will look at so-called "wicked problems" in chapter 6. These are the huge, complicated, and systematic issues mentioned earlier. Chapter 7 gives you a way to think about innovation targets. Ministry is different from business and we need a different set of standards in selecting problems. Then there are some ideas about innovative leadership in chapter 8. Leaders can create culture in a church, ministry, or other organization that is inherently innovative. We will delve into how they create an innovation culture, make decisions, view leadership, and empower teams. This is followed by a personal evaluation on how innovative you are in chapter 9. This section will focus on personal application of what we have learned. We will end our journey with a summary challenge in chapter 10.

Warning

Innovation, and particularly digital innovation, has tremendous spiritual implications for good and for evil. The collateral damage of innovation can bring great damage to people's souls. The Internet, originally designed to help scientists share information, has opened the floodgates of a global pornography pandemic. Once those floodgates are opened, it is impossible to close them again. Innovation can be a force for good but is often a force for evil.

The pace of technological innovation has overwhelmed theological reflection about its implication on our lives. The pace of technological change has outstripped our time to reflect on its use. With the changes wrought by COVID-19, for example, virtual versions of church and fellowship replaced physical gatherings. It happened with almost no serious discussion about the ramifications to Christian community. And there are many.

For example, the model of Christ was incarnation. He did not present Himself as a disembodied representation of Himself nor as a burning bush, pillar of fire, or other symbolic form. He was physically present as a human. God became a man and dwelt among us. There is a reason that the church is called His body. Technology can now project presence without physical presence. Is there really such a thing as a "virtual church"? It may take years or decades for us to really see what the pros and cons of these massive shifts have been. Is this era a

> **We must consider the impact of technology on both the meaning of our message and us as created beings.**

blip on the time line of our understanding of church or a watershed moment? We simply do not yet know.

The danger of what I call techno-paganism is real. Silicon Valley leaders like Ray Kurzweil and Peter Thiel are seeking to become immortal through technology. Elon Musk is building neural implants with the promise of "making the blind to see and the lame to walk." This trans-humanist[13] vision is redefining the way we will experience life. There is a rush to see who will be first to market, regardless of the consequences. We are ignoring the question of what *should* be done in favor of what *can* be done. As we talk about innovation and its partner, technology, we must consider the impact of technology on both the meaning of our message and us as created beings.

One way to do this is to avoid the trap that innovation is always technological. It often is and many of the examples in this book are technological. But ministry innovation can be about relationships, theology, personal discipleship, and similar, spiritually focused pursuits.

Another potential pitfall is to continuously chase after the latest thing. Innovation is not following trends. I have been doing work in global missions for many years now. Sometimes, when a new idea is introduced, old-timers like to say, "We've been through this before. It's just a trend that will pass." Sometimes this is true. Old-timers like me, however, are often first in line to critique an innovative ministry. So, while trend-chasing is not innovation, being set on "auto-critique" is not helpful.

A final warning is that, as Christians, we must recognize timeless truth that is not subject to innovation. We are not going to further enhance the gospel with innovation. We are not going to solve the problem of sin through innovation. Managerial practices will not replace biblical models of ministry. It is within the limits and framework of Scripture that we will find human flourishing. Innovation has an application for ministry but it is not the kingdom of God.

You, the Innovator

We started this chapter with a question: *Who are the innovators in the church today?* The best answer I can give is this—*you are.* Cartoonist Walt Kelly is credited with the phrase, "We have met the enemy and he is us."[14] If innovation is lacking in the eccliosystem, it is because we, its citizens, are not innovating. The crisis of innovation is not somebody else's problem.

I feel the frustration that others are expressing about how woefully inadequate our ministries are to create real innovation. If you are reading this book, I trust you sense that same crisis.

> One must not only innovate; one must be innovative.

Innovation always seems to be just beyond the horizon. Actress Marie Dressler once said, "You are only as good as your last picture."[15] She meant that people only remember your last contribution, not what you have done over a lifetime. Innovation feels a bit like this sometimes. Successes of the past are not sufficient for the current need. Thus, one must not only innovate; one must *be* innovative.

Nobody else is coming to save us from our lack of creativity and imagination. We are the cavalry. Let us mount up and ride in.

APPLICATION & DISCUSSION

Questions to Ponder

Here are some diagnostic questions to consider regarding innovation:

1. What do you see as the single most innovative ministry project in which you have personally participated?

2. What do you see as innovative in ministry today?

3. Do you agree or disagree with the statement: "There is a lack of innovation in the church today." Why do you feel that way?

4. Where do you think innovation intersects with theology?

TEAM EXERCISE & DISCUSSION

Homework:

Have each team member write a one-paragraph description of the biggest contribution your ministry has made to the eccliosystem since its founding.

Facilitated Discussion:

1. Ask each team member to read their paragraph and describe why they think it was the most important contribution.

2. Go around the room a second time, asking the team to discuss if the contribution stated continues to be the most important contribution.

3. Discuss how the ministry environment has changed since the founding of the ministry and what impact that has on the way the ministry currently serves its stakeholders.

The Calf-Path[16]
by Sam Walter Foss

One day, through the primeval wood,
A calf walked home, as good calves should;
But made a trail all bent askew,
A crooked trail, as all calves do.

Since then three hundred years have fled,
And, I infer, the calf is dead.
But still he left behind his trail,
And thereby hangs my moral tale.

The trail was taken up next day
By a lone dog that passed that way;
And then a wise bellwether sheep
Pursued the trail o'er vale and steep,
And drew the flock behind him, too,
As good bellwethers always do.

And from that day, o'er hill and glade,
Through those old woods a path was made,
And many men wound in and out,
And dodged and turned and bent about,
And uttered words of righteous wrath
Because 'twas such a crooked path;
But still they followed — do not laugh —
The first migrations of that calf,
And through this winding wood-way stalked
Because he wobbled when he walked.

This forest path became a lane,
That bent, and turned, and turned again.
This crooked lane became a road,
Where many a poor horse with his load
Toiled on beneath the burning sun,
And traveled some three miles in one.
And thus a century and a half
They trod the footsteps of that calf.

The years passed on in swiftness fleet.
The road became a village street,
And this, before men were aware,
A city's crowded thoroughfare,
And soon the central street was this
Of a renowned metropolis;
And men two centuries and a half
Trod in the footsteps of that calf.

Each day a hundred thousand rout
Followed that zigzag calf about,
And o'er his crooked journey went
The traffic of a continent.
A hundred thousand men were led
By one calf near three centuries dead.
They follow still his crooked way,
And lose one hundred years a day,
For thus such reverence is lent
To well-established precedent.

A moral lesson this might teach
Were I ordained and called to preach;

For men are prone to go it blind
Along the calf-paths of the mind,
And work away from sun to sun
To do what other men have done.
They follow in the beaten track,
And out and in, and forth and back,
And still their devious course pursue,
To keep the path that others do.

They keep the path a sacred groove,
Along which all their lives they move;
But how the wise old wood-gods laugh,
Who saw the first primeval calf!
Ah, many things this tale might teach —
But I am not ordained to preach.

2

SEE A PROBLEM
WORTH SOLVING

It isn't that they can't see the solution. It is that they can't see the problem.[1]
G.K. Chesterton

"Remember not the former things,
nor consider the things of old.
Behold, I am doing a new thing;
now it springs forth, do you not perceive it?
I will make a way in the wilderness
and rivers in the desert."
Isaiah 43:18–19

In the past few years, I have observed a marked increase in discussions around the topic of sustainability. These involve ministry leaders struggling under the weight of their current ministry operations. By "operations," I am referring to the functional systems and the people that run the ministry. Operations are originally designed to fulfill the mission. Over time, they can have the opposite effect from their original intention. They can produce drag on a ministry.

I recently spoke with a denominational leader on a video call.

Behind his desk were tall windows looking out at mountains. I commented on how incredible his office environment looked.

"We are out of here in a few months," he replied with a smirk, "and I can't wait. This building was great in its day, but we are moving our headquarters to an urban environment, closer to where our ministry needs to be."

Operationally, the suburban office made a lot of sense twenty years ago. Today, as the ministry seeks to reconnect with its roots, it is a hindrance.

Worse, operations create their own problems. Rules and procedure are created for good reason. When they fail, they are often solved by more procedural oversight. More money, more people, and more effort are required just to keep the existing ministry moving forward. A leader described to me that when he took over leadership, his first job was to "careen the entire organization and scrape off the barnacles." He was referring to the growth that used to collect on the hulls of wooden sailing vessels. They accumulated over time causing drag on the speed and handling of the ship. Every so often, the boat was careened; beached, turned to one side and then the other, as teams of workers scraped the hull clean. His phrase aptly captured the kind of renewal that many ministries need today.

We often think of scale as a solution to things like small budgets. That depends, though, on what you are scaling. If you scale operations, sustainability is more and more elusive. No business seeks to scale operations. Operations represent the cost of running the business. It is the part of the business you want to squeeze ever smaller. We often think that successful businesses are those with many employees. It is impressive to hear about companies with tens of thousands of employees. But that is the wrong measure of success. Revenues per employee tells a much more important story.

It is easy to mistake ministry growth for effectiveness. Growth should be considered with ministry outcomes as the primary measure of success, not ministry processes that make it happen. Churches that talk about the size of the congregations, buildings, and parking lots may be less effective in discipleship than much smaller congregations that are deeply impacting the worldview of their members. Growth and scale are not the enemy, but they are also not the solution.

When sustainability becomes the mission, the real mission suffers.

For legacy ministries, the challenge of the day has slipped from mission fulfillment to keeping the current slate of ministries up and running.

When sustainability becomes the mission, the real mission suffers. Sustaining something means to keep something at status quo. Leaders who dream of big goals, like the fulfillment of the Great Commission, do not have the luxury of sustaining their church or organization. If your ministry has a mission statement, go back and read it. I have never read one that says, "Our mission is to keep all the balls we are currently juggling up in the air." Yet, that is the unmistakable message behind this talk about sustainable ministry. Budgets, staff, and assets are a means to mission fulfillment. No more and no less. Your organization should be willing to burn itself out in pursuit of the mission. There is no promise in the Bible that a local church is supposed to last forever. Nor is there any indication that the worthwhile mission you are on today will be relevant forever.

Imagine what success looks like for a typical, growing ministry. It could be a church or just about any organization you might be leading. You have a strong following. You raised the funds necessary to operate and perhaps even built a building or purchased a property. It is now budget time. Ministry takes money and your budget has grown along with your ministry. This year, though, you want to explore a new project. Something new and innovative.

You realize, for the first time, that the creeping tentacles of operational expectations are beginning to squeeze excess funds out the budget.

The flexibility you had when growth was a few percentage points has been whittled down to nothing. You suggest to your staff that they consider some cuts to a few areas. They respond that they have done all the cutting they can do. In fact, they were going to ask you about cutting something. This is how innovation meets stagnation in the real world. This is how sustainability becomes the mission.

Another example involves risk. As ministries grow, they accumulate assets. Imagine, for a moment, a large ministry organization that sends people all over the world in pursuit of sharing Christ among the nations. They often send them to highly risky places. As they grow, they consolidate their operations onto a well-maintained property. By centralizing their operation, they cut costs. This asset, over time, becomes worth some millions of dollars. They are now holding on to something that makes them susceptible to a targeted lawsuit. The organization must be more careful about the freedoms they once extended to staff and missionaries regarding dangerous assignments. They do not want to take legal risks because they have an asset to protect. They say no to teams that wish to stay in the field despite local unrest. The type of risk-taking that created the hallowed stories of their founding is no longer possible. The precautions that have been put into place are understandable but also influence how well the ministry can execute on their mission.

Churches, as well, suffer from this risk aversion as they accumulate wealth. A budget of $250,000 for a small, struggling church is hardly a target for a lawsuit. But, for an expansive megachurch, multiple campuses, hard assets like property, and soft assets like curriculum, publishing, and media presence can contribute to growing liability. Further, many of these ministries are dependent on well-known pastors who, themselves, are perhaps the biggest concern for liability issues.

The Greek philosopher Heraclitus is credited with the saying, "You cannot step twice into the same river. Both the man and the river have changed." The same is true for organizations. Unfortunately, ministries can be like a river in another way. Without intervention, they run downhill. It takes a special leader to defy these organizational laws of gravity. If you saw water run uphill, you might consider it a miracle. So it is with organizations.

It is difficult for ministry insiders to see this slide. It is usually slow and decentralized across the ministry. These changes are slow-cooked, often over years. They subtly affect the culture of the ministry one small decision at a time. The best observers of this sort of slide are those who had once been insiders, left the organization, and then were invited back in. They remember what the former organizational culture was. They say things like this: "It felt more like a family back then," or "No, we never asked, we just did what we thought was right," or possibly, "Yeah, it was a different time."

> **Emphasizing growth over mission fulfillment mistakes organizational aspiration for mission fulfillment.**

GROWTH IS NOT A GOAL

Leaders often relay the message that growth is the goal. More donations, more people, more services, more everything. The thinking is that if doing X is our mission, then doing 2X is even better. Just as sustainability is about organizational survival, emphasizing growth over mission fulfillment mistakes organizational aspiration for mission fulfillment.

A political scientist named J. Q. Wilson once wrote, "Organizations tend to persist. This is the most important thing to know about them."[2] Organizations, like individual people, have a collective survival instinct. They begin to look out for their own wants, needs, and desires. In strange and unimaginable ways, organizations can make decisions that, to outsiders, seem completely unreasonable. They make these decisions because this invisible, collective personality that has grown in the ministry has become more demanding than the mission of the ministry.

Extreme examples of this in the ministry world can be found in child abuse cases conducted in churches, Christian schools, missionary schools, and other ministry contexts. History indicates a pattern that when such an abominable act is conducted in a ministry context, organizational survival takes precedence over the people involved, including the victims. Leaders lose perspective and circle the wagons, protecting the ongoing life of the ministry. Denominations are notorious for moving the predators from one church to another, seeking to quell the disruption rather than bringing shame onto themselves.

"More" is not a mission statement.

Paradoxically, ministries with "strong" cultures are the ones I find are most likely to fall prey to organizational groupthink. Core values statements, history about the founding of the ministry, distinct rites and rituals, and the use of insider language and acronyms create these strong cultures. These things matter to people who are members of the organization. They do not matter to those on the outside. In fact, they are often a turn-off. Outsiders care about mission fulfillment if that mission is truly focused on real problems.

"More" is not a mission statement. Your ministry exists for a reason. It does not exist for its own survival or for its own growth. When it does, outsiders have a unique sixth sense allowing them to smell organizational hubris and pride.

THE INNOVATOR'S DILEMMA

A problem we face as leaders is that the original mission is almost always overtaken by the way that mission is delivered. In 2005, the late Clayton Christensen wrote the book *The Innovator's Dilemma.*[3] He observed what happened inside businesses when they successfully developed a service or product and brought it to market. The dynamics hold true for ministries as well.

As a business has success with a new product, increased demand requires more organization. The delivery process is refined. There may be investment in the system that produces the service or product. People within the organization become convinced that their service or product—what they see as "The Best Way"—is the best or right solution to getting the mission done. Bureaucracy grows around its delivery and a self-perpetuating loop reinforces the value of The Best Way. New people join the team. Some are specialized and only participate in one aspect of the system that has developed. They do not have the perspective of the whole, but they are very good at doing what they know how to do.

In the business world, the innovator's dilemma reaches its peak when a new competitor enters the market. There is often an innovative improvement, and the incumbent organization, focused on delivering the Best Way, cannot adapt. They are experts at doing what they do best, not this new and novel solution. Their success has doomed them because they have become so good at what they do. The organizational culture affords no other means of delivery.

Do ministries suffer from the innovator's dilemma? Yes, they do. It is hard for us in leadership to see it, though, because often we are living inside the system that is suffering from it. Another reason it is difficult to identify is that our competitors are different. We are competing against worldview and cultural change. We may have developed culturally relevant ministries, but rapid change has now made our Best Way, whatever it might be, irrelevant because the people it was designed to serve are growing old, the next generation is always different from the former generation, and culture has changed.

The classic example from business is Seagate, a company that once dominated the hard disk industry. As customers moved from larger drives to smaller ones, they squeezed more and more profit from the factories creating hard drives. They got really good at creating 5.25-inch hard drives. Then the industry shifted to smaller drives using different materials. Seagate could not innovate fast enough. Smaller players, not invested in the same production facilities, took over and Seagate faded.

Local churches also face the innovator's dilemma. When you visit different churches, you begin to realize the extent to which our church models are copied from one another. Smiling door greeters, a couple songs, a warm greeting in which there is great effort to be sincere, announcements (or something like announcements that really are just announcements), a sermon with a specific application challenge, and a final song. The similarities between churches leads me to believe that this system, developed and used primarily by boomer church planters, is not keeping up with generational changes. It is a Best Way in need of a complete overhaul. As mentioned in the previous chapter, COVID-19 presented the church with a huge opportunity to innovate the worship service for a twenty-first-century audience. From my perspective, very few churches took advantage of these opportunities. Going online with the same format is not innovative.

Henry Cloud wrote a whole book on why some things need to end called *Necessary Endings*. Sometimes our ministries need to end. A few years ago, the organization I worked for took over a failing ministry that had been in its prime two decades earlier. Its approach felt old, its champions had retired, and the time had come for a necessary ending. We counseled some staff to move on, asked a few others onto our team, and shut it down. We held a final goodbye celebration, inviting past stakeholders, staff, donors, and those who had been served by the ministry. We remembered the former days and gave thanks. People cried, mourning the lost past as it formally ended. It was a healthy goodbye and freed up all involved to move on to new and more relevant ministries. Necessary endings can thoughtfully bless those involved.

Before moving on, one more example might be helpful. I was invited into a discussion about missionary deployment that was led by a significant leader in global missions. He had started a major missions organization. The topic of our discussion was the length of time that missionaries serve on the field. In the past few years, that number has dropped. When this leader started out, missionaries would go out for years. Today, this is rare. The question on the table was, "What can missionary agencies and churches do to send people for longer periods of time?" This question is also one which countless mission pastors have asked me.

I value long-serving missionaries. But I also know that nobody in our culture today takes a job that they plan to have for their entire life. Most people change careers multiple times, let alone stick with one job for a lifetime. Imagine an interviewer at a major company asking a potential recruit, "So, you are twenty-five years old. Are you ready to work for us the rest of your life?" It is not how we look at employment.

I suggested that this is the new reality of work, not just missionary work. After being scolded, kindly, I was lectured about the nature of missionary work. One must relocate to a new geographic area. There might be years of language and culture study before the work can begin. Finally, evangelism, disciple-making, and church-planting take many years. The work requires long-serving missionaries, I was told.

That is probably true in some places and cultures. The question on the table, though, should be, "What is the mission?" Is the mission to send missionaries for lifelong careers, or is the mission to see the church planted in all cultures? What if these leaders asked, "How can we re-envision the missionary's job in order to take advantage of shorter deployment windows?" When I suggested this, the group reacted with deep groans. Did I not understand the missionary task? I reminded them that Paul did not linger long anywhere he went. After much discussion, I realized that the innovator's dilemma was in full force. Nothing I said could dissuade them from a model in which the missionary would live on the field for decades before being fruitful. The largest potential missionary force lays outside the US and Canada; it is ripe for partnership and in need of funding. Yet, these leaders remain convinced that the solution that worked in 1970 is the best solution for today. It is a solution for some, of course. But it will not meet the need we face. Yes, there will be some pioneering missionaries that will go for a lifetime. We should encourage that. We should also see the potential for midterm missionaries who can bless thousands through indigenous partners. The goal remains the same; the means needs innovation.

Similarly, large, multicampus churches are the current rage. Just as the seeker sensitive movement came and went, so will this current form of church change. College ministry, youth ministry, what we mean when we say preach and teach, evangelism, small group ministry, worship forms, and pretty much every other category of ministry will need thoughtful innovation.

THE INNOVATION SPECTRUM

The good news is that the innovator's dilemma can be averted. Before we see how this can happen, let's look at where various ministries might fit on an innovation spectrum. You can evaluate your own ministry before looking at possible solutions.

THE INNOVATION SPECTRUM

| STAGNATING | SUSTAINING | INNOVATING | DISRUPTING |

Stagnating

"You don't get old and stiff. You get stiff, and then you get old."[4] The signs of ministry stagnation are easy for outsiders to spot. There is a struggle for recruitment and new staff. Budgets are thin, covering operations and not much more. If there are legacy funds, they are slowly being depleted over time. These ministries live off the momentum of a previous generation. The leaders are often fully convinced that the services and offerings of the ministry are valid and sufficient.

In the business world, stagnating companies do not survive long because . . . money. The horizon for ministries in stagnation is much longer. Because a ministry does not have the same metric as a for-profit corporation, there is less urgency. Stagnating ministries, it would seem, persist longer than stagnating businesses. Decades longer. All that time they are in stagnation they are depleting the church of precious resources.

I recently spoke with a newly appointed leader of a stagnating missionary agency. The previous generation of leaders had accumulated assets worth millions. They had purchased land for a camp and held onto it for over forty years in one of America's hottest real estate markets. It had been sold in the past decade generating these reserves. Each year they spent the savings to keep the doors open. They had over one hundred staff members and only two were under forty years in age. They had not sent a new missionary in years. The leader, much to his credit, was looking for an exit strategy that would honor the legacy while not wasting the resources on hand. That will be a painful but necessary process.

Unfortunately, this is not an isolated case. The United States and Canada are dotted with dying congregations symbolized by decaying church buildings. Urbanization, demographic shifts, aging, and a lack of visionary leadership has created a huge need to revitalize these ministries. Even in de-populated rural areas we find the skeleton of the church from a generation ago. What innovative entrepreneur is going to put these assets to work in new and refreshing ministry models?

Stagnation is survived only when the stakeholders of that ministry realize their predicament and make

> When leaders become detached from the problems they were originally called to solve, stagnation is on the horizon.

significant changes. Crisis is the friend of a stagnant ministry. It can shock people into confronting reality. Isaiah 43:18 (NIV) says, "Forget the former things; do not dwell on the past." This change of perspective is hard for those riding stagnating ministries to their grave, which they most often do. Helping people see the urgency of the situation is a prime responsibility for a leader in a stagnating ministry.

When leaders become detached from the problems they were originally called to solve, stagnation is on the horizon. This is often true in larger missionary organizations. Internationalization, the process of decentralizing the work into the field, has been the rage over the past twenty-five years. Through local empowerment, leaders have sought to bolster front-line workers. Unfortunately, when this happens, the home office staff grow distant from the needs of hurting, lost people. The organization sees the home office as a source of people and money. But, to raise up people and money, one must have a passionate vision. Since that vision has been largely pushed out to the field, the home office cannot fulfill their role well in recruitment or funding. This is one reason why I make certain to visit front-line ministry each year. It gives me a refreshing dose of Great Commission reality, where one can stand on a rooftop and overlook a city of millions with only a small handful of believers.

A pastor who started their ministry in neighborhood coffee shops and community events may now find themselves in their study preparing sermons for hours each week. What got them going in the beginning, exposure to people, has been exchanged for scholarly preparation. Over time, the church will emphasize pastoral preaching and teaching to the exclusion of contact with the world. National speakers often give examples of evangelism while flying on airplanes. I think this is because an assigned seat on a jumbo jet is their only chance to rub shoulders with the world. This is a sign of encroaching stagnation in that leader's ministry.

Leaders must infuse the urgency of the problem across the ministry. Structural changes, lines of reporting, how people are evaluated and rewarded, and many other facets of how we work together can be targets of innovation. This type of entrepreneurship is not glamorous but has significant potential.

Sustaining

I recently went fishing with a friend who is a nut for fishing. We were just offshore, exiting the channel and in big waves, when we spotted a mahi-mahi. We could see the green flash of the fish in the water as it circled a two-story, rusty buoy. The fish kept darting around to the other side of the marker when my friend cast toward it. He told me to steer the boat in as close as I could. It was *his* deep-sea fishing boat, and *I* was afraid of hitting that marker. The boat was jacking up and down on the waves in front of the wildly bobbing, barnacle encrusted buoy. I would get within a few feet and then back off the marker for fear of hitting it. My friend was standing on the bow. Each time I threw the boat into reverse, he would almost fall overboard, then flash a grin and a shrug at me. He was having fun; I was terrified. He yelled at me to get in closer, but I just could not do it. In frustration, he turned to me and said, "Hey, the boat is for fishing. I am fishing. Get in closer and don't worry about the paint!"

Many leaders talk with me about "sustainable models of ministry." This is most often about funding. There is a bit of a trap to be aware of, though, when it comes to sustainability. My guess is that you were not hired (or didn't found a ministry) with the goal of sustaining it. Instead, you were hired to solve a ministry problem. Perhaps the problem is the poverty of grace among the unreached. Maybe it is to see Bibles in the hands of all people. Or it could be to support the work of on-field missionaries. Regardless of what that mission might be, I have never read one that says, "Our mission is to keep this ministry open in perpetuity." That said, there is a balance to be struck between operational continuity and mission fulfillment. We need healthy organizational models to fulfill our ministry objectives. But when we exchange mission for sustainability, we get neither in the long run.

This is true for local church leadership. For example, you may be struggling as a pastor in a declining small town. Simply meeting each week might feel like a victory. But there are bigger victories to be had. There is life transformation in whoever it is that God brings your way. You can think about your mission in ways that the pastor of a large, urban congregation cannot. The influence in your small town is much greater than the megachurch pastor's influence in a city of millions. Do not let yourself drift into a sustaining mindset. Sometimes we have to scrape a little paint off the boat to accomplish the mission. Our ministry organizations were made for a purpose. Sustaining is a means, not an end.

Sustaining organizations probably make up the bulk of both churches and para-church ministries. A sustaining ministry works hard to deliver whatever ministry they have been conducting. During a past foundational era, typically led by a visionary founder or perhaps the leader directly after the founder, the ministry enjoyed the problems of growth.

I use the word "enjoyed" here on purpose. The problems of growth are the problems you want to have. How do you best take advantage of all the new opportunities around you? Where can we find staff and funding to keep up with the growth? How many services can we hold on a Sunday? Where can we find a place big enough to fit these people?

Problems for sustaining ministries are different in important ways. They are focused on extending past momentum. Why are our numbers leveling out? Is our operational budget growing faster than our income? Where are the young people? We have always been good at "X," how can we do more "X"? Leaders in sustaining churches and ministries will often discuss "the time before," when growth just happened. Now, it takes a great deal of effort to tread water, let alone grow.

Because of changes in our society, many, if not most, churches find themselves in the sustaining mode. It is because their Best Way has remained the same while the culture has moved on. Denominations are reporting declining numbers of members. Hundreds, if not thousands of congregations have church buildings, budgets and visions that were built during a time of growth. Now they are asking the question, "Can we sustain what we have?"

Mission agencies are not much different. One reason is historical. In the following table, compiled for the *Mission Handbook,*[5] we can see that most missionary agencies were founded before 2000. Over three hundred of the agencies that Missio Nexus researched were founded from 1980 to 2000. Then a steep drop occurred.

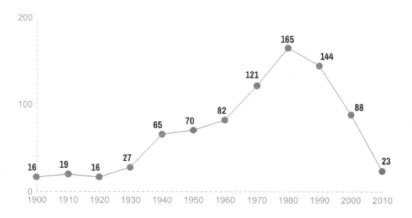

FOUNDING OF MISSION AGENCIES

Almost all these organizations have passed the baton from the founder's era to new leadership. In another study we conducted in 2017, we found that half of all missionary agency CEOs were in their first five years of service. Many of these leaders were handed organizations that had passed through an era of growth. These new leaders face the challenge of sustaining these organizations into the future. Unfortunately, both church boards and ministry boards often ask these new leaders to recapture the previous growth era rather than innovate or disrupt their ministry. The Best Way continues to live in their hearts and minds even though its relevance is fading.

An exciting facet of the US church is that church planting has grown over the past few decades. Unlike the mission agency sector, some parts of the country have dozens of new churches. The danger is that these churches are essentially clones of each other. I recommend that church leaders consider differentiation. The "3 songs, welcome and announcements, compelling video testimony, closing song" formula is all too common. I fear that many of these church plants are already facing the sustaining stage even though they are relatively young.

Globally, movements of churches planting churches is exploding. They do not use the Western model of church we are so accustomed to seeing. Groups are informally led by leaders whose primary role is to facilitate discipleship, not teach didactically. Is this a model for the West to consider? If so, I imagine the change will be hard, particularly for those who have no other model of church or historical memory of churches that meet from house to house.

Innovating

Innovating ministries are in their stride. It could be that they have created a new idea and are simply in that phase of their ministry development. It might also be that they are the rare ministry organization that has embedded innovation into their organizational culture. It is who they are, not what they do.

If there is any one marker of an innovative ministry, it is that mission triumphs over methodology. There is no confusion with means versus mission. The way that the mission is fulfilled is always secondary to the larger mission. Leaders embrace a static mission and a fluid methodology. People within an innovative ministry are clear on the mission no matter what role they fulfill. There is freedom about the how. Exploiting that freedom is where energy is created; a holy awe and a contagious sense of joy surround what God is doing.

I was visiting an outreach ministry in West Africa some years ago. The mission of this African-led initiative was to plant churches in the whole of West Africa, among every neighborhood and culture. Some of these were tribal cultures and some were staunchly Islamic. As we entered their main office, we were introduced to a woman who was answering the phone and receiving guests. As our small group of visitors went forward on their tour, I dropped back and asked her, "What do you do here?" Of course, it was obvious that she was the receptionist. I was making small talk. She answered, "I am a church planter." I smiled and nodded and went on upstairs.

> **If there is any one marker of an innovative ministry, it is that mission triumphs over methodology.**

When we arrived upstairs, we were shown a radio studio. I once again broke off from the main group and asked the sound technician, sitting in a glass-enclosed sound booth, what he did at the ministry. His answer? "I am a church planter." From there I asked others, and the answer was always the same.

Regardless of the role the person filled in that ministry, each person described themselves in light of the mission, as church planters. Their mission was clear. Even the taxicab driver, on the way to the airport, told us he was a driver by day, a church planter by night. Stop and think about this. What would happen in our own culture if every Christian saw themselves as a church planter?

C. T. Studd wrote,

> No wonder the Gospel spread like wildfire, first through Jerusalem, then throughout Judaea and Samaria, then through Asia Minor, Greece, Europe, and to the utmost limits of the worldwide Roman Empire.
>
> They didn't start a Missionary Society, for the whole Church was such, and all its members missionaries.[6]

It did not matter what role the individual had within the larger ministry. They all knew and understood that the mission was more important than their specific contribution. This allows for people to see beyond the imaginary walls of their own job description. The expectation is to fulfill the mission with whatever God-given talents and resources might be available. It is not to "do a job" but to be mission-focused.

There are other attributes of innovative ministries that will be touched on later. For now, the important idea for us to grasp is that mission is more important than means. For our purposes, we will define mission as the primary goal or objective of the ministry. The means or methods used to fulfill that goal are secondary and flexible.

Disrupting

"Disrupting" ministries create change. They don't simply react to the change around them. Here we can turn to our friend William Carey to understand why his message was disruptive. Rather than look at Carey's influence in India (which was substantial), let us consider why Carey disrupted our fundamental understanding of the Great Commission.

In 1792, the Protestant movement had been alive and growing for almost three hundred years. Martin Luther, a disrupter in his own right, had composed the 95 Theses that sparked the Reformation 275 years prior to Carey's booklet. In that time, the Reformation had taken root in Europe and transformed theology. Yet, this massive change had little influence on peoples and cultures with no access to the gospel message outside of Europe. The Reformation had done little to cast a vision for the cultures beyond Christendom's walls.

Then came William Carey's 1792 booklet, *An Enquiry into the Obligations of Christians to Use Means for the Conversion of the Heathens.* Like Luther, Carey was writing in an environment that was pregnant for change. He was not the first to write about the Great Commission, but his ideas came at a time of ripening. For disruption to happen, it must happen at the right moment in history. The "two Steves" (Jobs and Wozniak), creators of the first Apple computer, could not have built their garage prototype even a year earlier. In Carey's case, the massive British Empire, global travel, shipping, linguistics, and the concept of charitable support had all convened at the right time.

There was an intellectual void regarding the Great Commission. There were the beginnings of mission societies developing, but nobody had written a treatise quite like Carey's. His little booklet, accompanied by his personal commitment to go, was a watershed moment for the church. Missionary work, which the Catholic Church had been conducting all along, became a Protestant affair. Within twenty years of Carey's ministry, there would be hundreds of missionary teams sent from England, America, and many other places. His writing and ministry are a marker along a trajectory of disruption brought on by the changes of his day. He happened to be at the right time, at the right place, and acted.

Disruption occurs when an existing and commonly held understanding of how things work is displaced by a new idea, service, or product. In the case of ministry, disruption is typically not a product. Ideas are particularly disruptive. Carey's idea was simple yet profound.

Ministry disruption can also be service-oriented. Today, the evangelical church is dominated by a handful of celebrity pastors spawned by the megachurch movement. They have disrupted our concept of the local church in many ways. From massive buildings and huge congregations to multisite, simulcast services, these churches have an outsized voice in the contemporary church. There are less than two thousand megachurches in the United States among hundreds of thousands of churches. Yet, megachurch pastors dominate all churches due to their large footprint online, in bookstores, and through social media.

Disrupters create change. While innovators most certainly adapt and change to accommodate shifts in their environment, disrupters create that new environment. If this brings Jesus to mind, then you are understanding disruption.

CAN A MINISTRY CHOOSE?

As you evaluate your own ministry along the innovation spectrum, do you feel encouraged or discouraged? The innovation spectrum is a description of your ministry at a point in time. Where you are today does not dictate where you will be one year from now. As we will see, *you can choose what you want to be, even though the choice might be painful.* There are limitations, of course. Although it has been attempted, one cannot simply draw up an unreasonable future and expect it to happen. Yet, leadership is about making that choice and following through on it. Choosing begins with a realistic understanding of where you are today.

Because ministries are made up of people, they age. They do not, however, develop the same way we do as people. A ten-year-old ministry may be in its prime, or it might be an aging shell of its former self. Your current situation is affected by this aging process. As you evaluate where you are on the innovation spectrum, it helps to reflect on your ministry's maturity. If I ask a new ministry leader, "How old is your ministry?", they will tell me the answer in years. A very different question is, "How old are you in terms of a typical organizational lifecycle?" This latter question is far more important.

Churches age as well. In the model of church we practice today, entrepreneurial pastors start something small and, as the Lord blesses, grow it into something significant. Unfortunately for many congregations, the gifting of a startup pastor is different than the gifting needed to operate a large, complex church. Helping both leaders and their organizations understand the typical process of maturation for any organization or church helps leaders tremendously. They begin to troubleshoot the problems and see where they need to go to thrive. The framework for organizational lifecycles was introduced to the world by a Jewish refugee named Ichak Adizes.[7]

On a Sunday afternoon in 1943, Italian and Bulgarian troops flooded the Jewish quarter in Skopje, Macedonia. They went door to door, looking for Jews who were then sent off to concentration camps. Most were sent to Treblinka. Among those taken that day were a father and son, Solomon and Ichak Adizes. As they walked on the cobblestone streets under the watchful eyes of fascist soldiers, they had no idea what was ahead. More than seven thousand Jews were rounded up that day and put in the tobacco warehouse next to the train station to wait their eventual departure. The father, Solomon, paid a bribe to a Bulgarian guard, and disguised as Turks, they fled to Albania and, eventually, to freedom. Ichak Adizes would become a professor of organizational theory at UCLA, then at Stanford, Tel Aviv University, Hebrew University, and Columbia University. He has been awarded twenty honorary doctorates. His most important contribution was his research and book, *Corporate Lifecycles.*[8]

His theory postulates that all organizations go through a common aging process. Different stages of development require different leadership skills because the needs of the organization change. The early stages require entrepreneurship, risk, and unbridled growth. As that growth happens, it must be systematized. As the system overtakes the original goals of growth, the system itself must be tamed. These all require a different set of leadership skills, each with a primary contribution distinct from the others. There are few leaders that provide the right type of leadership across all stages of growth. My observation has been that far too many ministry leaders stay in place past their primary contribution. They hang on to their seat when they should relinquish it. Embracing the reality of the current need can free a leader to either step aside, rework the ministry around new realities, or remake themselves.

Founders typically have a high "problem orientation." They have seen a need and are focused on meeting it. If successful, the organization (or ministry) begins to grow. The growth state needs a leader who can systematize the work, providing for workflows and scalability. Then, as the organization begins to operate with high efficiency, they face problems of institutionalization. Antidotes to this dilemma include rediscovering original purposes, cutting bureaucracy, replacing leadership, and developing a sense of urgency in the team.

Both Clayton Christensen's *The Innovator's Dilemma* and Adizes' *Corporate Lifecycles* should stand as a warning to leaders. While the innovation spectrum does not dictate that you will someday lead a stagnating ministry, it will only be avoided with great care and diligence. Let me say it again, ministries run downhill. There is no better way to keep them from running downhill than for them to be focused on solving an important problem. The extent to which that problem is urgent correlates to the amount of effort the organization will spend going back uphill.

This brings us to the first rule for shoemaker-types of people. William Carey saw the injustice of entire cultures trapped behind enemy lines, with nobody taking the gospel message to them. This was an intolerable situation, creating a deep angst in his heart. Rather than rationalizing this injustice, he *saw the problem*. He let the status quo bother him to the point of action. Shoemakers identify a problem. Solving that problem becomes their mission.

> **Ministries run downhill.**

Shoemaker Rule #1: See a problem worth solving

Go read your ministry's mission statement. Does your ministry's mission address a real problem? Is it inspiring? Is it bigger than the boundaries of your church or organization? Does it make you wonder if you will ever achieve it?

Embracing a worthwhile problem drives you to do whatever is necessary to solve it. When solving the problem rises in importance, past all else, innovation and disruption have a chance. Listen to the disrupters of our day. Is Elon Musk building electric cars? Only as a means to an end. He has said many times that his goal is to transition the world from fossil fuels to renewable energy. Cars are just a part of the story. Was Steve Jobs creating a computer? No, he was making a computer that anybody could use. He was democratizing the computer. Henry Ford was not simply building cars. He was making a car that any American worker could afford to buy, thus changing the nature of the automotive industry. Up to that point, only rich people owned cars.

Problems are not always globe changing, but they must be real. Reed Hastings recalls when he first thought about founding Netflix. He had rented a video from Blockbuster and forgot to return it. They billed him for late fees. This felt unfair, wrong, and a terrible way to treat a customer. Netflix was designed around a different financial model in which there would be no late fees. Hastings disrupted the movie rental business by embracing the angst of late fees.

John Huss saw that the church had walked away from the Bible and literally gave his life to rectify this problem. Nicolaus Zinzendorf grieved that the church was not spreading the gospel and sent transformational teams across the globe. Luther never intended to launch the Reformation; he was addressing the problem of corruption in the Catholic Church hierarchy. His vision was to see a worshipping, faithful church at a time when indulgences and greed ruled the day. William Wilberforce saw the injustice of slavery and dedicated his life to eradicating it. From where he stood when he began, his efforts achieving this goal seemed impossible. Carey saw the masses of people with no witness for Christ and became their advocate. All of these were big problems begging for innovation and disruption.

What is the problem that sits at the core of your mission? We in leadership face many operational challenges. We worry about budgets, staffing, strategy, and sustainability. But these are not the sort of problems that drive vision. In fact, they make for lousy vision because they are internally focused on the ministry. People do not voluntarily give of their time, join your team, or spread the word about your work to keep your institution's doors open. People have an innate sixth sense that enables them to somehow know when leaders are moving from visionary leadership to sustaining (or stagnating) leadership. People within these organizations and churches see leaders as pursuing a self-serving agenda. The success of the institution is a poor substitute for visionary leadership.

Experience over a lifetime of ministry has led me to conclude that *good* leaders exhibit three characteristics. They are good communicators; they build teams of talented people; and they want to try new things. *Visionary* leaders add another element to this list. They identify and prioritize solving significant problems. The greatness of the problem is directly tied to the greatness of the vision. The institution they lead is a means, not an end. These are the innovators and disrupters.

Look at Pain Points

Think about the breakthroughs in your personal life and then in the life of your church or ministry. How many of them came at a time when things were going well? The markers of these breakthrough times might be a budget that is met through generous giving, healthy programs, good staff members, people engaging deeply, and personal margin in the life of the leader. These are the seasons of ministry we long for. But these are not the times of greatest growth.

Pain is the real mother of invention.

We learn through adversity. This is true for leaders, teams, organizations, and churches. Adversity is about problems. Adversity is where the solutions lie. If you want to have a breakthrough, it will almost always come with struggle, a problem, that needs to be overcome. Pain is the real mother of invention.

Some years ago, my wife and I were quite disappointed by the lack of discipleship in the church. It got to the point where I could simply not sit through another sermon and then watch people trickle out of a building with no significant life change. It created a longing for something more meaningful, better, and more challenging. We ended up starting a house church. It was the problem of "church-as-usual" that led us to take this step. Through it, we grew and were stretched in untold ways. We learned through that journey (and it was a trip) about our own attitudes toward community. We learned how our culture struggles with the demands of radical community that house church requires. We now know that church "models" are not the same as church life. That decade of house church will always be a mountain top experience for us as we reflect on our spiritual journey. This would not have happened had we ignored the pain point we felt in a traditional church. This is no indictment on the traditional church, by the way. This was our experience in that time. At other times in our life, the traditional church has played a key role.

You have no doubt heard the phrase, "Necessity is the mother of invention." I prefer to say, "Pain is the mother of disruptive innovation." What is grieving your soul to the point where you just cannot stand by any longer? We live with pain all around us. That means opportunity is all around us. There are countless problems to be solved. For disruptive innovators, this is a "target rich environment."

Pick a Right-Sized Problem

When Jim Collins and Jerry Porras published the book *Built to Last: Successful Habits of Visionary Companies*, they called attention to the same principal as having a BHAG, a "Big Hairy Audacious Goal." Among ministry leaders, BHAGs took off. Unfortunately, I have seen that BHAGs are often too disconnected from a ministry's reality. How many failed attempts could we count among those who said that they would "reach the world within this generation?" David Barrett and James Reapsome wrote a book in 1988 called *Seven Hundred Plans to Evangelize the World*. I imagine, since 1988, that number has climbed by a couple of thousand new plans, none of which have accomplished the goal of reaching the world. Huge, global problems that need solutions are going to be addressed in chapter 6, "Think Big." These big problems are worthwhile, and we should consider them. But, for many ministries, BHAGs should address problems the ministry can realistically affect, and often, they are beyond a reasonable scope.

Sometimes, solving small problems can have significant ramifications. A Minimal Viable Innovation may hold the key to a breakthrough. In the same book mentioned above, Jim Collins tells the story about Walgreens' evaluation of stores. They had been looking at sales data and comparing store managers against each other. Good managers were those with high margin stores. They were promoted and awarded. Management was looking to understand how they might better evaluate success. They made a small change. Instead of rewarding managers based on profit-per-store, they evaluated them on profit-per-customer-visit. Overnight, store managers no longer competed with one another. They began to cooperate in marketing, they called each other for advice, and they assisted each other through referrals for out-of-stock items. What had been a group of employees competing against each other became, instead, a team working against outside competitors. Because not all store locations have the same profit potential, they were able to identify highly successful managers despite their location. Profitability increased.[9]

No significant capital investment was required to make this change. They did not bet the farm and take the company in a totally different direction. Sometimes, the problems we need to solve are embedded in the guts of our ministries. Picking a right-sized problem is just as important as picking the right problem.

HOW PROBLEMS CREATE INNOVATION

Both stagnating and sustaining organizations replace bold mission with organizational survival. As we will see later, there is room for innovation around organizational survival, but that cannot be a primary purpose for existence. When a bold mission addresses a worthwhile problem, people care.

One way that we have sought to address a lack of alignment in ministry has been through the adoption of mission statements. Has this worked? It is probably a step in the right direction. Unfortunately, too often ministry mission statements are no more than business-speak, a check mark on a list of "best practices," or an attempt to satisfy the divergent agenda of people who were on the committee crafting the statement. Most staff, volunteers, and people served by the ministry do not know them. They do not understand the problem the ministry is trying to address.

As a part of my doctoral research project, I conducted in-depth interviews of missionaries covering many different topics about their organizations. These were all people giving their lives in cross-cultural service. Missionaries tend to be driven by bold mission. They have left home and hearth, after all, to take the gospel to the far ends of the world. If anybody would care about such things, I assumed, it would be missionaries. I was shocked that less than 3 percent were able to recite their organization's mission statement. The only successful ones were from one organization with a five-word mission statement that was clear and compelling.

Most mission statements are either too vague or too expansive. On the one hand are the myriad statements with the phrase, "To God's glory," embedded in them. Good for you! You are all about God's glory. So is every other Christian that ever lived. That is not a mission statement exclusive to your specific calling. All who are in Christ, share it. On the other end of the spectrum are the lengthy mission statements obviously edited by a committee to include everybody's pet position. These are hard to remember and lack focus.

> **Mission statements written around solving a problem are far more compelling than statements of activity.**

Mission statements written around solving a problem are far more compelling than statements of activity. One does not need to state the problem explicitly, but if innovation is a value, then the problem should be implicitly stated in the mission. The problem is best stated as a positive. If innovation is a value, then the statement should push your ministry past the bounds of what is possible today.

What would be a good mission statement for a car company like Tesla? "To lead the world in electric car technology" would be pretty good. But it is way off from the real mission statement which is, "To accelerate the world's transition to sustainable energy." You can see the much bigger picture than cars in this mission statement. Going to the Tesla website, you find solar energy for homes, battery technology, and cars as products in their portfolio. Selling cars is a means to an end and only one of many means.

Walmart is considered one of the most profitable companies in the world, if not *the* most. Is their mission statement "We sell lots of stuff cheaply?" No, it is "To help people save money so they can live better." Sam Walton lived in a rural community that was frugal. He knew that affordability was a problem for people who wanted to achieve a better lifestyle. He tried to solve the affordability problem for them and that became the mission of Walmart. Along the way, he reinvented discount shopping.

Judging from the outside, many churches appear to share a common mission statement that goes like this: "More butts in seats." That might sound harsh, but I have studied church mission statements and find a distinct gap between the stated mission and the reality of what is happening in the church. Churches prefer aspirational mission statements. I often read church mission statements that say, "We make disciples." Yet, pastoral teaching is the overwhelming priority of most churches. Discipleship takes a back seat to teaching. Small groups are required to discuss the pastor's sermon, not the issues of discipleship people encounter in daily life. Most of the corporate "worship service" is teaching. The church is evaluated by how many attend the service to hear the teaching. If the stated mission is discipleship, it is hard to see the priority in what is happening by the activities of the church. A mission statement must reflect reality, and in many churches, the mission statement is what they want to be but is disconnected from the operational reality of the church. This will not drive innovation.

Consider the mission statement of Christ Church of the Valley, in Peoria, Arizona. It is "To reach the valley for Christ." This is quite different than a generic statement about God's glory, bringing heaven closer, or the oft used "We make disciples." There is a problem inherent in this statement (the valley does not know Christ), the valley is the place where it happens, and it is outward-focused. I do not sense that this church is about themselves. Rather, it is about "the valley." I have never attended the church, but I envision a valley, a church, people who are without Christ, and a body of believers intent on reaching them.

Frontiers, a mission agency focused on reaching the Muslim world, has a difficult challenge crafting a mission statement. Muslims do not want to be reached for Christ. Thus, "With love and respect, inviting all Muslim peoples to follow Jesus" is a powerful way to address a problem with a positive statement. It is also memorable, short, and concise. It is also a *big* challenge, including "*all* Muslim peoples."

The tighter you wrap your ministry around a specific problem to be solved, the easier it will be to innovate solutions to that problem.

Blue Ocean Innovation

W. Chan Kim wrote the book *Blue Ocean Strategy*. In it, he contrasts what he calls "red water" as the competitive marketplace where lots of players are vying for the same market share (it is red because of the sharks and there is blood in the water!). Blue water is the open ocean where there is nobody present right now. It is open to you to wade in and set up shop.[10]

Can ministry innovation suffer from red ocean marketplace competition? Yes, of course it can. Planting a new church in a city where there are churches on every corner is a red ocean approach. Red oceans in the business world represent commodity markets. A commodity market used to mean a market represented by raw, non-manufactured goods. Today, it is more generally used to refer to markets in which the goods or services are easily reproducible.

When the first smartphone was introduced, Apple owned the market because they were the only player. Today, so many phone manufacturers are present that this is a commodity market. Online church services were once novel. Today they are more like a commodity service. Too often we consider something that is new to us to be innovative. When a product or service, including services in a ministry situation, becomes readily available, that product or service is not innovative.

There is plenty of blue ocean all around us. I think it is fair to say that the blue oceans are expanding for Christians today. I once heard Neal Cole say, "If you want to reach people for Christ you need to sit in the smoking section." Anyplace where you go and see no evident Christian community is a place for innovation. It is a blue ocean. Of course, there are entire cultures that have no Christ followers. Problems worth solving often entail going where nobody is currently working. By focusing on these challenges, we are forced up the innovation spectrum.

Summary

Stagnating, sustaining, innovating, and disrupting are descriptions of where organizations and churches may fall on the Innovator's Spectrum. Ministries, like other natural systems, run downhill. Their founding may have been solving a real issue, but over time the organization itself, its survival and culture, take more attention than the outward focus it once had. Before the ministry can innovate, it must identify a problem to solve that lays outside of its own organizational boundaries. This forces innovation and brings about rejuvenation. That can happen through rediscovery of an original purpose or the recognition that a new problem needs to be discovered.

APPLICATION & DISCUSSION

Questions to Ponder

Here are some diagnostic questions to consider about your own organization as it relates to the innovation spectrum:

1. When you look at your ministry through the lens of the innovation spectrum, where do you fall?

2. State your ministry's mission statement without referring to a copy of it. How many of your team can do this?

3. Restate your mission statement by finishing the sentence, "Our ministry solves a problem and that problem is _____."

4. Where do you place yourself on the chart of organizational lifecycles?

5. Does your mission statement identify a problem that you are seeking to solve?

TEAM EXERCISE & DISCUSSION

Homework:

Ask each person on your team to map, on the innovation spectrum, where they think your church or organization currently falls. Have these sent to one person, who will collate them onto one chart for the team to see when they gather.

Facilitated Discussion:

1. Ask each person to describe why they placed the ministry where they did.

2. Discuss with the team what conditions exist that keep the ministry from going to the next level. If you agreed that the ministry is disruptive, then discuss how you can keep it there.

3. What problem does the team see as the most important problem the ministry is seeking to solve?

3

RIDE THE WAVE OF
EXISTING INNOVATION

There is only one thing stronger than all the armies of the world:
and that is an idea whose time has come.[1]
GUSTAVE AIMARD

But when it was day, the magistrates sent the police, saying, "Let those men go."
And the jailer reported these words to Paul, saying, "The magistrates have sent
to let you go. Therefore come out now and go in peace." But Paul said to them,
"They have beaten us publicly, uncondemned, men who are Roman citizens,
and have thrown us into prison; and do they now throw us out secretly? No!
Let them come themselves and take us out."
ACTS 16:35–37

From the sixteenth to the eighteenth century, England established itself as the largest empire in human history. About 25 percent of the world's population lived under its dominion along with the same percent of the world's land mass. "The sun never sets on the British Empire" accurately described its global reach. A small island nation in Europe built this vast empire through sea power. Later, the East India Company leveraged this military might in subjugating Southeast Asia.

It is well known that the rise of Protestantism globally is interwoven with the remarkable expansion of the British Empire. What is less known is that missionaries like William Carey were themselves persecuted by the commercial interests of the East India Company. They opposed missionary work for fear that it would stoke anti-British sentiment among the Hindu population. Carey traveled to India on a Dutch merchant vessel because of this. His mission in India was in Danish-held territory. Like the coppersmiths found in the book of Acts, the British Empire was no friend of the missionary in India.

Despite this, Carey's mission would not have been possible just a few decades earlier. The rise of global trade and commerce, the ability to sail across vast oceans, breakthroughs in navigation, the Flying Shuttle (an automatic loom that enabled the formation of the global textile industry), and other technologies fueled the British Empire's growth. Carey's ministry happened during the beginning years of the industrial revolution. Carey's vision for global missionary work coincided with expanded opportunities for global travel. Carey's views were nurtured in an era when expansion globally was a new paradigm. He did not create colonialism, but he most certainly rode its ships to India, benefited from its ideas in his indigo factory, and elevated the dignity of Indians based on a philosophy of human rights imported from Christian Europe.

Colonialism is mostly understood today through the lens of its many evils. Yet, globalization, which is today's counterpart, is heralded by many as a human breakthrough. It will someday visit the same fate as colonialism and may already be in decline. The evil we humans create in one era are obvious to those living in a later era. We must acknowledge that Carey was locked in his own era and with humility recognize that we are as well.

Imagine what it was like for Carey to live when technological change would create new conditions for humanity that would alter the course of history forever. Now, stop imagining it—you are living in a similar era. Just as Carey rode the wave created by the technological and cultural change of his time, your ministry can ride the wave of techno-logical and cultural change today.

Shoemaker Rule #2: Ride the Wave of Existing Innovation

Shoemakers know that change creates opportunity. Rather than lamenting the passing of a bygone era, Shoemakers take advantage of these opportunities, molding their ministries around new realities. Change agents understand the times and exploit the new opportunities available to them. They ride the wave, harnessing its power, instead of fighting against it.

I am a sailor. Anybody who has spent any time at sea knows that overwhelming power contained in a wave. It is energy that is already moving in a direction. To redirect that energy would take an amazing deal of force. Harnessing that same energy, moving in a direction you want to go, creates the opposite effect. It works for you.

Let us consider an example, using a relatively concrete ministry activity, Bible translation. Here we stand, almost two thousand years since Jesus' ministry on earth, and the church has not been able to translate the Bible into the world's languages. To be sure, we have a good start, and the major languages of the world have pretty good coverage. But we have a long way to go before we finish the task. While there are more than two thousand projects underway, there are over seven thousand languages in the world. Just under 10 percent have a full Bible and about half of the seven thousand have a portion of Scripture.[2] The gap is significant. If you parse that just a little bit, you will find that the task is much larger due to other factors than just numbers. There are issues of quality, suitability, and age (languages change over time). The goal of having the Bible in all languages is elusive.

Why is this? The Bible was a controlled book, mostly kept away from people, for most of the past two millennia. Only experts could handle the text and when translations were done illegally, the brave translators were imprisoned, burned at the stake or worse. Before the digital era, all the work was hand done, and that work could be lost due to any number of reasons (about fifteen years of William Carey's work was burned in a fire, and Judson's was miraculously saved during his imprisonment). The Bible is not a short book, and the amount of time necessary to complete a translation has typically spanned decades.

The growth of the modern Bible translation era began when the process was systematized and refined in the last century. Wycliffe Bible Translators rose to become the premier translation organization with projects all around the world. Trained linguists carefully parse the text and produce translations that are contextually relevant, understandable, and academically rigorous. Innovative strategies and the use of computer-aided translation have drastically reduced the time to complete a translation. Yet, the overwhelming size of the task, the economic resources necessary to complete it, and changes within the cultures and languages themselves continue to keep the completion of the goal at arm's length.

In the past few years, a new approach has emerged using a crowd-sourced approach. Most Bible translation has been carried out by one or two linguists, who often had to learn the target language and culture to make the text both accurate and relevant to indigenous speakers. New models of translation are vastly different. Rather than working with one or two highly trained specialized linguists, a crowd of local language speakers is assembled. Many of these translators have little to no formal linguistic training. They rent a hotel for three weeks. The first few days of the gathering are a crash course on how best to translate the Scriptures using concepts developed by professional linguists over the past century. Then, the entirety of the New Testament text is chopped up into small, manageable pieces and assigned to groups of people. They head back to their hotel rooms and create a translation of their piece, individually, and then gathering in small groups later in the day to compare the text and improve it. The snippets are collected into books. In just a few weeks, what used to take many years to produce, a rough draft of the New Testament is ready for analysis. From there, specialists take over, refining the text. The time to translate the New Testament has been drastically reduced and, because the translators were target-language speakers, the final product embeds indigenous ideas more naturally into the final product. There is also a much higher level of local ownership because of their participation in the process.

Just a decade or two ago, what I have just outlined would have been quite difficult. Inexpensive computer technologies enable this sort of work. The combined contributions of Bible scholars, entire libraries that fit into a laptop, and systematic processes have come together to enable it. In fact, whenever you use digital technology, you are making use of many disparate innovations that have been pulled together into a technological system. When software components are built on top of each other they comprise a "stack" of technologies. Many of the modern systems we use on the Internet are built on top of a stack of free software that is available for you to use.

The Stack – Accumulated Innovation

We often do not realize how much the stack affects us when we use a product or service. Digital content delivery, from simple things like the webpage on our handheld device to high-touch services we enjoy are almost always stack-based. These smaller components are often free to use and widely available to everybody. Let us look at an example from the service sector, Airbnb.

Airbnb, hit hard in the COVID-19 pandemic, had grown to be the largest hotel chain in the world. They did this *without owning any hotels*. Airbnb not only avoids real estate costs; it avoids massive employment expenses as well. It has a database of available properties that literally spans the globe. Airbnb's infrastructure is built on top of tools that are smaller innovations, mostly free and easy to use, and available to you for free as well. Consider their stack:

- The Programming Language is Ruby on Rails (free to use)
- JavaScript drives most of the online interface (free to use)
- The webserver is Nginx (free to use)
- Redis is part of the database scheme and also provides security (free to use)
- Analytics are provided by Presto, Druid, and Airpal (free to use)

The only major part of their software stack is cloud storage, which they pay Amazon for along with a database program called RDS that Amazon also provides. Because the Amazon expenses are transaction based, this expense scales up and down as the market grows or shrinks.

Almost every piece of the stack used to create Airbnb is free to your ministry to utilize. Airbnb is a service. Most ministries are in the service business as well. This is an important way that technology works today. We assemble the component parts into something new. The innovation happens when we build it on top of existing technology. We exploit the system. We ride the wave.

At this point you might be wondering about how the stack can be used to serve people. Back in 2014, refugees began flowing into Europe. The numbers steadily grew, and the German government put out a call for people to share their homes. But how? Refugees Welcome International (which is not a faith-based organization) saw the overwhelming need for housing the newcomers. They created a small app that allowed any German to post their availability of their home to accept refugees. They could indicate how many, what gender they could be, and other conditions that a refugee might want to know (for example, how far the residence is located from public transportation). Similarly, refugees could post their need, how many were in their family, how long they needed assistance, and other items about themselves. The app caught on, and soon, thousands of refugees were able to find a place to stay while they figured out a longer-term solution for themselves.

As of this writing, the network has expanded into twelve European countries. They have partnered with other refugee resettlement organizations to expand their footprint. If you have been in a refugee resettlement camp you will appreciate the difference this effort makes. By using the homes of volunteers, the refugees have a much better transition experience and the strain on the government system is reduced.[3] I must ask the question you might be asking as well: "Why wasn't the church at the forefront of developing this platform?"

UnfoldingWord, a ministry based in Orlando, Florida, is also exploiting the stack. They are creating open-source translation tools that run on inexpensive Android computers, tablets, and handheld devices. They are also pulling together open-source tools that are not bound by copyright or permission standards that have inhibited broad Bible translation. Empowering believers from around the world in Bible translation, tools like this are marking an era of radical change in Bible translation. Crowdsourcing shortens the rough draft time frame. Mobile translation tools make it possible for indigenous groups to take these rough drafts and edit them for final, reliable, and solid Bible translations. The existing technology stack makes this all possible.

The stack offers us "big waves." The sport of surfing has developed two distinct forms. The one most of us know is when a surfer enters the water from the shoreline, paddles out, and surfs the breakers. The other form is called "tow-in surfing." Jet skis pull the surfers out into the huge breakers that lay offshore. They get the surfer up to speed and release them into waves that are fifty feet tall and taller. The extra speed makes this possible. Ministry leaders, often nontechnical end users of technology rather than technology disrupters, might consider a boost as well, before trying to ride these huge waves. The boost may come in the form of partnership, consultants, or training in the use of new tools.

THE BUILDING BLOCKS
OF THE NEW INNOVATION

The sharing economy might have been more appropriately named the "peer economy." When transactions happen between people without a middleman, it is a "peer to peer" transaction. We call it sharing because, in many cases, one person is sharing an asset they own with another person. With Uber, you share your car. Vacation Rental by Owner? Your rental property. People have always exchanged goods with one another in peer-to-peer relationships. But now, through the power of technology, it has become infinitely easier. Thus, a simple but useful definition of the sharing economy is when technology facilitates the direct exchange of goods or services.

The stack makes use of technology associated with the sharing economy. We use these new innovations all the time. Matchmaking, mass collaboration, and capacity utilization are different ways that the stack is applied within the sharing economy. These building blocks are not exclusive of one another but work together in varying degrees on different platforms.

Mass Collaboration

Mass collaboration happens when many people are empowered to provide a piece of the solution. When we think of crowd-sharing or crowdsourcing, we are talking about mass collaboration.

The organization I lead has a group health benefits program available for ministries. By aggregating our risk, we create a pool in which we share medical costs. Small organizations and churches can purchase insurance at lower rates because we act like one very big company. This is an old-school example of a mass collaboration.

Other ways that mass collaboration might work for ministries include:

- Rapid response volunteer teams for disasters can be pulled together from a wide array of churches with members having unique expertise.

- The funding of just about anything. Crowdsourcing can be applied to ministry work. For example, "Fund the translation of one Bible verse and together we will fund a whole Bible."

- The sharing of expert information within a network such as Wikipedia. A ministry application might be to share data about ministry progress on a city or country-wide scale to reduce duplication of effort and highlight areas of greatest need.

- Helping single parents with house projects by having an all-church volunteer day.

Any time we can bring the collective efforts of a large group of people together there is the possibility of mass collaboration. There are many ministry opportunities for mass collaboration. While it might be easy to see it in our local context, technology also makes broad scale, global collaboration possible as well.

Concerned that your ministry does not have the ability to collaborate like this? Imagine if your congregation decided to solve an issue together. Maybe it is a neighborhood cleanup program, a food pantry for the poor, or an educational coop. Now expand this to other churches in your area. Could your collaboration gain significant traction with a larger number of people? Can you create the mechanism for people to self-organize and collaborate around whatever problem you seek to solve?

> **Any time we can bring the collective efforts of a large group of people together there is the possibility of mass collaboration.**

Life Remodeled is a community development organization focused on the city of Detroit. Until I came across them, I was not aware that one third of Detroit's population lives below the poverty line. For many of us, the economic downturn of 2008–2009 is a distant memory. For Detroit, it was, and continues to be, an existential threat. With entire neighborhoods depopulating, the already stressed infrastructure lost jobs, revenue, and social cohesion. By 2012, sections of the city looked like war zones. Buildings, decaying and empty, were emblematic of the situation. Urban decay is a cycle that makes a city unlivable. How could one person even think that they could affect this sort of hopeless situation?

Chris Lambert, a Detroit church planter, was inspired by the television show *Extreme Makeover: Home Edition*, where volunteers gather and build a home for somebody who needs one. He adapted the idea to remodel homes in blighted Detroit neighborhoods. After a project debut, an onlooker noted to Chris that, while helping this homeowner was great, "It doesn't do anything for the rest of us." Challenged by the reality of this statement, Chris innovated.

This was an opportunity for crowdsourcing on a massive scale. Today, Life Remodeled brings together thousands of volunteers to remodel schools, rebuild buildings, remodel parks, create safe environments for people to travel to homes and schools, and upgrade the educational opportunities of residents. They do this by raising up an army of volunteers, creating a labor force to clean up, rebuild, and re-envision entire tracks of Detroit. Chris changed the model of their organization, included leadership outside of the faith sector, and partnered with local governments. He recently told me, "I have never had so many opportunities to share about Christ as I have now."

Mass collaboration makes it possible to improve the quality of life for one family or for thousands. Ministries are uniquely positioned to scale mass collaboration, particularly if they are willing to look outside of traditional sources for assistance.

Matchmaking

Some of the earliest applications of matchmaking are eBay and Craigslist. Matchmaking apps abound in many industry segments. The primary matchmakers are, of course, dating apps. According to industry data, there were 30.4 million online dating users in the US in 2019. This number is expected to grow to 35.4 million by 2024. One might think that it is all younger people using these services, but over half of the users are fifty-five years and older. One in six marriages is now started from an online relationship and that number is expected to grow.[4] Data like this shows how matchmaking is transforming how we find spouses.

The earlier example of refugees in Europe is matchmaking. Employment, hobbies, restaurant reservations, mortgages, consulting, and just about any service you can think of has the possibility of matchmaking. Matchmaking is simply finding a way to connect people with similar interests.

During COVID-19, food delivery services spiked. People wanted to quarantine and have their food delivered. One local area church I know of, Faith Assembly, put together a list of "collaborators" in the congregation that would be willing to deliver food to shut-ins. They organized an outreach in their community and began delivering hundreds of meals. Through the web of relationships in their congregation, they collected names and redistributed them to volunteers. These "masked agents of God" carefully prepared meals with guidance about sanitized food preparation, dropped them on doorstops, rang the doorbell and left, ensuring safety for those inside. Is this sort of innovation too small scale to be considered a breakthrough? Not if you were one of the shut-ins.

Capacity Utilization

Capacity utilization is about mobilizing otherwise immobile resources. The eccliosystem is filled with resources that are not fully utilized. Church facilities that are at full capacity for three hours on Sunday morning, but otherwise underutilized, are one example. So are educational buildings at seminaries and colleges, mission agency facilities, and just about any ministry building. An institution that has a facility that sits empty at any part of the week on a regular basis can utilize this capacity for ministry purposes.

Robin Chase, cofounder of Zipcar, writes,

> There are three ways that platforms make excess capacity accessible to others. They can slice it or aggregate it, in each case letting co-creators use excess capacity more efficiently. Or they can open it, enabling co-creators to generate entirely new ideas, processes, products, and services.[5]

Slicing excess capacity most often refers to making an expensive fixed asset available for smaller slices of time. People rent it rather than own it. Even money can be sliced. When I was a foundation board member, we struggled with the load of funding proposals. On-the-field missionaries needed smaller amounts of money, and we could not take the time to review the hundreds of possible applications for these smaller projects. We decided to fund a team of on-the-field workers, consisting of both foreign missionaries and indigenous church leaders. We gave them a large donation, and they vetted the many smaller proposals that were more helpful and appropriately scoped than a large donation would be. They sliced this donation into many smaller donations, did follow-up, and shared results with both our foundation board and other participants.

The team at Missio Nexus shares financial processing services with others. The company that provides these services "slice" their time across multiple ministries, freeing us from having to hire our own employees to process finances, saving us time and money.

Aggregating excess capacity, on the other hand, happens when a platform takes many different available resources and puts them together. Airbnb is the classic commercial example. They do not own any rental units but aggregate a list of people who do, providing the end user with a single catalog of options. When I need additional graphics services, I do not hire a full-time graphic artist. I use one of thousands available for hire on a per job basis using a website. These websites aggregate, or pull together, the massive professional capacity that is distributed around the world.

Platforms

The key to slicing and aggregating excess capacity is to make it easy. Technology based on community-oriented platforms in which the "buyer" and "seller" can easily connect with each other is one part of a platform. It would be easy to think that the sharing economy is all about new software that works on mobile phones. That would be a mistake: platforms are more complex than just the software that ties people together. One author has written, "We are no longer in the business of building software. We are increasingly moving into the business of enabling efficient social and business interactions, mediated by software."[6] It might be expertise in cross-cultural ministry, coaching for church planters, prayer, or a means of teaching the Bible. Ministries do not have to create these services in-house. Instead, they can find experts online and pay only for the services they need. Platforms like RightNow Media are providing these tools on a global basis.

A single mom in your congregation might need tax advice. A recently unemployed teacher could benefit from a resume review. A young thirteen-year-old boy might be fatherless. A new homeschool co-op needs a meeting space just three hours per week. Each of these situations presents the opportunity for making connections that serve the body. Platforms are the means to connecting these dots.

What are the factors that should push us toward greater platform ministry in the near-term future? Obviously the almost complete penetration of mobile technologies in the West plays a role. Along with this has come changes in our own behavior and the sorts of things we are willing to do digitally. Just a few years ago our behavior was different. COVID-19 has pushed us much further in this direction. A few years ago only the technologically astute used Zoom. Now, elderly people use it to connect with their families, sometimes throughout the day. As people turn to their phones for answers, the church needs to be present. Giving, teaching, Christian education, and outreach will migrate toward platforms.

What does a shift toward platform ministry look like in the real world? Education in general is in massive flux and missionary education is no different. The rise of marketplace missionaries and other, nontraditional missionaries has risen sharply over the past two decades. The route of Bible college, seminary, and the missionary candidate is becoming less common. This in turn affects the amount of theological education that candidates have as they join agencies. Different approaches have been adopted to address this, most often in the form of a standard list of classes an inspiring missionary must take before going overseas. This takes time to administer, including ongoing follow-up, encouragement to finish in a timely manner, and a system for tracking each individual and their requirements.

These people are interested in getting overseas in a reasonable amount of time. That time is often set by their fundraising time line, which takes about twelve to eighteen months. Traditional theological education is packaged in semesters. Even some nontraditional, online courses are delivered in semester packages. People must choose between accredited coursework and nonaccredited coursework. Courses at a seminary typically cost more than $1,000 per course.

Biblemesh has stepped into this gap. They have created a set of classes that are designed from the ground up to be online. Working in tandem with Zondervan publisher's academic division, textbooks are indexed to coursework. Using a "best of the best" approach, the classes are taught by leading experts in their field and proctored by qualified educators. You might think, "Many schools are attempting this," but there are a couple more elements that make Biblemesh different.

Typically, payment for a seminary course is an up-front arrangement.

The student writes out their check and the class begins. Nontraditional students do not work on a semester schedule and like open-ended time frames. Unfortunately, this does not motivate students to get the work done in a timely manner. Biblemesh charges per month for the course. The price point is set low, at $250 per class per month. Motivated students can finish the class within two months, reducing the cost of the class while encouraging them to finish on time. Most students will pay half of what a traditional institution charges for the course.

Biblemesh classes are not accredited. However, the Biblemesh team has signed partnership agreements with a broad range of seminaries who will consider these classes to meet degree requirements. Thus, time and effort spent in a Biblemesh class can be later transferred into a conventional seminary. This has an important secondary outcome. Schools that would otherwise be in direct competition with Biblemesh are now trusted partners.

A final element makes Biblemesh unique. Organizations can craft their own certificate programs by working with the Biblemesh team. Our association, for example, is currently creating a Missio Nexus Missionary Preparation Certificate Program. Within the next few months, any member missionary agency will be able to suggest this program to their candidates as they seek to prepare them for long-term cross-cultural service.

The Biblemesh platform is an example of using a digital strategy to satisfy the needs of multiple stakeholders. The student receives high quality, decentralized, work-at-your-own-pace theological education. The cost to the student is substantially reduced from traditional models. The organizations sending the students have a "plug-and-play" certificate-level program to offer their candidates. Finally, theological institutions that would otherwise be competitors are partners.

Scale

To be successful, most platforms require "scale" to be successful. Scale here is not simply about size. Scale refers to the ability of the platform to grow large enough to make the offering worthwhile. If you called an Uber for a ride, but there was no car close by, you would be discouraged from calling Uber a second time. But because there are so many drivers, the wait is almost always short. One of the challenges that platform creators face is getting to scale fast enough to make the platform attractive to enough users before their start-up capital runs out.

Scaling is largely dependent on what economists call "network effects." When more people are using a product or a service, the value of the product or service goes up. If everybody in your office uses a particular video conferencing tool, then it is more important for you, too, to be using that same tool. But if half of them use one system and half of them use a competing product, then the overall usefulness of video conferencing decreases. My parents recently got their first smartphone. Why? Because everybody else in the family was using a smartphone app to communicate with each other. The network effect, even in a group as small as a family, made the value of owning the phone greater.

Network effects and scale work together as powerful influencers in our daily lives. There are many social networking sites, but Facebook reigns because everybody is there. This could change quickly (just as MySpace) but not without a significant number of people changing their affiliation. Only two phone platforms exist (iOS and Android) in the West. China is seeking to create an alternative. If (or more likely, when) they grow larger than iOS and Android, the network effect will be substantial. Wikipedia works because there are no alternatives.

One of the challenges of scale is that whatever you offer, the cost of that offering must be compelling, or close to nothing. Scaling physical products costs more as the volume is scaled. The cost of connecting people relationally, however, is virtually free. If I create a platform that can connect two people, the cost to connect two thousand is not two thousand times more. Ministries that offer high-touch, human-centric services will not scale easily. The question you should be asking yourself is, "What scales in the space of spirituality?"

Oneway Ministries, located in a Chicago suburb, is scaling prayer for the world. Through the creation of media that highlights every nation in the world, they seek to be on the computer screens and phones of all Christians. RightNow Media is seeking to scale Bible teaching. New forms of the church, from multisite to simple churches are attempts to scale ministry by making it more accessible and in reach of more people.

Monopoly Effects

Have you ever wondered why there is no serious competition for Facebook? You can thank monopoly effects for this reality. Who wants to be on MySpace when all the cool kids are on Facebook? Platforms encourage monopolies by their very nature. This has elevated "first to market" strategies in the business world. As Zoom has positioned itself to be the dominant player in virtual meetings, Microsoft has feverishly worked to present their product, Teams, as an alternative. They are investing much of their future in Teams and understand that they need to be in the top spot for longevity. The number of vendors offering similar tools will consolidate down to just a handful in the next few years. Webex, the previous incumbent and pioneer of the online conferencing platform, is in a distant third place as this is written. By next year, this market segment will look different, but one thing is guaranteed, whoever becomes the leader will enjoy monopoly effects.

Are there monopoly effects in the church due to platform dominance? Perhaps Life.Church's Bible application would be one. A strong competitor is Logos, with a completely different model. Whereas the Bible app is a broadscale, free offering, Logos is a platform built for Bible scholars that carries a higher price tag.

Some economists argue that monopolies are, at times, important and helpful. For an example, consider the local water utility. There is not much evidence that monopolistic platforms have developed in the evangelical world. One exception might be RightNow Media. Billing itself as "the Netflix of Bible teaching," RightNow Media has thousands of

Bible studies, sermon series, original series, and event recordings all on one platform. With a single login, a person has access to a huge library of material. While RightNow Media's own team creates some of the content, the majority is obtained through partnerships and agreements with hundreds of ministries. Their reach is now going global, with teams on two additional continents and material being produced in those contexts. (We will cover their story in chapter 4.)

In the wake of the 2020 election, social media platforms highlighted the downside of unregulated monopolies. It has become clear that there is incredible power in monopolies. Perhaps muting monopoly effects in the eccliosystem is, in the long run, healthy for the church.

Trust

Imagine I am talking with my nineteen-year-old daughter on the phone as she travels across her college town. During the conversation, she casually drops the fact that she had just gotten into a stranger's car for a ride. As a responsible parent, shouldn't I ask her, "What are you doing?" or question this arrangement in some way? Five years ago, I would have. Today, not so much. Because she is taking an Uber across town.

In a short amount of time, our culture has moved from trusting in institutions (and the regulations that governed them) to something altogether different. We now look to platforms like Uber, Sittercity (providing babysitters), and Waze (giving road conditions and directions for driving) to give us the sense that transaction is safe. Each one uses a different trust mechanism.

> Our culture has moved from trusting in institutions to something altogether different.

With Uber, you can read reviews about the driver before you get in the car. You can check to see if the person pulling up to give you a ride is the same one as the image on the app. They ask me, "Ted?" and I ask them, "Mary?" and we know we have connected. If you are really concerned, you can order a higher-grade ride that includes a higher-grade of vetting. On some platforms, like Amazon, there are reviewers with reputations that enhance their feedback and give you a greater sense of trust. Do you read Amazon reviews of products before you buy? These reviews have become more important than the product descriptions. If others are saying that the item does what it says it does, you buy. Reviews have become an expectation for most online purchasing processes. Their purpose is to build trust.

In addition to reviews, Sittercity has a lengthy profile that is checked against other online sources. That profile includes a vetting process because the potential risk is so much higher for Sittercity than it might be for another platform. A preselected set of options is presented to parents based on what they have identified as important to them. The profile is made to match the specific concerns of the parent. Identity verification, track record, and a personal interview are a part of this profiling system.

Today, even though it is controversial, many employers check Facebook listings about people they intend to hire. Facebook is a profile; a documented means of understanding who a person is that can be quite detailed. Many platforms contain some sort of identity check and some are quite extensive. Twitter offers a means to verify a person's identity. LinkedIn has built their entire platform around a person's profile. Some platforms verify financial transactions before you can use them.

Waze, which lets drivers report on road hazards to other drivers, uses crowdsourcing to establish trust. As a user, you are prompted about the veracity of what it reports in real time. As you drive along and see a car on the side of the road, you are giving the option of saying, "Yes—it's still there," or "No—there is no hazard." Over time, these sorts of self-correcting systems become very reliable. The more one uses Waze, the more they realize that accuracy belongs to the community, which encourages better reporting. This becomes a self-reinforcing loop that further reinforces trust.

This cultural shift in what establishes trust in our minds has made the sharing economy possible. For many years trust in the ministry world has been established by institutions. The church itself was a trusted institution. Somebody raising personal support for their ministry would include the name of their organization in their fundraising materials. That name lent credibility to their efforts and assured the donor that this was a legitimate ministry. While new forms of trust have emerged, these older forms, which were institutional in nature, have eroded.

Another way that trust is established is through regulation. When you purchase food in the grocery store, do you think about how safe the food is to eat? For the most part, we simply trust that the government has monitored the production of the food. The debacle in Flint, Michigan, over its tainted water supply in 2015 is an example of just how trusting we are in government oversight and how harmful it can be if that trust is violated.

In a transaction that is peer-to-peer, there is often no regulation governing the quality or safety of the goods and services. This is the fault line on which Uber was successfully forced out of Austin, Texas, in 2016. Taxi companies formed a political coalition that would require ride-sharing services like Uber to submit to the same regulations as they did. In almost every other case before Austin, Uber had prevailed. The issue of rider safety was one of the reasons why they failed in Austin (the other was regarding their treatment of their employees). Uber decided to withdraw after losing a referendum on the issue, choosing not to do business in Austin rather than submit to regulation.

For decades, accredited education was considered a must, a seal of approval that the educational services being rendered met a minimal quality and the student met basic requirements. As we move more toward self-directed education, there is no institution providing the trust factor. Many educators are struggling with this new reality.

We live in an era where MOOCs (massive open online courses) are offered by top professors to hundreds of thousands for free. This has given way to "digital badging," in which organizations offer online credentials that a course has been completed. Google recently announced new certificate level programs, self-directed and nonaccredited. The company will look at them as equivalent to a four-year degree despite their nine-month completion time line.

The disruption in education is tied to trust. Leading schools, including Bible colleges and seminaries, were a brand that carried credibility. This area is ripe for innovation. It is a paradox that trust in the digital era is increasing for service providers while trust in traditional institutions has been declining. Even churches have reviews on different platforms. Reading them reveals not only how people perceive the church, but also what is important to the reviewers. These reviews no doubt have an effect on people who are considering whether or not to attend a particular congregation.

Blockchain

Peer-to-peer systems cut out the middleman and make direct connections between people. Bitcoin, the original application of blockchain technology, has already upset the financial world and promises to deliver more disruption in the years ahead. For most laypeople, it is difficult to understand the technology that makes Bitcoin work. Yet, that same technology, blockchain, has great ministry potential.

Blockchain allows for the tracking of transactions in a secure way. Things like international payments can be secured and controlled by both the sender and the recipient in a secure manner. At some point in the near future, a ministry is going to find an innovative way to send money directly to ministry partners in restricted access countries. This will undercut hostile governments and decrease transaction costs.

The most discussed cryptocurrency, Bitcoin, is an application of blockchain for money. But blockchain technology can also be applied to other processes. Imagine, for example, a foundation that has a block-chain of all granted funds and organizations. Donors would be able to see the sources and ultimate destination of funds and how they were used. The blockchain could be programmed to automate transactions. For example, it is common for foundations to give "matching grants." When a ministry raises a certain amount of money, the foundation could be notified by the blockchain and the grant released.

It gets more interesting when we move from major donations to small donations. Most foundations are not able to administrate small grants. Often, small grants can be the most important forms of giving. Imagine an evangelist in Africa who needs a bicycle so that he can visit villages in the bush. Foundations would typically not consider this need because it is so small. Blockchain software, however, does not care about the size of the grant. Thousands of small grants could be administered through a blockchain system. Audits of projects, historical giving patterns, and other data points could serve ministry funding on a global scale while enabling small grants to be given at scale.

Fractional ownership using blockchain can represent real property. Ministries could make assets available to each other in partnerships where buildings, down to very granular resources like rolling media carts, could be tracked and shared.

Thus far, I have seen no ministry apply blockchain in a way that delivers on its promise. By the time this book goes to press, however, I think it is highly possible that this will change.

USE THE NEW TOOLS

Many of the examples provided here are not in the domain of evangelism, discipleship, or church planting. Churches and other ministry organizations have been mostly absent from the use of these revolutionary tools.

It is worthwhile to think about the nature of the church. On planet

Earth, there are few social networks as large and expansive as the church. The church has possibly the largest volunteer force in history. Geographically dispersed throughout the world, there is no political country that does not have at least some group of believers. Resistant to persecution across the two thousand-year arc of its history, the church is a survivor. Its dispersed and decentralized leadership structure makes it difficult for even large and aggressive dictatorships, like the Chinese Communist Party, to shut down.

> The church is unmatched in the potential for mass mobilization to solve humanity's biggest challenges.

Even though there remains a significant missionary challenge in the world, the church is unmatched in the potential for mass mobilization to solve humanity's biggest challenges. Imagine if William Carey were alive and well today. What would be the big problems he would see and solve? Certainly, he would be riding the waves of innovation's new tools. By leveraging these tools, Shoemakers will bring innovation to the church. The entrepreneur should be warned, however, that there is a price to pay. I learned this price myself when Missio Nexus began to focus on a problem of significant magnitude.

In late 2016, I attended a webinar on an obscure topic called "Association Health Plans." Changes in insurance regulation had been introduced by the Trump administration. I was a member of an association of association presidents, and they offered this overview of the changes. One of the action steps was to conduct research on how Missio Nexus ministries were providing health care. We decided to focus on the one-third of our membership made of smaller agencies (these tend to have the biggest struggle in finding affordable health care). We were shocked to find that 65 percent of them offered no health care plan for their employees at all. One question asked if they would be interested in Missio Nexus investigating ways to purchase health insurance as a group. All but one agency was interested. We had identified a need within our community.

Insurance is an old-school example of scale and collaboration. By combining our risk, we can purchase health care at a predictable cost. Small mission agencies, churches with staff of two to fifty, and student ministries have a challenging time purchasing health care. By coming together, Missio Benefits could offer a plan that lowered costs for most ministries and churches. Rules for religious organizations exempted us from onerous state-by-state regulation. This was "real" insurance—not medical cost sharing, and for most organizations and churches, provided a significant cost savings.

Or so I thought.

We put together a small team of volunteers from our members who helped us develop a "request for proposal" document. I began to educate myself on how these insurance plans work. While there were new rules, they were being fought over in the court. But I learned that Missio Nexus could qualify as an association of churches and their ministries. We created Missio Benefits.

In July of 2019, we were set to launch. About one thousand people had signed up for Missio Benefits. Many were missionaries living overseas. We had an arrangement with two health care networks, one domestic and one global. We had contracted for the onboarding systems and it was operational, very easy to use, and we had gotten many different churches and organizations to sign up. Things were looking great.

Or so I thought.

Literally days before we launched, our global insurance partner threatened to back out, uncertain of the regulatory carve out we were utilizing. I contacted a law firm. After explaining the situation to them, they told me it was their responsibility to inform me of the possible penalties for proceeding. If we were found to be out of compliance, it was a felony in the third degree and the state could level substantial fines against us. I was scared. We had collected hundreds of thousands of dollars in premiums and people were starting to visit their doctors. On July 3, late in the day, our global partner pulled out of the program. We were already live.

The next two weeks were tense. The Lord provided for the missing piece through our domestic partner. They took a step of faith with us, trusting that we would obtain regulatory permission and agreed to be our global network. Because of the lag between a visit to a doctor's office and the billing, we were able to reorient our systems before any bills came due. In the meantime, we were called into the insurance regulator's office for an interview. It was confrontational. They did not know what to do with us because of our unique approach. Regulators have a set of categories into which businesses must fit. They were pushing us into one of those categories, but it was not the one we needed to succeed.

My prayer life exploded over those days. I thought about the lone missionary family, visiting a hospital with an emergency in some far-flung part of the world. What if they were denied coverage? What would happen to Missio Nexus if we ran afoul of the law? How did we expect to financially survive this mess? Had I made a colossal mistake?

"Regulatory entrepreneurship" is a phrase that writers have used to describe new paradigms of business that challenge regulation. Sometimes, as in our case, the laws on the books are not designed to handle the situation at hand. For example, what happens when somebody dumps a few truckloads of electric scooters in your city and tells people to just leave them "wherever they find them"?

Leading scooter company Bird did just that to the city of Bakersfield in 2020. Hundreds of scooters were positioned across the city overnight. Residents woke up to both a new form of transportation and discarded scooters, blocking sidewalks and making handicapped access difficult. The company contacted the city that very morning, offering to talk about their plans. By that time, they were hopeful that customers would help them force a favorable policy and create scooter-friendly regulations. In some cities, this strategy has worked, while in others, the scooter companies have been banned.

Or how about a car company that releases self-driving features to the public when there are no rules governing how these cars should work? The pace of change today is more rapid than government regulators can be in addressing unseen issues. Our insurance program was under fire because it had developed in an area where the law was not clear.

Fortunately, the regulators gave us time. They allowed us to operate while we clarified our position with the Internal Revenue Service. Through that process we learned that we held the right kind of government registration to operate a "church plan." In the long run, the state not only allowed us to continue operating, they also wrote a letter indicating that they had reviewed our plan and agreed that we had the right to operate, giving us a defense if challenged in other states.

Missio Benefits will struggle for survival. The health insurance market is volatile and even now threatens its existence. But this is a lesson for the budding Shoemaker. Innovation at the edges is difficult. You will be misunderstood, you will be accused, and you will question yourself. Many days I asked in prayers, "Was that You or me coming up with this idea, God?" Any of us can use the new tools of innovation. Most of us will not, though, because it is hard. Had I known at the outset what lay ahead, I cannot say that I would have proceeded as I did. Innovation is hard work with no guarantee of success and there is real risk of failure.

Summary

Each era carries new opportunities for innovation. Understand what those opportunities are and work within them instead of against them. The digital era has introduced new ways of business, made possible by the computers in our pockets. Mass collaboration, matchmaking, capacity utilization, platforms, and scale are all new concepts that ministries can consider in reshaping the world.

APPLICATION & DISCUSSION

Questions to Ponder

1. How does your ministry utilize new tools? Have you considered creating new tools, and if not, why not?

2. Can you think of services in the community you are seeking to influence that your ministry might provide, enhance, or partner over that are currently inaccessible to people living there?

3. What examples of mass collaboration in ministry have you experienced?

4. What platforms exist in your ministry sphere?

TEAM EXERCISE & DISCUSSION

Homework:

Ask each team member to make a list of the processes in your ministry that might be ripe for innovation. This list can include things like new member orientation, delivery of services, or back office procedures.

Facilitated Discussion:

1. Have each team member share the items they considered ripe for innovation.

2. As a group, create a prioritized list of these items based on feasibility that the team could execute the priority.

3. After agreeing to the list based on feasibility, create a second prioritized list, but this time focus on how big a difference that innovation might make to the ministry.

4. Using both lists, attempt to choose one item for further consideration.

5. As a group, discuss theological ramifications for innovation.

4

BE BIASED TO ACTION

I never worry about action, but only inaction.[1]
Winston Churchill

Then they said to one another, "We are not doing right. This day is a day of good news. If we are silent and wait until the morning light, punishment will overtake us. Now therefore come; let us go and tell the king's household."
2 Kings 7:9

It is probably unlikely that William Carey ever saw himself as an innovator. He saw a hole in the dike and stuck his finger in it. The problem—the lack of gospel witness in India—that he decided to do his best to solve. He rode the wave of colonialism, not unlike modern missionaries have ridden the wave of globalism, which took him around the world.

WHO CAN INNOVATE?

I have heard many bold statements made about the nature of innovation. I understand that speakers and authors like to be provocative about their topic. Innovation, however, comes in many forms, through very different people, and in unique ways. Before we can answer the question, "Who can innovate?" we will dissect some innovation myths.

Myth 1: Innovation Is for the Genius Inventor

When I think of innovators, Elon Musk comes to mind as one of the most important contemporary examples. First, he makes millions on a company called PayPal. Then he starts Tesla to solve global emissions, and then SpaceX in order to colonize Mars. He not only looks up at the stars, but down, underground, as well. He founded The Boring Company to dig tunnels to eradicate congestion in cities and increase high speed travel. OpenAI is another "hobby" through which his team is developing a neural implant to interface digital devices with the brain. Elon Musk can innovate at the genius level.

But I do not think we should adopt Elon Musk as our model innovator. Innovation happens on a large scale through gifted people like Musk, but it also happens on a small scale, one little innovation at a time. The cumulative effect of these innovations, added up over time, is revolutionary. To understand innovation, we must shed some of our preconceived notions about it, starting with the Genius Inventor concept.

Let us agree that there are genius inventors and that they have been highly influential. Edison, Tesla, Einstein, and Musk come to mind. They apply genius level minds to problems and deliver results. They are, however, responsible for only a tiny sliver of the millions of innovations we encounter each day.

Was William Carey an innovative genius? I think he was, but he did not start out that way. He began as a humble shoemaker with a burden. Time, tenacity, and a lifetime of pressing on for the kingdom built his contribution to history. He chose simple obedience and took the next step.

Myth 2: Innovation Comes from the Margins

Perhaps the most common trope about innovation goes like this, "Innovation always comes from the fringes." Along with this way of thinking is the suggestion that "one must look to the margins and the misfits" to find innovators.

Hogwash.

Pull out a piece of paper and something to write with. Just do it. Off the top of your head, without overthinking it, list the first four innovative companies that come to your mind. I am going to make a very educated guess that at least two of your companies are on my list: Google, Amazon, Microsoft, and Apple. If you are under thirty-five, then you might have Tesla or SpaceX there as well. Now, ask yourself this: Would you consider any of these to be "fringe companies"? Of course not. Yet, people continue to press this idea that innovators are all bohemians.

It does not matter if you are a lean start-up, a small to medium-sized enterprise, a megachurch, or a house church. You might be mainstream. You might be avant-garde. It does not really matter. You can innovate. We see examples of innovation today from every sector of industry. Is it too much to ask that we also see it from every sector of ministry? Our first hurdle in being innovative is overcoming this mantra that we cannot innovate because we are not "fringe."

Myth 3: Innovation Is Invention

Yet another misleading mental frame we often hold about innovation is that it is about originality. We see innovation as invention. It might be invention but, most often, innovation is different. Innovation is arranging existing components in a new way, combining things that already exist to create something that does not. It might be using something in a new or novel way.

Henry Ford did not invent the car. He did not invent the assembly line. He did not invent marketing. But he innovated in all three areas. He designed and built an affordable car at a time when cars were only for rich men. He used innovative, efficient systems to reduce production costs. Instead of hiring sales staff, he developed a chain of dealers to scale his marketing presence. Henry Ford combined existing inventions into an innovative ecosystem designed to sell cars to the growing middle class of America. That is very different than Edison, who invented new things.

> Innovation is arranging existing components in a new way, combining things that already exist to create something that does not.

Too often we limit innovation because we see it as a lone inventor, working in a lab, testing this and that, for hours on end in pursuit of a single breakthrough that will change the world. Then, in a dramatic presentation, the invention is revealed, the world is changed, and the genius lauded for his cleverness. This is not how innovation typically happens.

Most innovation is borrowed, not original. Think about innovations in the church. The church growth movement was an innovation introduced by Donald McGavran. He took the lessons he learned while working as a missionary and applied them to the US context. McGavran's ideas were imported from India. Yet another church innovation, the missional church movement, came from Indian roots as well. Lesslie Newbigin returned home from India to England where he similarly imported ideas from the mission field. He did not intend to start a movement, but many of the original ideas in the missional movement came from his writings. Adapting concepts from foreign cultures created innovation in the church of the West.

My late brother graduated from college with a degree in industrial technology. While he was technically astute, he did not interview well. He struggled to land that first engineering job. As days turned into weeks, and then months, his wedding day approached. He needed a job and took one soldering parts on an assembly line in a factory making guided missiles. Day after day he saw the parts go by in front of him, as he did his best to keep up. He began to reverse engineer the circuit board in his mind. He identified the inputs, the outputs, and what the various components were contributing to the design. One morning he took out a piece of paper and drew out a schematic of the circuit, revising the number of parts to reduce manufacturing costs. His foreman looked at this drawing with some concern. These were supposed to be secret designs. He ordered Jim to sit down and wait while the little drawing worked its way up the chain of command and back down to the engineering department.

By the close of the business day, Jim had been promoted to junior engineer. He took existing components and reworked them in a new and innovative way. During his career, he would go on to both invent and innovate. He held numerous patents in the field of cardiac pacemaker technology and was a highly active engineer until his death in 2020 from brain cancer. One of his personal treasures was a box of old *Popular Science* magazines. He believed that by looking back at old inventions he could rework them into something new and appropriate for our day.

LIMBox is an innovative solution to help people who are amputees. If you were to lose a leg in an accident, war, through disease or other calamity and you lived in a rich nation, chances are pretty good you would get a prosthetic device. In the United States, this would cost you about $15,000. Insurance, family, or local charities would help you if you could not afford that. Not only that, but Western nations have made great advances in providing handicapped access. Contrast that with somebody living in an impoverished nation. Not only is the cost exorbitant, but life depends on walking. There is no service to deliver you to school, your job, or even the grocery store. There is no car in your household.

LIMBS International has put everything needed for a prosthetic in a single box. The total cost is $600 and they can assist you with that cost if you are unable to pay it. They combine this with a fitting service and six weeks of rehabilitation to make sure you can use the new prosthetic leg. There are forty million amputees around the world today. Imagine the life change that comes inside of a cardboard box.

Each component of the LIMBS International offering was in existence before the LIMBox. What they did was combine the low-cost hardware with partnerships to provide the fitting and rehabilitation. After gaining valuable experience on how best to serve amputees, they developed a new prosthetic knee that became the cheapest, most durable, and stablest prosthetic of its kind. This development became the prosthetic kit called LIMBox. By training others, the staff of three multiplies their efforts across the world (forty-nine countries when I spoke with their CEO, Oscar González, in 2020). The innovation came about by putting these components together into a life-transforming package of hardware and service.

Myth 4: Innovation Is about the Breakthrough Idea

Closely related to the confusion between innovation and invention is the false narrative that innovation is the result of a "eureka moment." Rarely does a single breakthrough innovation produce life-changing results. Most innovation happens in small increments over time. We need to avoid pitting incremental innovation in opposition to innovative disruption. Disruption, in fact, is often the accumulated effects of incrementalism. Because the pace of innovation has sped up dramatically, we can easily mistake incremental innovation for singular breakthrough events.

Most often, innovation occurs when people do the hard work of thinking, organizing, and executing.

Amazon is an example of a company that innovates incrementally but whose accumulated innovation is disruptive. I recently had a conversation with a twenty-three-year-old about the Amazon Kindle. "Do you mean," she asked me, "that Amazon invented the Kindle?" She did not believe me when I told her that Amazon started out as an online bookstore. Merchandise and the Kindle device came some years after its founding. I have on my desk the original Kindle, released on November 19, 2007. It is a clunky little white device with a chicklet keyboard and a goofy roller for moving a cursor that sits to the right of the screen. Lying next to it is my newer waterproof Kindle Paperwhite, backlit, thin, and about half the weight of its older sibling. Incremental devices in between have led to this newer machine. Ten years from now, who knows what they will be producing, but I am pretty sure there will will be an incremental invention that makes it better than either of these two.

Thus far, we have seen that innovation is usually not only the domain of the fringe and outcasts, the product of a genius inventor, invention, or a miraculous breakthrough. All of these can happen, but most often, innovation occurs when people do the hard work of thinking, organizing, and executing. Even what we see today as explosive, disruptive innovation is really the result of hard work and incremental advance. Steve Jobs's new phone did not appear out of thin air. It was the accumulated, incremental innovation of thousands, probably millions, of much smaller discoveries. The silicon chip itself is the product of many innovators. The touchscreen, battery technology, wireless system, the manufacturing processes, and more were all incrementally developed. Jobs, like Ford, put the pieces together and created an entire ecosystem from parts that were creatively spliced into a new whole.

Anybody Can Innovate

I find this encouraging. This revelation means that anybody can innovate if they are willing to be creative and do hard work. There are no special skills, hidden gifts, or certifications required. There are those who walk among us, of course, who see what the rest of us often miss, people like my brother, who are wired to recombine, dream up new things, and invent as if it were a personality trait. For most of us, though, it takes a decision to act. A commitment to innovate. A willingness to make big changes, or small changes that will, over time, create big changes.

Innovation has many sources. It does come from the margins, sometimes. It is the product of the genius inventor, occasionally. Breakthroughs do happen, and they are innovative. But incremental innovation is by far the most promising, the most in reach, and the best bet for most leaders. By trying new things, failing, and trying something else until a solution is found, we innovate. By systematically using our most important muscle, the brain, to do the heavy lifting, we innovate. By seeking the Lord, on our knees, asking for wisdom with a view toward fulfilling the calling He has placed on ministries, we innovate.

There is another part of Jim's story that our family likes to tell. As a young boy, ironically, Jim struggled with math. He almost failed the fourth grade. My mother went to meet with the school principal. He asked my mother if Jim could be put in a "special class" for kids who were lagging behind (which my mother rejected out of hand). Jim could not memorize multiplication tables. Four or five years later, something woke up in him, and he became a math wizard. Ultimately, Jim earned prestigious research awards as a scientist in medical devices. His focus was on frequencies, waves, and how pacemakers could adjust to the heart's changing condition. It was all math. Remembering his early struggles and the premature judgments made against him became all the more meaningful when he proudly presented these awards to my parents, who never lost faith in him.

Who can innovate? I would not count anybody out. We can all innovate. Innovation can happen in your ministry if you are willing to work at it. It is empowering to realize that just about any motivated leader can initiate innovative change. For sure, we are not going to build rockets to take people to Mars, at least not most of us. But starting where God has placed us, we can, like William Carey, stick our finger in a dike. Some us will lead dramatic, disruptive innovation, but we must take initiative to make it happen.

Shoemaker Rule #3 – Be Biased to Action

Innovators are biased to action. Many people are not satisfied with the status quo. But innovators (and innovative ministries) take action to change the situation. William Carey did not just write about the lost in India. He moved his family there to address the situation.

The titans of tech know that action and innovation are correlated. The Kindle eBook reader created by Amazon came out of a culture with a bias to action. Amazon's culture is reinforced by a set of leadership principles, one of which is "Bias to Action." They ask candidates applying for jobs about it. They ask managers about their bias to action in review sessions. They reward action taken when it is the wrong action because failure too often reinforces inaction. They use data but realize that "analysis paralysis" dooms projects to inaction. They want the whole team, well over half a million of them, to be biased to action.

Action can take many forms. It might be big and disruptive. It might be as simple as asking for help. Regardless of its intensity, action breaks the status quo.

Inaction in ministry organizations is created in a myriad ways. The "nice-ness" of Christian ministry may cause somebody to stay silent in a meeting when a critical voice needs to be heard. The way we relate to leaders might include an over-spiritualization of their wisdom, causing us to acquiesce to a bad idea instead of fight. Sometimes ministry structures create inaction by placing problems in somebody else's area of responsibility. Instead of taking action, we shrug our shoulders and let somebody else take care of it.

Before COVID-19, when I was contemplating writing this book, I held a couple focus groups with ministry leaders to ask them about their ministry culture. One question was, "What leads to inaction on your team?" Here are some of the things I heard, distilled down to four summary statements:

- Contentedness, the sense that things are moving forward and there is no need to make change.

- Uncertainty about what to do or ask. Overall lack of direction and empowerment about moving forward.

- A fear of looking inadequate or misinformed by asking the wrong questions or inappropriate questions.

- Problems that lay outside one's job description, leading the person to conclude that it is either not their problem, or that it is inappropriate to comment on or meddle with the issue.

These can be stated in more common ways: "All is well. I am not sure what to do. I don't want to look dumb. It's not my job." Leadership can address each of the four areas. If people are content with the status quo, then the leader needs to help them understand what a better future looks like. If they are uncertain about what action to take, leadership can empower them with a clear view of the team's direction. Social fear means that trust is not healthy on the team. Once again, a leadership issue. Finally, turf wars, silo-ing, and organizational hierarchies are created by leadership. They can be uncreated as well. Inaction flows from how leaders lead. If you desire more innovation in your ministry, develop a bias to action across the ministry team that changes these dynamics.

> If people are content with the status quo, then the leader needs to help them understand what a better future looks like.

How a Bias to Action Becomes Toxic

Having a bias to action does not mean throwing away prayer, thinking, caution, or analysis. The whole next chapter is devoted to a systematic innovation method that requires serious data gathering and analysis. A bias to action means first acting to gain understanding and *then* taking action. It is not a license to run rough-shod over others and implement plans that put the ministry and its effectiveness at risk.

A bias to action becomes toxic when there is a lack of trust and open communication. For leaders, there is a problematic deference to upper level leaders instead of truth-telling. When we see ministry scandal by high level leaders, behaviors that most of us would shun were often overlooked by the team surrounding that leader. The team could not openly and honestly express their views instead choosing to remain silent out of deference to the leader. Consider that if this dynamic is at work on issues of scandal, it is even more at work on less significant issues. It affects the everyday decisions of teams.

In a ministry context, one practice that must be considered is deep reconciliation. This may include revisiting painful events and allowing people to mourn them. Sometimes repentance is called for. In the Old Testament, we see many examples of group repentance as a sign of a true return to God. The story of Ezra is a good example of a leader lamenting and calling for repentance on behalf of the nation. When leaders have a bias to action that passes over or dismisses past hurt, trust is diminished. Innovation requires high levels of trust and thus calls us to a higher standard of trust building as leaders.

Groups can also create incorrect bias to action. The Abilene Paradox explains how leaders who otherwise are smart people, make terrible group decisions. Management guru Jerry Harvey describes a scene in which a family in Coleman, Texas, in the days before air conditioning, discuss their afternoon. They are sitting on the porch in scorching heat, when the father-in-law says, "Let's all go to Abilene!" Nobody wants to go, but nobody wants to throw cold water on the idea. One after another, they positively but guardedly support the proposal, secretly wishing that somebody else will torpedo the idea. Nobody does, and they climb into the car for the hour long drive across the dusty plains, have a mediocre meal, and drive home. Riding along in silence, they are all brooding to themselves about how they wished they had just stayed home. Finally, the mother-in-law breaks the silence and says, "I wish we had all stayed home." One after another, they agree that going was something they never wanted in the first place. Even the father-in-law states that he did not want to go. He suggested it because he thought the others may have wanted to go. As a result, they blame each other for the bad decision and end up in a heated argument.[2]

The way a group develops a bad call to action looks like this:

1. Group members have a private view that they do not share out of an assumption that others do not agree with them.

2. A plan is put forward, often because it is assumed to be the desire of others in the group.

3. Maintaining agreement takes precedence over expressing opposing viewpoints.

4. A poor decision is made, serving nobody in the group.

5. Afterward, blame is assigned to others, leading to future hesitation in suggesting that the group act or execute a plan.

Group decisions in which trust and openness fail from the beginning are most likely to create a ministry culture of inaction. Group decisions require transparency. Leaders who do not create this sort of environment will not get the input necessary for good decisions. Humility, particularly on the part of the leader, goes a long way toward alleviating the problems in the Abilene Paradox. Another important aspect of good group decision-making is an understanding of the personalities and natural tendencies of each team member. I have introduced the concepts behind the Abilene Paradox to teams that I have led. Then, when we are making a decision, I ask the team, "Are we going to Abilene here?" After a few chuckles, there is usually an affirmation that all are on board or we revisit the decision. Innovation requires good team decision-making skills.

Purposeful Incrementalism

The low-hanging fruit for action in innovation is experimentation. Experiments, even very small-scale experiments, create incremental innovation which, over time, creates the large-scale innovation we often dream about. Experiments, comparing two things with a small change between them, highlights the effectiveness of the change. It gives us hard data about the better way forward. While we recognize the importance of experimentation in science quite readily, ministry experimentation is a bit more obscure.

In 2005, while I was working with Pioneers, one of my team members, Jeff Samuelson, was overseeing the recruitment and mobilization of new missionaries. He was looking for ways to increase the effectiveness of his team. Missionary recruitment is a difficult task. The "ask" is to leave behind family, friends, and the familiarity of, well, just about everything, to go to a foreign place. Often, you and your message are not welcome. The best recruiters have been those who have previously served in overseas missions. They are able to tell the stories and challenges of the field to prospective workers. They can also see the weaknesses and strengths of new candidates because they have been there and done that.

This was Jeff's dilemma. Through traditional advertising means, Pioneers had collected a few thousand names of potential missionaries. These were mostly unqualified leads and needed vetting. How could he multiply the workforce to recruit more missionaries when the number of experienced missionaries with the desire and time to do the vetting was a bottleneck?

Jeff and his team looked at data regarding the deployment of missionaries. A window emerged which showed the lag between when a person inquired about service, and when they went. It was about two years. Jeff wondered if that gap was significant and how it might help in discerning how likely a person was to decide to be a missionary. "Let's start asking everybody we talk to if they are students," suggested Jeff, "and if they are, what year they are in right now." They marked this in the database with each call, seeing the results accumulate and testing the hypothesis that they could ferret out high potential candidates. They brainstormed new questions and tested them.

Not every question provided actionable information. But they kept going, and they documented the results. Soon, they had a short list of five questions that accurately identified which people were serious about long-term missionary service, which ones might be in the future if given time, and which ones were most likely to never make it. These questions could be used in conversations at churches, over the phone, or in email. They were designed to be conversational, not at all like a survey.

As Jeff thought about the process, it dawned on him that contrary to how things had been done to date, anybody could ask these short questions. It did not take a seasoned, experienced, missionary. He proposed that a new team be pulled together of volunteers willing to simply ask these five questions, make a note in the database, pray for the person on the other end of the phone, and move on. They marked the correct "next step" in the database as they finalized the call. High potential candidates were reserved for the precious, limited time the qualified missionary recruiters had.

Looking back, most innovation seems obvious. When Jeff took these steps, however, it was controversial. In the ministry culture of our organization, only qualified recruiters with field experience spoke to candidates. This ensured that there was both sufficient recruitment (encouraging the person to take the next step) and screening (making sure only the right people were appointed as missionaries). The idea that anybody could be on the phone doing this was contrary to the carefully constructed system.

At this point innovation was at risk. Within the staff there were questions about the approach. Three influences conspired to make it stick, though. There was a strong value for innovation and leaders provided support for it. The incremental nature of the innovation, testing the questions, trying new ones, and then repeating the process, lent credibility to the process. Results soon began to speak for themselves. Funding was granted to hire the screening team (known as "the phone team" in the early days). Answers to additional questions like, "Have you spoken about your missions interest with your church leadership?" helped honor other organizational values, such as local church involvement. The overall care given to each person was able to grow and the quality of the candidates along with it.

> **Innovations that allow for an initial slow adoption are often more successful than those that require sudden change.**

How innovative was this new system? The average mission agency size in the US is under ten people. Pioneers regularly recruits a few hundred *new* missionaries per year. There are reasons beyond the recruitment process, but the process developed fifteen years ago continues to be a contributor.

Incremental innovation, based on experiments, reduces risk. It gives people time to get on board as changes are introduced slowly over time. Even though the story line is not as exciting as we might hope, being open to change and adapting to what lies before you is a good first step. Innovations that allow for an initial slow adoption are often more successful than those that require sudden change.

I introduced you to RightNow Media in chapter 3. It is the largest distributor of online, Christian teaching materials in the world. It was not always that way. Marty Mosley founded a media ministry after graduating from Liberty University back in the days when Jerry Falwell was a household name. Marty had a heart for missionaries and began traveling the world, documenting their incredible stories on VHS tapes.

When I first met Marty in the mid-2000s, his ministry, Bluefish TV, had shifted from missionary stories to small group, video-based Bible study materials. Bluefish TV was among the largest distributors of church media in the United States. That was back when media either meant television or something you could hold in your hand. They had an impressive marketing group that would reach out to over 300,000 churches per year. I remember listening to one of their staff members call and describe the quality of their Bible study material to the church. Rather than ask for the church to purchase the material on the phone, they sent a box to the church with return postage. One could evaluate the series and then decide to buy. This innovative distribution model drove their growth, along with the highly creative, relevant, and professional video Bible studies with accompanying group discussion guides. They were a ministry that was in a strong growth position and riding high.

In 2009, Marty decided to make room for a younger generation of leaders. His twentysomething-year-old-son, Brian, was full of energy and ideas. They had put together a young leadership team. Marty resigned, and the board of Bluefish TV appointed Brian to lead the ministry. When I heard the news, I was a bit shocked. The ministry was in its prime. Marty, who stayed engaged as a team member rather than a team leader, went out on top. Unlike many leaders, he did not stay past his "sell by" date. When I asked him why he left the top spot when he did, he shrugged with a smile and said, "It was their turn." That was all the explanation I ever got out of him.

That same year, Netflix was still mailing DVDs. They had started streaming services in 2007, but it had not yet caught on. The church market on which Bluefish TV was focused was quite happy to get DVDs. A church youth group meeting in 2009 would use a DVD player hooked up to a television to watch the Bible studies. The business model was prospering, and additional ministries were being launched.

One of them was called RightNow Training. Scott Mosley, Brian's brother, was also on the staff. He was married to a schoolteacher, and she was taking part in online training. "Let's try this with Bible teaching," Scott suggested, and RightNow Training was born. They envisioned a Bible study platform that was fully modifiable. The technical team began working on a platform to stream training. While none of this seems innovative now, let me remind you that it was 2009.

Over the next two years, RightNow Training began to take up more bandwidth from the larger organization. The DVD distribution model, still the cash cow, took resources because the DVDs and workbooks were hard copy materials that required production, storage, postage, and restocking. Brian decided they couldn't afford to keep both in place. They had to decide. Would they become a streaming media company or continue to sell DVDs? In retrospect, we all know the right answer. In 2011, with most of their income generated using DVDs, it was not so clear. But it was the decision Brian and the team made. They pulled the plug on their faithful cash cow and looked to the future. All the various teams were pulled into a new brand and identity: RightNow Media.

They suffered losses for a few months while they reworked the sales team around the new paradigm and ramped up digital resources. Some churches doggedly refused to switch to streaming, and they lost customers. As they digitized and posted new material, things began to pick up. Today, RightNow Media is the largest ministry that delivers streaming Bible teaching on video. The distribution model preserves a core value: that the church should be at the center of local ministry. RightNow Media's primary customer is the church, not individuals. The church makes the service available to its members. The training modules are incorporated into the accounts of each ministry. For churches that want to develop their own training, they can post it to RightNow Media. This can be shared widely or just with their own church.

When I interviewed Brian for this book,[3] I pressed him to show me how RightNow Media was innovative. His humble response was that RightNow Media developed over time. While we like stories in which a singular, heroic figure overcomes all odds to deliver on a personal vision, this is not the typical path for innovation. With each change in the environment, Brian and his team adjusted to meet new challenges. Today they are looking at going global. There is also a possible shift from group to individualized learning as mobile devices continue to displace larger screens. I have no doubt that RightNow Media will continue to adapt, incrementally innovating as they go. They have it in their DNA.

Incremental innovation is not always possible. In 1967, Sweden changed from being a right-hand drive country, to a left-hand drive country. Decisions like that must be made all at once. RightNow Media had to make a jump to the online world. Their story is one that should give every innovator hope. They experimented with training, saw the future, and then pulled the plug on the old model.

Intentional Experiments

Experimentation is the partner of incremental innovation. Testing, adapting, and adding process improvements are the bread and butter of major tech firms. Experimentation in the business world has, for the past few decades, centered on big data. In fact, big data has taken over from the scientific method as the preferred means of experimentation.

Science has emphasized systematic observation, the identification and isolation of variables, changing those variables in controlled settings, and then observing once again. Changes either support or deny the validity of a hypothesis. The scientific method allows us to test *theories*. Unfortunately, *real life* is different. Running scientific experiments in a social or human system is difficult. Isolating and controlling variables when people are in the mix is complicated. There are ethical questions at stake and people do not take kindly to being a test subject. Or do they? You may be surprised to learn that you take part in hundreds of experiments each day, using big data approaches.

In 2008, *Wired* magazine wrote an article that set the scientific world on edge. The title was "The End of Theory: The Data Deluge Makes the Scientific Method Obsolete."[4] It brought out into the open a discussion that data scientists had been discussing behind closed doors. Because we now have so much accumulated data, we can short-circuit the scientific method and learn directly from real life interaction.

Imagine the amounts of data about human behavior that a company like Google has. It is truly mind-boggling. Unless you take extreme measures, tech companies know all the basics about you and most of the particulars as well. It is not just Google. Microsoft, Facebook, Apple, and Amazon are in on things as well. Any of these tech companies can sift through their databases and discover who we are, our habits, our choices, our politics, and just about anything else they want to know. All without ever running a single, testable hypothesis through the scientific method.

Ministry leaders can begin thinking about big data right now. The steps to utilizing it are simple: gather, analyze, act on it.

For the social sciences in particular, big data mining is a gold mine of information.

The proponents of the scientific method have not gone away quietly. They insist that correlation is not causation. But for much of what we want to know, we do not need scientific experiments. If we see everybody buying gym equipment after January 1, we cannot scientifically prove that New Year's resolutions result in new spending habits. But if we are selling gym equipment, so what? We are never going to be Google, but ministry leaders can begin thinking about big data right now. The steps to utilizing it are simple: gather, analyze, act on it.

Gathering data is often as simple as asking for it. At Missio Nexus, we conduct dozens of surveys each year. We survey organizations about compensation (we publish an annual compensation survey for ministry leaders), what fundraising is working and what is not, how ministries adapt to challenges like a pandemic, the racial makeup of our members, and so on. Most of these are freely available to our members for their own data awareness. But our staff also utilizes them to make decisions. In the next chapter you will learn about personas, descriptions of our primary stakeholders. These were developed in part by looking at data.

The sources of data collection can be quite unusual. I maintain a list of ministry CEOs and each month publish a "CEO Only" newsletter. This is one of the most important touchpoints we have with a primary constituent, maybe our most important "customer." I send it direct from my own email address so that these leaders can easily hit reply if they want to offer feedback or ask me any questions. One month I was asked, "How often do CEOs travel?" We had never conducted a survey on this topic. I then realized that I had a great way to use live data to find the answer.

Each month my CEO newsletters generate a fair number of out of office notifications. I began counting these replies and adding them to a spreadsheet. I can tell you which months are best to hold CEO events and which months should be avoided. I have a solid statistic on how much of the time an average CEO from Missio Nexus is on the road. They spend just under 40 percent of their time traveling. One way I knew that COVID-19 was impacting our membership was when, in April of 2020, that number dropped to almost 0 percent. Over the next few months, there were almost no traveling CEOs.

List your stakeholders to determine what data you should be collecting from them on an ongoing basis. Congregants, congregants that give, funders, and people in your community are all potential sources of data that can drive innovation. Financial tracking is ripe for data analytics because they usually represent the most complete data sets in your ministry. Sometimes, connecting data sets transforms your understanding of the data you have. I once mapped the churches in our missionary agency that gave to missionaries against a data set that held the size of the congregation. This showed that churches tend to be more generous to missionaries per capita as they grew to about 1,200 people and then it decreased. Churches in the 4,000 and up range give the least per congregant, even less than very small churches. What data do you have that, when connected to other data, suddenly becomes actionable? Do not fall into the trap of thinking that analytics is only for your website. Analyzing data can be a difficult task, particularly if you do not have a large data set. In an increasingly technical world, leaders need to be trained on how to ferret out and utilize data. Presenting the findings is also important, with dashboards (summarized views of ongoing processes) being a helpful way to communicate. One way to identify what type of data to collect and analyze is to draw a dashboard that represents your "dream dashboard." How do you work backwards to collect that information?

A few simple principles for data collection will make the results more accessible for analysis later. Use the same tool as much as you can for all data collection. Most ministries have databases of members, a different system for financial records, spreadsheets, and contact lists on mobile devices. Customer Relationship Management software platforms like Salesforce like to say that they become the "one source of truth." In managing data sets, having one repository is important. If you collect data in different buckets, you will forever be trying to stitch them back together to find connecting points.

Another principle is that all data should be timestamped for future comparison. When people ask me, for example, if COVID-19 affected the number of missionaries deployed, I would need to compare data across years to come up with an answer. Regularly snapshotting data helps with this. For comparative data, make sure that you do not change the questions being asked if it can be helped. Changing questions makes comparison impossible.

For digital outreach via the Internet, there is a wide array of experiments that can be conducted. A/B testing, in which a variation between two pieces of communication are contrasted, is an example. It is astonishing to watch how different webpages, displaying the same information, can garner significant results. In fact, each time you do an Internet search, the tech giants are doing experiments so subtle that you usually cannot identify them. With every search, they are collecting data on what you like and what you pass over.

Stefan Thomke, in the book *Experimentation Works*, recounts how a Microsoft employee changed the length of the title in a listing of search results. The experiment resulted in a net increase in sales of 12 percent for the ads associated with the longer titles. Longer titles meant that the results showed up in more searches because there were more words and thus more likelihood that the article would satisfy a search. This amounted to an additional one hundred million in annual revenue for Microsoft.[5] Not a bad discovery.

Have you ever seen the little happy and sad faces that are buttons that you can press that are often located in airports? These "smile kiosks" are also nonscientific data collection points. But they work. They alert staff to potential problems like long waits, customer service issues, or how well a doctor informs a patient about their care. Because they are simple and take two to three seconds to consider and vote, they work. Simple and human-centric.

Leaders like data. It makes them feel like their decisions are on firm ground. We should be cautious, though, in thinking that data is the only driver for decisions. Data, particularly big data, gives leaders a sense of confidence but it has limitations. Limitations are any restrictions on how we collect data. The methodology almost always affects how we understand that data.

All research has limitations and knowing them makes our use of the data more appropriate. The presidential polling of the past decade should alert us to this fact. Big changes in society (like smartphones and television viewing habits) have undercut pollsters' ability to provide us with accurate predictions of elections. Being aware of limitations does not undercut the importance of data, but it might undercut your interpretation of it. Data is almost always incomplete. Researchers are biased. Analytics are often done with an end goal in mind, rather than simply letting the data tell the story.

Because ministry is people-focused, we need to develop empathy.

Fortunately, empathy is at the heart of a revolution in innovation called "design thinking." That is where we head next.

Summary

There are many assumptions about the nature of innovation, and it comes from many different sources and people. If we stop thinking of innovation through these assumptions, we realize that anybody can innovate. It is not only the domain of the super-creative, the genius, or the breakthrough discovery. Often, innovation is incremental and discovered over time. Encouraging experimentation will unleash innovation that, over time, becomes significant.

APPLICATION & DISCUSSION

Questions to Ponder

1. Of the four assumptions about innovation (innovation comes from the margins, innovation comes from a genius inventor, innovation is invention, or innovation requires a breakthrough discovery) which has influenced your thinking on innovation the most?

2. Do you consider yourself to be an innovator? Why or why not?

3. Can you think of any innovations that are in your ministry because of learning over time?

4. How often do you purposefully make changes in your ministry to test them out? Can you give an example?

TEAM EXERCISE & DISCUSSION

Homework:

Ask each team member to write down an answer to the following question: "When I consider whether or not our ministry has a bias for action, I think we (are OR are not) biased to action. An example I would give to illustrate this is _____."

Facilitated Discussion:

1. As a team discuss how hard data informs the decisions that you make as a ministry.

2. Discuss whether most frontline workers in the organization take action when a situation may lie outside of their clear

area of responsibility. Are there examples? What implications does this have about a bias to action in the ministry's culture?

3. Can members of the team identify any issues or problems that have existed for longer than they should? If so, why are those problems present and how does this affect mission fulfillment?

4. Discuss how free people are in the organization to experiment and test out new ways of working, ideas, or processes.

5

EMPATHIZE,
THEN STRATEGIZE

When we honestly ask ourselves which person in our lives mean the most to us,
we often find that it is those who, instead of giving advice, solutions, or cures,
have chosen rather to share our pain and touch our wounds with a warm
and tender hand.[1]

HENRI NOUWEN

For we do not have a great high priest who is unable to sympathize with our
weaknesses, but one who in every respect has been tempted as we are,
yet without sin.

HEBREWS 4:15

As a missionary who has visited many countries, I have learned that Jesus is the best way to open any conversation about spiritual things, regardless of the person's background. They might be from a religion hostile to Christianity, like Islam. They might be secular, completely indifferent and with no interest. They might be ethnically tied to a religion like Hinduism. They can be Buddhists, void of the concept of beginning and end. It does not matter. The reason? Because when you talk about Jesus, you talk about an empathetic leader and everybody loves an empathetic leader.

133

JESUS, OUR EMPATHETIC LEADER

The incarnation itself is an act of empathy. God becoming a man. Jesus moved to tears by the mourning over Lazarus's death. Jesus suffering as we feel suffering. He was one of us, not an out-of-touch elite who was above His followers. Empathy is an avenue into the hearts of people unlike any other. It creates understanding.

Innovation and empathy walk hand-in-hand. When seeking solutions for the problems that people face, we must begin by understanding the problem. A failure to do so at the outset creates a cascading chain of failure. As we build the wrong things, our hopes, investment, and expectations for it being the right thing compound like interest. By putting empathy at the beginning of our innovation we create understanding. This opens the door for solutions that meet real needs.

Unfortunately, as we have seen already, ministries that have developed a solution double-down on that solution even if it is no longer serving the needs of the stakeholders. Like people, organizations and ministries often see themselves as what they do. This leads to exchanging the mission for the way you accomplish this mission. Do not underestimate the power of your ministry's methods to blind you to its mission. The original founder's solution was highly innovative and met a need *when it was launched*. Empathy building is not explaining that methodology to a new audience. It is understanding the new audience in a way that drives new solutions. My experience is that when faced with disruptive change, ministries revert to what they know best. This cycle becomes self-defeating. A powerful way to break that cycle is by understanding deeply the people whom you serve. This is empathy.

I enjoy the television series, *Undercover Boss*. The plot is almost always the same. The CEO goes undercover and becomes a frontline worker. They wear a wig, dye their hair, grow a moustache, or obscure their identity in some other way. When they show up for work, they are greeted by one of their own employees whose job it is to orient them to the ways of the company. Most often, they are doing menial labor. Why do we so enjoy seeing the boss do menial labor?

The CEO may discover that the employees must supplement meager tools with their own paychecks because not enough or the wrong things are provided. They might find out how ineffective corporate training programs are. They may be surprised to discover that safety measures are inadequate or simply ignored. They observe how sales are done, food is cooked, products are displayed, buildings are maintained, and many other aspects of the business. One hundred percent of the time, they are shocked by what they learn.

This education extends to the domain of the employees as well. Like all people, they suffer from medical challenges, debt, divorce, a lack of education, missing rent payments, and so much more. They aspire and dream for a better life. They have ideas for how the business can be better managed. Many seek promotion and want to be leaders. Of course, at the end of the show, the disguise comes off. It is now time for the employees to be shocked. The wealthy CEO solves many of their problems by writing checks, handing out promotions, and ordering up changes. Sometimes, they even make serious course corrections for the whole firm.

This is empathy building. By dropping down to where the "little people" live, the big-time CEO sees what he could not see from his corner office. The problem, of course, is that the boss should not need to go underground to develop this kind of empathy. Do not be too harsh on these bosses; at least they are trying. This is a challenge that all leaders face. The higher up the food chain we go, the farther down we must reach to understand the grassroots. This is not just a leadership issue anymore, either, but organization wide. Specialization creates silos, which makes it difficult to see the big picture. Turf wars, played out with smiles and niceties, affect ministries no differently than secular companies. Like *Undercover Boss*, understanding can be created by having staff work in other departments. This is an exercise in empathy, helping employees see the work through somebody else's eyes.

Stakeholders each have their own perspective and need to be understood. You should make an online donation to your own church or organization sometime. What is the process like? How does it communicate thankfulness? What can we do to make it better? Only by walking through the process, becoming a donor, can you fully understand what a giver's experience is like. This is empathy building.

Why is the *Undercover Boss* story line so compelling to us? Because we all have worked in organizations with leadership who are not empathetic. They treat us as a means to an end. Seeing the hierarchy leveled feels good but more importantly, everybody likes to be understood. Empathy is understanding.

Shoemaker Rule #4: Empathize, then Strategize

Empathy drives and informs innovation. When leaders discover the conditions under which stakeholders labor, they identify problems. I have observed leaders who have not taken a donor call or visited with a potential missionary candidate, gone out to dinner with a congregant, done a hospital visit, or any number of simple things that should be happening in our ministries all the time.

In the 1990s, a way of thinking about problem-solving was called *design thinking*. It laid out a simple system for how to create products that serve the needs of the person buying that product. Design thinking as a discipline that has grown since that time and is perhaps the dominant form of innovative product development in the business world. It has expanded past physical products to include services, training, events, and processes.

Design thinking is considered by many to be among the most transformative approaches to innovation we have today. What is exciting for ministry leaders is that design thinking can be used to create innovation in churches, Christian organizations, schools, or just about any kind of ministry you can imagine. In this chapter you will get a very brief overview of design thinking. As you read, keep in mind that this innovation framework offers as much as you put into it. Do not let this brief introduction inoculate you to the possibilities it provides.

Rob Wassel, a leader at my former employer, Pioneers, is the founder of the Seeds Global Innovation Lab (Seeds). Seeds utilizes design thinking to help ministries think through next-level innovation. Their vision is to equip the global missions community (as well as churches and businesses) for the emerging world. Rob and his team have visited innovation labs in corporations across North America. What they have found is that design thinking, while it has permeated the business world, has hardly touched ministries. Working within Pioneers and across the spectrum of churches, foundations, agencies, and other ministries, Seeds gives organizations a common definition and language and mindset for innovation.

Innovation teams in corporations often use design thinking to initiate innovation. They may send that team out to troubleshoot and innovate when a product, process, or service is not working well. An airline, for example, discovered a problem in their cargo delivery system. They dispatched their innovation team who used design thinking to change the process. That is not how Seeds works. Instead, Seeds focuses on training your team to employ design thinking so that you can develop a culture of innovation, as well as facilitating your team through design projects. Their philosophy is that innovation needs to be embedded throughout the ministry, and not simply be a project that is run by people in a lab that are disconnected from the end user. Both approaches are valid but the outcomes are different depending on the organization's structure and leadership framework.

When Rob first conceived Seeds, he thought that projects would be at the center of the work. However, as he and his team innovated on their own model, they realized that an innovative ministry culture was a better outcome for decentralized ministries. They still conduct project-focused innovation labs, but more often they are also passing on the potential of design thinking through virtual and face-to-face courses.

Seeds is not the only innovation lab that ministries are utilizing today. In most cases, however, design thinking is the primary activity. In my research, I have concluded that a subset of design thinking, called *service design* is perhaps a tighter fit for ministries to consider. Service design suggests that product development is different enough from designing services that a separate approach should be considered. However, on a practical level, there are few differences between design thinking and service design.

Design Thinking

Design thinking is an innovation process with five stages:

THE FIVE STAGES OF DESIGN THINKING

Step 1: Empathize

The foundation of design thinking, and where much of the innovation occurs, is in this first stage, empathize. Empathizing helps overcome the problems that the innovator's dilemma creates. If you recall, when we develop a solution to a problem, we organize around that solution. We create rules and policies to make it more efficient and effective. We hire with that solution in mind and we develop systems to support that solution. When the environment changes, we have a ministry designed around a solution instead of the problems found in the new environment. Empathizing with the people whom we are serving takes our focus off the solution we are perfecting and reframes our thinking. We are put back into the original state we were in when we started: creating a solution to a problem that our stakeholders care about.

Numerous innovation experts have told me that the biggest problem ministries face in implementing an innovation ethos is not understanding how design thinking helps them. Rather, it is an unwillingness to let go of the status quo. Because many of us were influenced by the history and tradition of the ministry, we assume that others will be as well. It is a dynamic that I call, "Believing in your own brochure." It is important to be committed to the mission and vision of our ministries. It is also important to see them through

> The biggest problem ministries face in implementing an innovation ethos . . . is an unwillingness to let go of the status quo.

the eyes of those we seek to have join in that mission. Empathy building includes setting aside our assumptions about the current situation and seeing them from a fresh, stakeholder-infused perspective. It is hard work.

For ministry leaders there are many ways to increase our empathy. Subject matter experts (SMEs) are people with specific knowledge about your ministry area. An SME can assist your leadership team in teasing out assumptions you might have about the topic you are studying. Examples in the ministry space of SMEs are research firms, church growth and development experts, and consultants. Always remember that when you use a consultant, they carry their own biases into the project. Your goal is to empathize with your stakeholders, not with the consultant.

Identifying the stakeholders is key. The seeker-sensitive movement, led by Willow Creek, saw the unchurched in their community as the primary stakeholder in their future. They redesigned the church around this person. I understand the theological objections to this, as well as the evaluation of the long-term effects this has had on discipleship. Yet, Willow Creek identified its stakeholders and was committed to understanding and designing services around them. This sort of intentionality is what leaders need to consider as they seek to innovate.

Perhaps you have identified low-income tenants in a difficult neighborhood to be your primary stakeholder. You want to understand their situation so that your church or organization can serve them better. You face many obstacles in getting real, firsthand information about this group's perspective. There will be cultural issues, economic factors, historical challenges, and many other factors limiting trust. To fully understand this sort of situation, you may need to do what Jesus did and move in. Spend time listening to and developing empathy from the inside out. Involving them in the process from the very beginning, allowing them to innovate on the solution, will make your innovation that much more relevant.

Make a list of all stakeholders. Consider the problem you are considering tackling from each of their perspectives. Funders have different objectives from those utilizing a service. Congregants are different from those outside of the church. Administrative staff have a different agenda. By mapping out the stakeholders early on, a greater understanding of the problem emerges.

Other, more formal methods of data collection are interviews, focus groups, surveys, and direct observation. All can play a role in developing empathy.

Personas are a powerful tool for building empathy. The first leader that I personally observed using a persona to communicate how to design ministry was Rick Warren. "Saddleback Sam" was the prototypical resident of southern Orange County, California. Saddleback Sam described who Saddleback Church was seeking to reach. Saddleback Sam is a well-educated male who loves both his job and his community. He is white-collar, skeptical of religion, prefers the informal over the formal, and prefers large groups over small ones. At a conference I attended when Warren's book, *The Purpose Driven Church*, was first published, Saddleback Sam's various attributes were described in detail. Warren then connected those details with specific elements of their ministry. Saddleback Sam was informal. So, Rick Warren wore Hawaiian shirts when he preached. Saddleback Sam liked to "test" church anonymously. So, nobody pressed a newcomer for their name or contact information.

This is how a persona can be translated into pragmatic ministry.

Since those days, plenty of critics have come along, critical of Warren for Saddleback Sam. The point here is that personas help us visualize who we are serving. They create empathy. Missio Nexus has developed a set of personas to represent different stakeholders. One of them, for example, is the CEO. Here is how we have broken down this persona:

Persona	My Goal: I want to lead my organization well.		Resources Most Used
	Demographics **Average Age:** 50s **Gender:** M – 90%+	**What I Need from You** Keep me informed of things and people I should know to lead my organization.	• CEO Monthly • CEO Retreat • OnBoard • Book stream • Podcast • Research • Mission Leaders Conference
CEO	**Key Attributes** • Learning on the go • Travel-heavy schedule • Considers their situation or organization unique	**Common Tasks at MissioNexus.com** • Register and attend a face-to-face event • Register and attend a webinar	**Pain Points to Consider** • Limited time • Fundraising for the organization • Sustainability issues

Each of the boxes notes things that we need to be aware of as we develop services for them. For example, a chief pain point for a CEO is *limited time*. When we create material for CEOs, we are sure to include summaries and shortcuts so that they can quickly digest the information. I write a monthly CEO email, and I write it direct from my inbox, without using a mailing list company. This way, CEOs never have to search for my contact information. They have it each month and can easily reach out to me by hitting "Reply." Did I come up with this solution? No, one of my board members, a CEO receiving the letter, suggested it.

In our case, we have defined several important personas (church mission leader, primary administrator, office staff of an agency, field staff of an agency, and mission educator). We seek to drive our offerings based on these personas, with each having unique offerings.

A board member once asked, "Why aren't our personas more diverse?" The assumption was that if we want more diversity, we should have more diversity represented in the personas we use. This question led to some long discussions about how we use personas. Rick Warren used Saddleback Sam because he wanted to draw him into his church. Before designing services, we had better understand not only our current "customer" but also the persona that God is asking us to consider in the future.

Empathy mapping is another method for understanding stakeholders. Typically, four quadrants are labeled with the terms, "Says, Does, Thinks, Feels." People participating in the exercise use notes to add to the map until a picture of the persona begins to reveal itself. They help with understanding the motivations, desires, and pain points that a stakeholder may have.

Before we develop strategy, we must develop empathy.

A "journey map" or an "experience map" is an important component of service design. Imagine you are designing a service for a newcomer to your church. What do they see from the street before they come in? How are they welcomed (if at all)? As they roam through the building, what images are evoking reactions in their hearts and minds? By mapping this journey through the perspective of an outsider, you can design a new experience that delights them.

Of the five steps in design thinking, the most important step is the empathy building. Understanding who you are serving will make the other four steps more accurate, more relevant, and more likely to yield innovative breakthroughs. It takes effort to build empathy, and even more effort if one has well-established assumptions that must be discarded as new understanding is developed. Leaders who see themselves as experts about their own ministries are particularly vulnerable to this dynamic. Before we develop strategy, we must develop empathy.

Step 2: Define

After you have a good handle on whom you are serving, you can develop a problem statement. These statements, sometimes posed as questions, lead to strategy. Defining the problem is not as easy as one might think. When starting a design thinking process, one must be open to the real problem being different than the assumed issue at the outset. That is why some innovators like to say that this stage is "refining the problem," instead of defining it.

One way to refine your understanding of a problem is to reframe it as a question. Perhaps your church has noticed a disturbing trend. New people sometimes come to weekly worship services but never join small groups. You started an empathy gathering project and surveys have revealed something interesting. Newcomers that do not join a small group within four months of their first visit never join a small group. Instead of seeing the problem as "Many newcomers never join small groups," you can reframe it with your new data. "What if we designed a newcomers' onboarding process that helps them join a small group within four months of their first visit?" This has taken a problem and defined an innovative path forward.

Missio Nexus, as an association, is made up of members supporting and leading causes within a broad definition of the Great Commission. A leader may write to me and ask, "I would like to develop a network around reaching children in unreached people groups. Can you help me?" Too often, our response was vague and impractical, even though we were sitting on perhaps the largest database of missionary contacts in the world. I began to formulate some ways we could meet this need.

At a board meeting I opened a conversation about the problem. Board members listened and then began to ask questions about the proposal. From my perspective as an insider, I felt I was answering these questions adequately, but I could sense growing confusion in the room. I described a data system that allowed leaders of causes to connect with members. Online forums. Event support and other services designed to help these leaders. But it was coming across like a big mushy mess of initiatives with no overall coherent strategy. It was, in fact, a big mushy mess of initiatives with no overall coherent strategy. That is where outside groups, like boards, help to define problems. I knew there was a problem worth solving, but I could not yet define it well enough to create the solutions needed.

Refining your problem includes dealing with the realities of your situation. If you have no budget, then the solution will be different than if you have a pile of cash to spend. In research, any constraints are called limitations. Your project no doubt has limitations to consider. These may be money, time, staff resources, or the culture of your ministry. As mentioned earlier in this book, there is a time for "blue ocean" strategy where you think outside the realm of current realities. This is not how innovation works using the design thinking paradigm. If you are designing an event, the date of the event could be a limitation that shapes the solutions you derive. Prayerfully consider these issues and make sure your team understands them. Failure to do so will waste time in the long run.

Step 3: Ideate

The image of an empty whiteboard and a box of markers comes to mind. For extroverts, this is the fun stage. Whereas traditional whiteboarding means to let any idea flow, in design thinking, we have set the stage; it will be informed by the work we have already done. The list of stakeholders, personas, empathy maps, limitations, and other tools should always be informing the ideation stage. Put the problem as you have defined it on the whiteboard first and then review all the collected material.

Ideation in a group happens best when the environment is conducive to open sharing based on the data. Remember that innovation can come from anybody. If you can recruit stakeholders to assist in this stage, the outcomes will more closely match their needs. Be careful about letting senior leaders drive the conversation as others will submit to their ideas. Subject matter experts can also be problematic if the rest of the group looks to them for answers. There should be plenty of space to write, walk, and converse during ideation. The facilitator needs to make sure that the focus stays on the problem and does not bog down. This requires redirection at times, reminding people of the various stakeholders, constraints, and other pieces of information. At some point, as major solution sets begin to evolve, the facilitator can lead the group toward more specific definition of the solution.

One popular methodology for the ideate stage uses the acronym SCAMPER[2]. Keeping in mind the targets of ideas, services, products, or processes, you can:

- Substitute one of them for another
- Combine two of them in a novel way
- Adapt one of them for a new use
- Modify one of them
- Put one of them to a use other than its current use
- Eliminate one of them
- Reverse two of them

Suppose, for example, you were seeking to innovate on something small, like how you thank the speakers who were at your recent conference. You have been sending an honorarium check to them in the mail along with a thank you note. Could you substitute this for something else? Perhaps, instead of an honorarium, you send them a high-end microphone for use in online meetings (Missio Nexus did this very thing and were amazed at the positive response). Perhaps you send them a less expensive gift, combined with a slightly smaller honorarium. This is a small example but shows how elements can be reconsidered in new ways for an innovative service touch.

Design thinking facilitators can use any number of strategies for collecting the results as they develop. These may include Post-it Notes, bulleted lists, different voting schemes, and other creative methods. The group can rank ideas by popularity, relevance, and other attributes. The group can get loud and raucous as ideas emerge. The goal is to walk away with a tangible innovation that can be tested via prototyping.

Step 4: Prototype

When Missio Nexus was formed in 2012, it was through a merger of two historic mission associations. The leadership decided that they would shift the model of the association from a trade association (representing the organizations, with a goal to create a healthy industry) to a professional association (representing individuals, with a goal to advance their careers and effectiveness as employees). Included in this shift was a leap to a new financial model, favoring church and individual memberships over organizational memberships. The goal was to broaden the membership through growth into sectors that were not a part of either of the two former associations.

> It is far better to test new ministry models before making a leap, ensuring that the innovation will be effective.

It was a leap of faith that took considerable courage to enact. Unfortunately, it did not work out quite as expected. The less expensive memberships did not produce the growth that had been hoped for. The reduced organizational fees did not produce the income necessary for continued operation. While some of the program enjoyed a healthy bump in size from the previous era, the economic model was not working. When I took over leadership in 2015, we turned back these changes about halfway. We raised organizational dues, but not to the former levels. We continued with individual memberships but charged more for them. Within a few years, the financial model was working again.

The changes that had been initially implemented were experimentation on a grand scale. It was risky and bold. In hindsight, prototyping the new model first could have saved some pain. It is far better to test new ministry models before making a leap, ensuring that the innovation will be effective. Prototyping gives the opportunity for course correction at minimal cost.

Ministry prototyping can take many forms. New service offerings can be run on a short-term basis, tested, adjusted, and retested. Different ways of giving, new missionary models, approaches to team leadership, and digital approaches to ministry can be prototypes. It can be applied to just about any size project. In the context of a formal design thinking lab, wireframing, process diagrams, storyboarding, physical models, and sometimes games contribute to the prototyping stage.

At each stage in the design thinking flow, one can revert to an earlier stage. Design thinking processes are often drawn showing arrows pointing back to earlier stages. If prototypes are considered unfeasible for any reason, the team may go back to the ideate stage. If there are issues in understanding the problem, a return to more empathy gathering may be in order.

Step 5: Test

When I held my first position at Pioneers, I was eager to try something new to fund overseas ministry. I proposed a giving catalog, like the annual catalogs that relief and development organizations often use. This time, though, we would highlight field projects for missionaries. I worked with the communications team and a catalog was developed. With an example in hand, I asked my boss to fund shipping them out to all donors. At the time, that was some tens of thousands. "No," he wisely replied, "let's run a test first." We printed about five thousand catalogs and distributed them to donors. It raised less than $1,000 in total, a loss of about $15,000. I was disappointed, but much less so than if we had sent them to all donors. This is failing in a way that does not devastate.

User testing precedes a product, process, or service launch. Projects tend to gain additional empathy at this stage, which may lead to another return to ideation or another step in the process. While the best tests are with near-final outcomes, holding lightly to the proposed solution is important. Testing formats include direct observation of a person using the proposed innovation, after-action feedback, success via measured actions taken (for example, did the person take the next action step), and delayed follow-up (used to test how well something was understood and remembered). For digital products there are testing services, companies that will do the testing for you. They can set up the test and systematically record how the testers use it or perceive it. Concept testing, very applicable in a ministry setting, puts the concept in front of a prequalified audience.

If you are looking for a practical means of innovating in your ministry, design thinking provides an easily accessible framework. If you can diffuse these ideas through the church or organization, better yet. Imagine what your ministry might look like if all your staff were constantly innovating in their service area. From administrative staff to those discipling, mentoring, and teaching, there is always room for more innovation.

WILL IT WORK IN MY MINISTRY?

When Helping Hurts,[3] by Brian Fikkert and Steve Corbett, has helped thousands of leaders understand poverty from a new perspective. I recently called Brian[4] to ask him about how he developed the innovative ideas behind the book, which starts with a big, important question: "How do we understand poverty?" He explained to me that as a young man he heard different worldviews in the answers to this question. The economists he had studied said that people were material beings, so their solutions to poverty were primarily material in nature. (Brian was himself a professor of economics at Maryland University.) They essentially left out the spiritual nature of human beings. When Brian asked church leaders about poverty, a standard answer was that sin affected their situation and they needed to repent. Brian didn't believe either perspective got at the complexity of the problem, which gave birth to his quest to address poverty from a more holistic perspective.

Moving to a role at Covenant College, he joined a community that emphasized the kingdom of God. The kingdom sweeps up both the material and spiritual. An organization was launched to help churches develop a more complete view of poverty based on the whole person and their network of relationships. The Chalmers Center was created to diffuse this innovative approach to the broader church, both at home and abroad.

I described to Brian the outline of this book. He lit up when I mentioned design thinking. Even though I was trying to get him to explain the past innovation he has initiated, he was overflowing with joy about the current innovation projects he is focused on. The Chalmers Center has taken the five-step approach, created an innovation team, and is using these ideas to further transform communities.

He told me about members of a very poor church in Togo, West Africa, the seat of the voodoo religion. The Chalmers Center ran a simplified design thinking process with the church members. As these extremely poor Christians listened to the people in the village, they began to see their communities' biggest problems through their eyes. One challenge to the quality of life in the village was unmaintained roads. The group ideated on how they could contribute, then they dug a few holes, replaced some dirt, and prototyped a means of addressing the problem. They were soon rebuilding larger swaths of the road system. Soon the whole village came out and pitched in to help. A witch doctor from a neighboring village saw what was happening and offered the church members land in his village so they could plant a church there.

This is how design thinking can help ministries innovate around real problems to spread Christ's kingdom.

If you are still convinced that design thinking is a business methodology and not a ministry methodology, consider Community Bible Study. Their international director, Keith Sparzak, planned on attending an innovation lab shortly before the COVID-19 pandemic hit. Impressed by what he told his team about the lab, four members of the senior management team decided to go through the week-long course together with him. The experience was so positive for all five that the decision was made to put an additional dozen department directors and key leaders through the course. From the senior management's perspective, the expense of doing so was well worth the return on investment. For everyone in the ministry to have a common language and understanding of how to think about innovation—to create a culture of innovation—was deemed critical for the long-term viability of Community Bible Study.

When the pandemic struck, their ministry was particularly challenged. Community Bible Study gathers groups of people to study the Bible. They had 680 groups, meeting face-to-face. They were a forty-five-year-old organization who had never thought about online, virtual Bible study. As far as they knew, there never had been a group that met virtually through their ministry. It was antithetical to the view of how life transformation works. It was what is called a paradigm shift. Within weeks, using the newly instilled commitment to innovation, they converted all but a couple of these groups to online Bible study groups.

One might think, "The whole world went online; that is not innovative," and I think that is fair. However, the speed and the means of launching this internal revolution *was* innovative. Keith told me, "Our goal was to birth and nurture a culture of innovation. Then COVID-19 happened. It was the test that pushed us to use these new tools."[5] Now, Community Bible Study is using design thinking in other ways, including a project that will enable them to globalize their offerings in a way that honors and better serves indigenous cultures. They also have recently developed and launched a project for oral learners, which is already seeing significant success.

Summary

Empathy is the cornerstone of innovation. It makes it possible for us to envision the problems that need innovation. Ministries often sabotage their own ability to problem-solve by seeing the situation through status quo solutions. Design thinking is a step-by-step system for innovating on products, processes, and services. The five steps are empathy building, defining the problem, ideating about solutions, prototyping solutions, and testing solutions.

APPLICATION & DISCUSSION

Questions to Ponder

1. Can you describe a time when your organization was not understanding a problem that you saw?

2. What are some examples of personas that might help you and your team understand your stakeholders?

3. Can you explain the difference between design thinking and a meeting called to whiteboard an innovative idea?

4. What problem in your ministry do you think would be a good candidate for a design thinking process and why?

5. Can you think of any projects that have failed in your ministry that might have gone differently if there had been more empathy gathering before launching?

TEAM EXERCISE & DISCUSSION

Homework:

Even though your ministry probably has many stakeholders, ask each team member to list who they think is the most important stakeholder and why. Have them bring this answer to the discussion.

Facilitated Discussion:

1. Have each team member share who they think is the primary stakeholder for the ministry and why.

2. List the stakeholders on a whiteboard and ask the group to prioritize the list, keeping your mission statement in the foreground of the discussion.

3. Discuss how well you think the team understands the primary stakeholders you have defined. What sort of research might be necessary to understand them better and why?

4. Create a specific plan to empathize with your stakeholders.

6

THINK BIG

Some problems are so complex that you have to be highly intelligent and well informed just to be undecided about them.[1]

LAURENCE J. PETER

And Jesus rebuked the demon, and it came out of him, and the boy was healed instantly. Then the disciples came to Jesus privately and said, "Why could we not cast it out?" He said to them, "Because of your little faith. For truly, I say to you, if you have faith like a grain of mustard seed, you will say to this mountain, 'Move from here to there,' and it will move, and nothing will be impossible for you."

MATTHEW 17:18–20

The first time I heard the phrase "wicked problem" I assumed it referred to problems with an evil root. Things like human trafficking and drug addiction naturally come to mind. But then I learned that academics use "wicked problem" in an entirely different way. Wicked problems are, simply put, problems that are extremely difficult to solve.

These are such things as racism, environmental issues, poverty, equality, political division, and so on. Human systems are typically more prone to being considered "wicked problems" than nonmaterial systems that engineers seek to solve. Often, a solution to one part of the problem creates other problems elsewhere.

In the realm of the Great Commission, we have gigantic, wicked problems that are going mostly unsolved. These problems will continue to go unsolved unless the church can invent, innovate, and collaborate in unprecedented ways. It is, in my view, highly unlikely that this will happen without a serious kick to our collective creative pants.

WHAT IS A WICKED PROBLEM?

The phrase "wicked problem" first appeared in sociological literature in the late 1960s. C. W. Churchman wrote in the *Journal of Management Science* that wicked problems "are ill-formulated, where the information is confusing, where there are many clients and decision makers with conflicting values, and where the ramifications in the whole system are thoroughly confusing."[2]

For our purposes, we will consider issues in the Great Commission to be "wicked problems" when they meet this criteria:

1. Difficult to define, including incomplete or contradictory data

2. Multiple stakeholders, often with conflicting or competing agendas

3. Numerous root causes that must be addressed in tandem

4. Complexity beyond the scope of individual problem solvers

5. No stopping rule or final solution

Most large-scale sociological problems are difficult because they are wicked problems. Consider something like health care in the United States. What does it mean to offer "affordable healthcare"? To some people, the answer is obvious. But to others, it is a difficult question. Basic primary care would solve many medical issues. However, for those with life-threatening illnesses, basic primary care is not a solution. Some say we should socialize medicine, guaranteeing a collective minimum. Yet, the US has pioneered more medical advances through capitalist incentives than any other nation *many times over*. Inexpensive prescription drugs enjoyed in other countries are often the result of price controls. These price controls are possible because Americans pay more for these drugs, creating the incentives for their development. But is this good? The astronomical cost of some of these drugs makes the overall health care system in the US very expensive. Moral dilemmas will only increase as higher costs drive life and death decisions. These questions define the problem even before appropriate solutions can be sought.

There are also multiple competing stakeholders in any health care system. Doctors, nurses, hospitals, insurance companies, and patients are primary stakeholders. Secondary stakeholders are researchers, administrators, regulators, and many others. The competing agendas of these disparate stakeholders create misalignment in solving health care problems.

Complex sociological systems cut across problem definitions and stakeholder categories. No one company or institute can possibly create adequate solutions. Massive cooperation and collaboration across the sector are necessary to align solutions appropriately. This is one reason that so many people look to the government for solutions; there is simply no other way to force this sort of collaboration. Yet, singular solution providers create their own problems. Government solutions are rife with examples of unintended consequences and failure. Idealized solutions such as socialized medical systems have created rationed health care, diminishing doctor populations and growing bureaucracies.

Additionally, providing primary care (and sometimes even advanced care) to people is often treating the symptoms of disease and not the underlying health issues. For example, the health crisis among Canada's aboriginal population has not been solved by socialized medicine. There are root causes for these health issues stemming from addiction, poverty, and historical and cultural issues. Providing access to health care does not take away these root causes. In the United States, the incentive to sell opioids has created health issues as companies have been quick to turn a profit despite the outcome. The capitalist solution for health care is a significant contributor to this epidemic of drug addiction.

Definitions, agendas, complexity, root causes, and ambiguous resolution all combine to make health care delivery a wicked problem. Our language betrays the wickedness of this issue. We often avoid using phrases like "*solving* the health care crisis," preferring "delivering *better* health care."

But not all wicked problems are global in scope. Sometimes a wicked problem exists on a much smaller scale. It might be as simple as the development (and subsequent adoption) of an organizational mission statement. Size does not make a problem wicked. In fact, it might be that a focus on the largest of these problems *requires* many smaller wicked problems to be solved concurrently. Your own church, company, or organization might be facing a wicked problem that is specific to your situation.

CAN WICKED PROBLEMS BE SOLVED?

There is a long list of wicked problems in our world today. Besides health care, terrorism, environmental degradation, climate change, gun violence, and poverty come to mind. One that most of us would not include on the list is cigarette smoking. It was not long ago, however, that cigarette smoking in the US was a wicked problem.

In 1954, 45 percent of American adults smoked cigarettes.[3] Stop and consider a world in which almost half of all the adults you know smoked cigarettes. That was reality in 1954. The health effects of smoking are well-known and the cost to society was enormous. Smoking mothers affected their unborn children. Teenage smoking was rampant. Lung cancer was the leading cause of death. For most Americans, the smoking culture of just a few decades ago is now unthinkable. That is because in 2018 that number fell to 16.[4] One percent would be better, for sure, but to cut that original number by two-thirds is an outstanding public health achievement.

The Surgeon General in 1954, Leroy Burney, was a smoker himself. He knew that Americans saw tobacco as a part of everyday life. Unlike today, nobody knew that smoking was linked to cancer. Burney began to worry about the issue and ordered his staff to comb through eighteen different studies in 1956. The head of the research team delivered the results: tobacco was killing Americans. A year after the research had begun, on July 12, 1957, the Public Health Service issued their verdict. "Excessive cigarette smoking is one of the causative factors in lung cancer."[5] By including the word "excessive," Burney was laying down a fig leaf in hopes that the tobacco industry would not explode.

But explode they did. Powerful and well-financed tobacco interests denounced Burney, the report, and government intrusion into the private sector. They formed research teams to prove the safety of tobacco products while simultaneously discrediting opposing studies. Looking back in history it is laughable to think that people did not see through this "smoke-screen." However, medical research itself was being transformed by the search for answers around tobacco.[6] Large-scale population studies were in their infancy. Even though doctors knew by experience that smoking was killing their patients, the proof was framed as arbitrary and political. In fact, there was no proof by today's medical standards. The truth was, at the time, somewhat complicated.

In 1958, the Tobacco Institute was formed as a trade association representing the companies behind big tobacco. One of the first of its kind, the Institute collected research favorable to the industry and created advertising not just for one company but the entire industry. A favorite tactic of the Institute was to publish white papers to counteract the medical research that was piling up against tobacco use.

To understand the magnitude of this effort one can visit the website Truth Tobacco Industry Documents where over fourteen million written documents are archived.[7] Among this horde of documents are thousands of white papers. Within this archive is a memo from 1969 highlighting conference proceedings. The unnamed author writes, "Doubt is our product since it is the best means of competing with the 'body of fact' that exists in the mind of the general public."[8]

Just as important as creating doubt was the attempt to manage legislation. The Tobacco Institute made huge payments to politicians. The very people elected to look out for your best interests were paid handsomely to do just the opposite. There were many stakeholders in the tobacco game, from the farmers, the industry, politicians, and smokers themselves. Each had a different agenda for the promotion of tobacco.

During World War I, volunteer organizations formed a brigade to collect money and cigarettes to send to troops fighting on the front lines. One such effort called "The Sun Fund" collected 137 million cigarettes in just two months alone.[9] General Pershing himself called for people to contribute to the war effort by saying, "You ask me what we need to win this war. I answer tobacco, as much as bullets."[10] Historians point to World War I as the pivotal event leading to mass acceptance of smoking by Americans.

The root causes of smoking are many. Why do people smoke despite the overwhelming evidence against it? The negative effects of smoking are delayed for years. The immediate physical response is pleasant. Our politicians have promoted it. The social pressure to smoke is strong in many communities. The culture's tolerance and support of smoking has been huge.

The Surgeon General's 1954 pronouncement included the word "excessive" because he knew just how complicated the issue had become. The science behind health issues lacked conclusive broadscale research studies. Perhaps one way to understand this complexity from the 1954 perspective is to look at the status of diet research today. It often seems that one study advocating low-carb diets, as an example, is immediately countered by another study warning against them. The lack of settled science, cultural embrace, widespread use, huge sums of money, politics, uncertainties about addiction patterns, and so forth presented a tangled mess for the anti-smoking movement.

What was the goal of the anti-smoking movement? This seems obvious now: reduce smoking rates. But at the outset there were many possible goals. Included in a long list of possible options are making smoking safer, shutting down the tobacco industry, educating the public, researching the hazards of smoking, changing cultural norms and mores, ending political lobbying by the Tobacco Institute, advertising about the effects of smoking, reducing the number of young people exposed to smoking through regulation, taxing cigarette consumption, and addiction research. Where would one start when looking at a problem this big? As we shall see, binary thinking about solutions is an obstacle that must be overcome when considering wicked problems.

Difficult to define. Multiple stakeholders. Complexity. Numerous root causes. The tobacco problem was filled with all of them. Yet smoking rates have fallen precipitously and continue to fall. Globally, smoking rates are down in most countries, with stark exceptions in Russia and Eastern Europe.[11] The heart disease rate in the United States is in decline. Cigarettes are heavily taxed. Numerous studies have proven the damage that smoking causes. The tobacco industry was sued under federal racketeering laws and forced to pay enormous settlements. The anti-smoking movement has been one of the most successful campaigns in modern history.

It is premature to say that smoking has been "solved" (not knowing when a problem has been solved is itself a descriptor used for wicked problems). Yet the transformation of the issue shows that wicked problems are not immutable. We can effect change in our quest to solve wicked problems. The list of solved wicked problems could include traffic deaths (substantially reduced over the past decades), serfdom (this system held most people in economic captivity for hundreds of years), and air travel. Medical breakthroughs have become commonplace.

As mentioned in chapter 1, William Carey took on *sati*, the practice of widow-burning. This Hindu practice was widespread in his day. It is based on the story of the wife of Shiva, Sati, who set herself on fire to protest how her father treated her husband. It is an ultimate act of loyalty to a husband. There were many reasons for *sati* to exist. Women who had no children to support them killed themselves rather than become dependent on others. Society pressured women to undertake this gruesome act and even young widows performed it. Carey opposed it and worked to eradicate both the practice and the factors leading to it. He felt that if the church could assist in caring for these women, one part of the problem was solved. He pressed government officials to ban the practice and enlisted others in his efforts. It took many years for *sati* to eventually die out. Even into recent decades it has occurred, with the Indian government passing legislation against it in 1987. Carey, a common shoemaker, was a part of solving this wicked problem.

Tracking the geographic footprint of missionaries, Robert Woodberry demonstrates how Protestant missionaries have tackled wicked problems wherever they went. They impacted global literacy rates, spurred the printed word globally, educated millions through the creation of entire school systems, increased the economic well-being of the cultures they served, and paved the way for liberal democracy.[12] The gospel contributes to the solution set of just about any large-scale wicked problem.

Yesterday's Wicked Problems

Carey, like Luther, did not set out to launch the massive change that would come. Yet, he is credited with a breakthrough in reframing the commands of Christ theologically and practically. Innovation, like pregnancy, sometimes seems like the inevitable culmination of natural forces set in motion by an invisible hand. Of course, we know whose hand that is.

As we look back on the history of the church, it can be hard for us to see that innovation has played a significant role. That is because innovation, once it happens, becomes obvious. Consider these five watershed moments in global church history:

1. Rediscovery of the Great Commission by William Carey

2. Bible translation as a missionary task

3. Democratized fundraising to pay for salaries and ministry expenses

4. The reframing of mission around unreached people groups

5. The indigenization of mission and field leadership

We have already covered Carey's remarkable breakthrough. Stop and consider that from the opening pages of the book of Acts forward, we see a missionary movement. That movement was not birthed by triumphant leaders with a solid track record of success. Imagine the broken hearts of the disciples, hopes and dreams dashed, and the fellowship broken. From the start, a handful of activists changed the course of history.

Bible translation, now assumed to be a goal of the larger global Christian movement, was once extremely rare. Those few who ventured to attempt it could be hunted down, burned at the stake, and their life's work destroyed. Cameron Townsend, working among the peoples of Central America, realized that Christianity did not penetrate deep into their worldview. While they often had a veneer of traditional Christianity, by translating the Bible into their indigenous language they could become acquainted with the gospel. Along with Bible translation, Townsend focused on health care, literacy, and education. He was a driving force behind the formation of Wycliffe Bible Translators and the Summer Institute of Linguistics (SIL). Today, modern Bible translation can be understood as a relatively recent innovation in Christian mission.

Another innovation surrounds how missionaries were funded. Denominational agencies of the late 1800s were dominant. They hired missionaries and the career path was much like a pastor. One went to the denominational theological school, was ordained, and then sent out. As missionaries' zeal grew and more people wanted to become missionaries, a significant change occurred. Financial support was given directly to missionaries, usually through a board or other governing body. The extent to which this has changed global outreach is hard to imagine now.

Missio Nexus was formed in part by a merger from two long-standing mission associations. One of them, the International Foreign Missions Association, was started because these upstart mission organizations were not allowed to join the "big boys" when they met. Was this the idea of any single person? No, it was not. In fact, the practice had been around for some time but not significantly exercised. With the advent of growing evangelicalism, a realization of the wider world, cheaper travel, and more affluence the support-raised model took off. Today, we can hardly see why it was ever novel. While we may see Internet-based crowd-funding as a new form, the same concept, individuals pledging financial support, has created a disruption in missionary sending.

In 1974, at a conference in Manilla, Ralph Winter pressed his thoughts about the nature of the missionary task. At one time missionaries focused on the coastal areas. Then they went inland (hence the names of several older missions, like Sudan Interior Mission and China Inland Mission). Winter suggested that the Bible's framing is around ethno-linguistic people groups. Today, this is the dominant idea in understanding the missionary task. It serves as both a metric (how many of these groups have been reached?) and a rubric for strategy (where should we send missionaries and deploy resources?). This was a disruptive idea that continues to reverberate through global Christianity.

Another significant missions breakthrough was the empowerment of indigenous leaders. This seems to a modern mind like a given. Is not the goal of missionary work to leave behind a functioning church? When first pressed by innovators such as Henry Venn and Rufus Anderson, it was highly controversial. Mirroring public attitudes about indigenous people and their abilities, mission leaders initially opposed the concept. It took pioneers like John Nevius to put these ideas into action. Today, no missionaries would dispute the importance of the three self-principles of self-propagation, self-government, and self-supporting churches. At the time, it was a breakthrough innovation.

Each one of these five innovations were addressing huge, significant problems. They answered the following questions: "How do we motivate the church to take up mission?" "How do translate the Bible into thousands of indigenous languages?" "How do we fund a large missionary force?" "What is the goal of a missionary?" And, finally, "How can we empower indigenous people to lead their own churches?"

The Reformation stands out as a unique period of Protestant innovation. It was a time of theological rediscovery, ushering in a departure from traditional church structures and an expansion of Bible preaching, reading, and studying. The conditions for the table had been set. Luther lit the match and ignited the fire. Part of solving a big, wicked problem is to solve it when the time is right.

Today's Giant Problems

The phrase "wicked problem" as used by academics is not about defining problems on a good to evil spectrum. The word "wicked" referred to the difficulty in finding workable solutions. However, many human problems do indeed reflect evil and are a sign of humankind's fallen condition—racism, greed, sexual dysphoria, addiction, loneliness, and many others. They are the fertile soil in which the gospel must be planted.

Slavery, long gone as an American construct, continues to cast a long shadow over the US culture and church. How many more generations will come and go until we feel that racial issues are not impacting us? The church, itself divided at the outset of the Civil War between northern denominations favoring abolition and southern denominations favoring slavery, has continuously harmed its testimony on race. Whether we look at segregation in the church, the lack of black missionaries, or the chasm between political views in the white evangelical church and the black evangelical church, racial issues continue to divide. Innovation is needed to solve this wicked problem.

Eighty percent of the church's global wealth is tied up in the US and Canada. At the same time, valiant pastors, missionaries, and other leaders struggle with a lack of both ministry resources and personal resources. What will it take to unleash these financial resources where they can do great good?

The train wreck known as the sexual revolution has killed millions via abortion, made marriage less common than singleness, and rewritten basic assumptions about human identity. Our sons and daughters are easy prey to pornographic substitutes for real intimacy. Children, not yet mature enough to comprehend their own sexuality, are manipulated by parents and society who are feeding them hormones and performing gender surgery at younger and younger ages. Sexual dysphoria has become a major life issue for many. How are Christian leaders innovating on this crucial challenge?

Addiction, perhaps the biggest killer of young men, is a scourge on society. Suicide follows accidental death as the number two reason for death among American men. It beats all medical conditions including cancer and heart issues.

These are big problems. These fit the definition of wicked problems. How can we innovate to bring the gospel's power to these giants?

TAKING ON A WICKED PROBLEM

Health care is a classic wicked problem in any society. Having lived in many different cultures, I have learned that people defend the system in which they live regardless of the problems. No system is perfect. Yes, I have lived in countries with socialist systems and the level of service, immediacy, and availability of treatment does not compare with the US system. Yet, the US system is horribly broken and in need of major overhaul.

I mentioned earlier that Missio Nexus started an insurance program that was very difficult to get off the ground. The ongoing issue of rising health insurance costs is a classic wicked problem. All five attributes listed above are present. Perhaps the most difficult hurdle is that there are multiple stakeholders with competing agendas. We ran into these problems, and they were difficult. While health insurance costs will continue to be a problem, we are contributing to a future solution set.

Tools for Wicked Problems

Wicked problems like these will not be solved using solution sets for typical problems. In studying successfully "solved" wicked problems, a few strategies do emerge.

Collaboration at Scale

Collaboration needs to match the scope of a wicked problem. For example, you will not significantly change the addiction problem in your city if you simply look at your own neighborhood. The next step may be to ask other churches to draw a similar radius around themselves and join you in the fight.

Problem solving will include reaching across traditional barriers to cooperate. We might find that the best collaborators are not other ministries, but business and government leaders. Denominational allegiances, historical divisions, and simple relationship neglect are not helpful in addressing large-scale issues.

EveryCampus is a movement that has overcome organizational border walls. York Moore had recently been appointed to a position with InterVarsity Christian Fellowship to develop creative partnerships. Soon after, he was at a conference when, upon exiting an elevator, he bumped into the newly appointed Cru leader for collaboration. Over pork chops they began to talk on a question that often leads to collaboration breakthroughs, "What is something we could do together that we could not do on our own?"[13]

InterVarsity and Cru are among the largest of campus ministries. Despite this, they are only present on a small slice of campuses globally. Just in the United States, there are over four thousand campuses, and over half of them have no known student ministry. Could these two organizations reach the rest of these campuses and see a ministry started among all of them? It did not take long for York to recognize that no, they could not. They needed to collaborate with a much larger number of campus ministries to accomplish this task. EveryCampus was born.

I recently spoke with Jon Hietbrink[14] who told me about their directory that highlights where campus ministries are needed.[15] This is a collaborative data source for anybody seeking to strategize about where to launch a student ministry. It lists by state the campuses where there are gaps. Today they are conducting prayer walks and looking at how to mobilize student leaders from and to these schools. The collection of data across organizations is an example of how collaboration can fuel a vision. What data could be collected from others about your sector of ministry?

Develop a Shared Understanding of the Issues

Gathering stakeholders early and often as the problem is being understood makes it much more likely that solutions sets can be found. Stakeholders have different perspectives when it comes to wicked problems. Some gain, some lose by the status quo. Building trust between these stakeholders makes it more likely that solutions will emerge from the group.

As a part of this process, it is helpful to map connections between stakeholders and how they affect each other. The more you can document the problem, the more likely it is that empathy is built between stakeholders.

Developing a shared understanding of the issues does not happen overnight. It may take months or years and will only come within the crucible of ministry.

Author Carolyn Custis James started a ministry for women leaders in the early 2000s called the Synergy Women's Network. Women who were working in ministry had few opportunities to gather and talk about their experiences. In 2004, Synergy held a national conference, one of the first of its kind, connecting women in ministry leadership. The next year, they agreed to focus on a future in which women are recognized as God's image bearers and seek a "Blessed Alliance" with their Christian brothers. Since that time, numerous other gatherings have occurred, authors have further delineated the issues that women face in leadership positions, social networking has emerged to support women in leadership, and the number of online resources available has exploded.[16]

Women in ministry leadership face myriad issues, from the practical to the abstract. Through a season of discernment, allowing many to participate and contribute, a kingdom-focused, shared understanding created a vision (a preferred future) for women in ministry leadership. Today, Synergy is more of a movement than an organization. Its influence has spread into various streams of the eccliosystem, recognizing the potential of "more than half of the church."[17]

Reframe the Problem

In the case of Missio Benefits, the wicked problem is the US health insurance system. We reframed it and rescoped it to our community. It has the potential to be one of the largest group health plans in the US. It may drive down health care for ministries nationally. We publish our rates on a public website, allowing them to be used as bargaining chips against existing policy providers. We charge no fees on ancillaries (additional types of policies) and reduce brokerage fees substantially. We hope the market will respond and the program will assist both Missio Benefits subscribers as well as lowering costs for those who do not use our service.

One way to identify wicked problems is to listen for excuses that are conversation ending. For example, why do mission agencies pay so much for health insurance? Because the US health care system is so messed up. End of conversation (usually). Why have we not translated the Bible into all languages? There are just too many of them. The same goes for unreached people groups and cultures. Why is addiction ravaging the neighborhood around our church? It is the total breakdown of society. These are all excuses that stop us from thinking deeper about the problem.

> One way to identify wicked problems is to listen for excuses that are conversation ending.

If your city suffers from an epidemic of addiction, your church may feel helpless to solve it. You might feel like the proverbial "drop in the bucket." But, if you reframe the problem around the two-mile radius surrounding your church, the problem becomes more tangible and realistic. In each of the cases above (health care, translation, reaching unreached cultures, and addiction) leaders reframed and rescoped the problem definition into actionable plans.

Identify Root Causes

The root causes of wicked problems are never singular. There are multiple conspiring factors that make them difficult. Often, these root problems are hidden or obscured and difficult to identify. Unlike natural systems in which cause and effect are easily observed, social systems, like the eccliosystem, are much more nuanced and complicated.

Over the past few years, I have observed how root causes are often neglected. The US health care industry has better technological tools than any other on the planet. Yet, the costs are very high. One reason is that the system does not easily identify root causes. Patients often see multiple doctors that work in different specialties. Sometimes these doctors are unaware that other treatment is being sought. The patient might even be prescribed medications for different ailments that are not to be taken together. The Missio Benefits insurance plan has a company that analyzes claims. When they find a person with multiple conditions, they can initiate communication with them about their health status. If the person desires, a doctor or physician's assistant researches the entire situation, calling on those medical professionals who have served the patient. They seek to identify the root cause of the illness. Often, there is unregulated stress, family problems, addictions, or other underlying causes creating physical ailments. It is not rare for a patient to enter the program taking fifteen to twenty different prescriptions. After a consultation, that number can drop to four to five. This holistic view of a person's health can fast-track their healing while reducing costs to them and the insurance program.

While Missio Benefits seeks to mitigate the results of a wicked problem by addressing the root causes of a person's health care, the bigger wicked problem is, of course, the system itself. With close to 350 million stakeholders, this is a big one. That does not even include the billions globally who benefit from the overpriced US system through drug and treatment development.

Too often, our networks, denominations, social class, race, and other factors keep us from working with those best situated to identify root causes. It is more likely that root causes are identifiable when a wide array of stakeholders are sharing information. In the example above, the system provides little motivation for a single doctor to share information. Health care regulation, in the form of privacy laws, makes medical record sharing difficult. Legal liability works against sharing patient information. This was never designed to be the case. Yet, the way the system has developed harms holistic care. Uncovering these unintended consequences is how innovation breakthroughs can happen.

Give Freedom for Many Solutions

Wicked problems will not be solved by any singular solution. Instead, there will be many different approaches. As I have observed hundreds of leaders, particularly young to mid-career ministry leaders, I have seen that many universalize their model of ministry. Because it worked for them, they assume it will work for others. Because it flourished in their context, they assume it will flourish in other contexts. This is, of course, usually not the case. In a world of growing diversity and an exploding number of subcultures, universal solutions will be less and less effective.

At times, our solutions will be in direct competition with one another. Perhaps your church believes in inviting people to join the existing congregation while another sees church planting as the best way forward. There are arguments for both, but in the end, the best overall approach is probably to encourage both. Even in the pages of the New Testament we see rival leaders using different means. "What then? Only that in every way, whether in pretense or in truth, Christ is proclaimed, and in that I rejoice" (Philippians 1:18).

The passion with which we pursue our objectives can hinder collaboration with others who are equally as passionate, but with different strategies. Often, those who are most likely to be our allies become our enemies. Dartmouth psychologist Judy White has coined a helpful term to describe this paradoxical truth. She calls it "horizontal hostility."[18]

Horizontal hostility happens when zealous leaders require conformity from others. If others do not conform, they are judged to be "worse than the enemy." Collaboration requires forming coalitions with like-minded people. But if "like-minded" becomes too narrow, there is no room for diversity in the selection of strategies and solutions to achieve the goal of the collaborative effort. A split occurs not over the "what" (the objective of the potential collaboration) but over the "how" (the strategy that will be used to achieve our objective).

In the book *Originals*, Adam Grant describes horizontal hostility using women's suffrage as an example.[19] We all know the name Susan B. Anthony as the leader of this movement. But another name is less well-known, though she was perhaps just as influential. Lucy Stone, some argue, was the original movement leader. But Stone and Anthony, though both fervent for women's voting rights, could not agree on the strategy to accomplish the goal. They became bitter rivals. Had they learned to work together, it is likely that women would have had the right to vote much earlier. How well we collaborate matters.

Within ministry movements I see similar horizontal hostility. History, in fact, is littered with denominations, churches, mission agencies, and leaders who will not work together. The organization I lead was formed when two historic missionary associations merged. They should have merged decades before. There were differences, though, that blocked this from happening. It was not until a new generation of leaders arose (combined with the fear that both associations were becoming irrelevant) that there was a breakthrough.

Among groups pursuing church planting strategies there are two approaches. The first is the traditional model (teach a missionary to preach and teach, empower them to lead the work, and trust that the healthy church will someday reproduce as the missionary hands over the church to trained indigenous leaders) and those with a newer, movement model (teach a missionary to coach and empower nationals from the beginning, encourage inexperienced leaders to multiply churches from the start, and trust that they will mature as they experience fruitful ministry). We will cover this more in the next chapter. Both groups value church planting. Both would claim to empower nationals. But, because the strategy to get there is different, they will not work together. One side has started campaigning against the other group, creating division in the missions community. This is horizontal hostility.

Similarly, churches in many cities and towns do not work well together. Even though the spiritual health of the people around them is their objective, their strategy is focused on their congregation. Fortunately, this has improved in recent decades. Yet, there is very little real collaboration between

> We feel good when we invite others to join us in our fight. We also need to be willing to join others in theirs.

most congregations in the same geographic area. I realize there are real differences at times. Doctrine does matter. But note how the doctrines that mattered in 1980 are not the ones that matter much today. We need to be careful not to divide over secondary issues.

Horizontal hostility can also be found in the pages of Scripture. In Philippians 1:15–18 (NIV), we find Paul writing about those who preach Christ out of envy and rivalry. They were other preachers of the New Testament era "stirring up trouble" for Paul. Paul suggests that it does not matter, so long as Christ is being preached.

One final note on collaboration at scale. We feel good when we invite others to join us in our fight. We also need to be willing to join others in theirs. Sometimes I find that there is a group of people who see themselves as primary catalysts and will only be the initiator. It is important that we learn to live on both sides of the collaboration invite.

Invent & Innovate

Now that the problem is better understood by all involved, different problem-solving teams can employ innovative approaches. This is different from a hackathon, where everybody is working on the same project together. Wicked problems, because of their wide scope, may take years to solve. Empowering different organizations, churches, and the whole eccliosystem to solve it in the best way they see fit is often more powerful than designing a singular solution.

In my role as the head of an association, I often attend association management events. As we make introductions, I have learned that our association is distinct from others in an important way. Most associations are formed as collaborative efforts among competitors. In our case, we are an association of cooperators. In fact, Jesus gave us the specific command to work together. But collaboration does not mean that the solution set will be unified. Different teams, with different views of the problem, can each employ their own solution. It is the accumulated efforts of the whole group that make the difference.

There may even be competition between these entities. Human nature is to pit one thing against another. But leaders need to embrace "both/and" thinking. At this early stage, pick an objective that your team can tackle while simultaneously communicating the larger vision. This larger vision is motivational.

Let us take an example using orality. Orality is an anthropological term referring to the way that some people and cultures understand and relate to the world through spoken words. It may or may not mean that the people are literate, but most of the time, reading is not widely practiced. Some observers think that we are moving toward a more orality-based world as screens, icons, and emojis are taking over communication.

In literate cultures the younger generation is moving away from reading, and in non-literate cultures a high percentages of the population do not have the benefit of reading. Global statistics reveal that 63% of the world population do not read because they are either illiterate, functionally illiterate or visually impaired. Another nearly 20% can read but prefer to learn through non-textual means. A whopping 82% of the world, approximately 5.7 billion people, are oral preference learners.[20]

Set aside for a moment the idea that orality is a problem to be solved through literacy. That is a lengthy discussion past the bounds of this example and almost always the reaction of the literate person, like you. For now, be aware that many people in the world are oral learners. It is a reality that we must contend with for good communication. It is a missiological issue when applied to the communication of the gospel.

When first observed some decades ago, there were few resources available for teaching oral cultures outside of recorded materials. Even then, a didactic approach to teaching was used, and most oral learners are storytellers. Storytelling makes information more memorable to the listener.

Oral approaches to communicating the gospel go back in time, but the *Jesus* film is the modern day "first strike" weapon. New Tribes Mission, in the 1970s, began looking at storytelling using the Scriptures in a systematic way, later taken up by Southern Baptist missionaries and others. In the 1990s, several consultations were held. As researchers gathered and discussed the situation, they began to realize the large scale and massive problem that orality presents.

Further, it is a subset of much larger wicked problems such as complete cultures with no gospel witness and declining biblical literacy in the West. To keep from losing the focus on orality, the first network of like-minded oral practitioners was created in the 2000s—Oral Bible Network (OBN) whose focus was to create an oral Bible. At the same time, another network developed under the auspices of Lausanne. In 2005, these two networks joined to form the International Orality Network (ION).

ION has defined the problem and initiated massive collaboration. The root causes for orality are not what you might think. Literates often see the root cause as a deficit in literacy. This fails to capture the nature of why some people communicate orally. Innovative training programs, best practices models, publishing, and other steps have undergirded the movement. The problem that oral learners do not have access to the gospel, is far from solved, but there is a solid first step toward that end. It is a wicked problem the eccliosystem is addressing.

CONSIDER NEW WAYS
OF PARTNERING WITH OTHERS

Big problems, stretching problems, and wicked problems will force innovation. If you are serious about them, they will also force partnership. The examples in this chapter have all involved collaboration. It is astonishing to me that today, with the problems we face in the world, that most ministries are not devoting more energy, finance, and human resource at partnership. Local church pastors should take note. A question

I often ask when I meet new pastors for the first time is, "How are you working with the churches in your area?" If they are doing anything at all (and they most often are not), the answer is usually, "We meet once a month for prayer." The most positive thing I can respond with is, "That is a good start." Prayer is important and I am glad that is happening. But I challenge pastors to take on at least one significant community problem and work with others in solving it for their city.

John Fletcher, when he was the International Director of Pioneers, was speaking to the leadership team of Pioneers in 2005 in Brazil.[21] As they thought about the future, he posed a question:

> "Where and how can the vast resources of the global Church and of Pioneers International Fellowship be fused together into a powerful synergistic whole for the expansion of the gospel and the Church among the unreached?"

My challenge to you is to rework this question around your God-ordained purpose:

> Where and how can the vast resources of the global church and [your ministry here] be fused together into a powerful, synergistic whole for the expansion of the gospel and the church for [your God-ordained purpose here].

Shoemakers think big. Thinking big forces innovation.

Summary

Wicked problems are, by their very nature, difficult to solve. Unlike innovation within an organization, they often have variables outside of your control. Tools for addressing wicked problems include developing a shared understanding of the problem, reframing the problem, large-scale collaboration, and identifying and tackling root problems.

APPLICATION & DISCUSSION

Questions to Ponder

Here are some diagnostic questions to consider about your own ministry as it relates to thinking big:

1. What wicked problems (see the list of factors that define them) exist in your ministry sphere, geographic region, or internally in your ministry?

2. Are there typical excuses that keep you from addressing a wicked problem in your ministry?

3. How is your ministry currently partnering with others? Make a list. Are you satisfied with this list?

4. Are you working with others outside of the eccliosystem to solve problems that people in your community face?

5. Does your mission, vision, and set of core values empower you to tackle wicked problems or do they keep you from doing so?

TEAM EXERCISE & DISCUSSION

Homework:

Ask each person on your team to make a list of the three most pressing problems in your sector of ministry. These should be scoped to the entire ministry and encourage people to think big.

Facilitated Discussion:

1. Have each person on the team present their prepared list.

2. Together, create a prioritized list of the three most pressing problems that most of your team agrees on.

3. Ask your team to discuss the question, "Are we working on these problems and why or why not?"

4. Have the team consider the problems considering current priorities and strategies. Consider the budget and the strategic plan in light of these big problems.

7

IDENTIFYING
INNOVATION TARGETS

Management is doing things right; leadership is doing the right thing.[1]
PETER F. DRUCKER

*See, I am doing a new thing! Now it springs up; do you not perceive it? I am
making a way in the wilderness and streams in the wasteland.*
ISAIAH 43:19 (NIV)

Business and ministry have a fundamental difference. The ultimate
metric in ministry is not profit. We measure ministry less by black and
white metrics. If, for example, you are in a discipleship focused ministry,
how do you measure success? Jim Collins, writing in the monograph,
Good to Great and the Social Sectors, warns us that ministry must not be
treated like a business. "We must reject the idea – well-intentioned but
dead wrong – that the primary path to greatness in the social sector is
to become 'more like a business.'"[2] In selecting targets for innovation,
ministries have a more abstract set of issues to consider than most business leaders do.

LEARNING FROM OUTSIDE YOUR DOMAIN

As mentioned earlier, I had to wrestle with how to price Missio Nexus membership when I first came into my role as association president. I had multiple conversations with board members about this as I considered a drop in prices. I had created multiple spreadsheets with different scenarios and was presenting these approaches to various board members. A typical conversation would end with something like this: "Ted, the issue is not pricing. They want to pay the price. But they only want to pay it if there is value in the offering, and that's the real issue."

> One of the best ways to find innovative ideas is to get an outsider's perspective.

This was the real issue. People do not mind paying for value. I had to stop altogether and reassess. My intuition had been telling me for some time that we were charging a segment of our membership too much. The seeds of that idea had been planted in a survey, months before, about why a member had not renewed. I let that seed grow into a nice, fat thesis about pricing. I had then marched out in search of the data to support it. This type of confirmation bias leads to bad decisions. It also inhibits innovation. My board had an outsider's perspective and I needed to hear it.

We all expect that as limited beings we have limited perspective. What we often fail to recognize is that as we become better at what we do, we create mental models that become, themselves, limiting. One of the best ways to find innovative ideas is to get an outsider's perspective.

An innovation lab at a major hospital once told a friend that the solutions to the biggest health care problems will not come from within the health care sector, but outside of it. For that reason, the lab seeks partnerships and shared learning opportunities with other industries.

Ministry leaders should similarly seek out insight from outside of the ministry space.

The Innovation Taxonomy

There are several helpful "taxonomies" intended to categorize types of innovation. One that is particularly helpful for business is found in the book, *Ten Types of Innovation: The Discipline of Building Breakthrough.*[3] Rather than utilizing a model designed to increase value to *customers* (thus increasing revenues), the following taxonomy is designed to generate value to the *kingdom*. A church, mission agency, or other ministry can use it to evaluate if any of these areas are ripe for innovation.

When I make the distinction that ministry innovation is different from business innovation, businesspeople scoff. These are the same, they argue. Creating value for people is agnostic as to why you are doing it. I do not agree. Value in the kingdom is not the same as value to a consumer. Kingdom value may have little value to the consumer. The Bible is filled with examples that defy the value proposition. Isaiah was not very effective as a prophet. He preached to an audience that did not respond to his message. That was the point (God was using Isaiah to demonstrate the hardness of the heart among the Jewish people). Jonah, on the other hand, provides us with a picture of a reluctant prophet who had a bad attitude about those to whom he was sent to "provide value." Yet, his ministry was highly effective from the value standpoint. Suffering and martyrdom are hard to figure out if the measurement is increased value, yet they are among the most valued elements of Jesus' ministry (and the ministry of countless saints in church history). Nobody would say that we should treat our spouses using the value construct from the business world. If we did, our relationships would become transactional and void of the beauty and mystery of love.

Innovation in ministry can go in directions other than the value proposition commerce offers. This should be freeing to us even though it makes the pursuit less concrete. A taxonomy is a useful way to categorize information. The following taxonomy can be used to evaluate different types of ministry innovation.

THE INNOVATION TAXONOMY

OUTCOMES	WHO DOES THE MINISTRY SERVE?
Stakeholders	Understand and service stakeholders in creative, new ways.
Collaboration	Work with others to solve ministry problems.
Evaluation	Define, understand, and evaluate ministry goals.
SERVICE	**WHAT DOES THE MINISTRY DO?**
Experience	How people experience your ministry.
Identity	How your ministry is perceived by others.
Relevance	The cultural relevancy of your ministry to others.
ORGANIZATION	**HOW IS THE MINISTRY ORGANIZED?**
Economic Engine	How expenses are paid for or eliminated.
Structure	Alignment around your ministry purpose.
Methodology	How you execute on ministry purposes.

Outcomes

Outcome-based innovation focuses on **who the ministry serves**. Outcome-based innovation in a ministry is aimed at identifying the people being served and seeks to serve them better, innovating on outcomes. Sometimes, ministries do not understand who they are serving. If they have the right audience in mind, they are often serving them in ways that are not relevant to them.

Stakeholders

Stakeholders represent anybody involved in a ministry. This seems like an easy to identify target, but it is not. Who does your church serve? The people attending or the people not attending? The board of elders? Perhaps it is the community in which the church resides. Of course, the answer is that it serves all of them. There are few innovations, though, that will serve such a disparate group of stakeholders. Ministry organizations are faced with a similar dilemma. Do they serve the donors, the missionaries, the churches sending the missionaries, the board of directors or the people they are seeking to reach?

Stakeholder innovation means a narrowing of the focus on who the ministry serves and ways to deliver that service. Life.Church is a multisite church that is based in the Oklahoma City metro area and has dozens of locations throughout the Bible Belt and across the nation. From this Midwest base, they serve a stakeholder that many churches would never dream they'd be able to serve. On July 10, 2008, Apple opened its App Store with five hundred apps, two hundred of which were free to download. The world had never seen anything like it before. A place where small programs could be instantly downloaded onto your phone. Among those two hundred free apps was the YouVersion Bible App, the only Bible app available on day one. As of this writing, the YouVersion has almost a half billion unique downloads worldwide. How many churches do you know that can claim to have this kind of reach across the globe? YouVersion is unique in that it was a "first to market" app. Today there are competitors, but none compare to YouVersion. It also has a kid-friendly sidekick, Bible App for Kids, that has more than 65 million downloads.

Imagine it is late 2007 and somebody has just asked for money from your church budget to develop an app.

"A what?"

"An app. A small program that will run on your phone."

"My phone?"

"Yes, your phone will soon be able to run programs."

"Cool. But why would we want to use church resources for this? Who does this serve in our congregation?"

YouVersion was innovative, not only because Life.Church saw that a new era was coming, but because they decided to serve somebody outside their church walls, the many people globally who want to read the Bible. They decided to serve people outside of their direct line of influence.

Life.Church generously serves the Global Church in other ways as well. They give away tools related to church metrics, youth and children's programming, leadership development, training in many different areas, staff development, and a means of putting any church online. When COVID-19 hit, thousands of churches who would otherwise not be able to easily go online, utilized their resources to offer virtual services. These tools are free. When they developed these items for their own use, they did so in a way that would enable them to share the tools with the Church at large. If they had seen their primary stakeholder as themselves, they would never have innovated in this way. Reframing who your stakeholders are opens a wide vista for innovation.

A few years ago, the mission agency Frontiers questioned how they were being understood by Muslims, the people they were seeking to reach. As they examined their own communication, even internally, they realized that they were sending a message inconsistent with their mission. They innovated on their mission statement, which is now, "With love and respect, inviting all Muslim peoples to follow Jesus." This mission statement respects an important stakeholder for Frontiers.[4]

> Reframing who your stakeholders are opens a wide vista for innovation.

As you seek to innovate, who is your primary stakeholder?

Collaboration

Collaboration creates innovation through scale, resourcing, the mixing of attributes from different collaborators, and creativity. By working with others, you bring more people into the equation. By working with those who have different resources than you, you combine strengths. By collaborating, everybody gains the advantage of creative ideas from different perspectives.

Because we covered collaboration in chapter 6, we will move on for now. As a reminder, collaboration seeks to answer the question, "What is something we could do together that we could not do on our own?"

Evaluation

Evaluation has to do with the judgments we make about how and what we do in our ministry. Goals are inextricably linked to evaluation. Often, the goals we have are unspoken and only through careful examination do we understand even our own motivations.

Changing how we evaluate can lead to breakthrough innovation.

We all work under assumed standards each day. When I meet a pastor and ask about their church, I almost always get a reply that is related to the size of the church. They will tell me how many people attend weekly services. This is a helpful way for us to socially understand the type of ministry and the scope of the ministry that the pastor oversees. But it is a terrible rubric for evaluating a ministry and we all know it. Goals set the stage for how we think about the work we are doing.

Similarly, I recently spoke with a leader frustrated by the emphasis on missionary sending. New forms of missionary service, from entrepreneurial business start-ups to taking jobs in multinational corporations have become commonplace. He was challenging the notion that we should ever count missionaries and think that it means anything significant.

Poverty alleviation has been greatly affected by evaluating who we are serving. It summed up in the age-old phrase, "Give a man a fish and he will eat for a day. Teach a man to fish and he will eat for a lifetime." Is the goal of a ministry to feed a person, or is it help that person feed themselves? It would seem obvious that giving away food, water, shelter, and other things to alleviate poverty is less strategic than investing in people to make that gift unnecessary. Yet, a significant amount of direct aid is given away every year. To be fair, there are situations in which direct aid is appropriate. Yet, evaluation of how aid affects those who receive it has transformed the development community.

No matter where you go in the world, one reality remains constant. If somebody in a household has a job that provides for that household, poverty rates decline. For this reason, groups like Join the Journey have turned to new forms of micro-enterprising to alleviate poverty. Adam Cole, the founder, has a vision to create a massive peer-to-peer giving network for entrepreneurs. Small scale loans make possible business ventures that you can fund straight from your phone.

Yet another area under massive change surrounds orphan care. We have all seen pictures of institutionalized orphans. A movement to stamp out orphanages within the next decade seeks to replace these institutions with foster care. Instead of seeing a parent-less child as somebody with needs for food, shelter, and education, this new movement sees them as children who need parents. By placing them in homes an entire system is disrupted.

Subtle shifts in goals have significant consequences. Planting a church is a very different goal than planting reproducing churches. If you plant a church, you will serve a congregation. If you seek to reproduce churches, then you will be working with leaders to encourage that reproduction.

Sometimes removing metrics that have been traditionally used in your ministry helps spur innovation. Examples might include counting how many people attend church services (a poor metric by any measure, no pun intended), how many missionaries are sent (does not speak to effectiveness), or how many people visited your website (does not evaluate action taken). As long as these metrics are utilized people will focus their efforts in this direction.

When the goals are changed, there is great opportunity for innovation. What might you measure that would lead to innovation?

Service

Service innovation is aimed at improving *what the ministry does*. The delivery of your service to people is like the Marshal McLuhan observation about media: the media is the message. The form of a medium becomes part of the message and influences its meaning. Similarly, service becomes a part of how people experience the kingdom through your ministry, influencing how they perceive and understand the kingdom.

Experience

What kind of experience do people have when they interact with your ministry? It is a broad question, encompassing digital presence (your website, mobile, email, social media and similar representations of your ministry), physical touch points (from architecture to how events are organized), and spiritual sensitivity (do people sense the Holy Spirit in relationships, communications, prayer, and how you care?). Churches must pay special attention to the experience they provide to those whom they serve. Too often in evangelicalism, we have put truth and doctrine too far ahead of how we communicate and live out that truth and doctrine.

Despite what you might think about the seeker sensitive movement, it was innovation focused on this attribute of experience. The leaders went to great lengths to identify church service elements that would upgrade the experience of an attendee. They wanted to communicate that people were welcome. Sermons were adapted to an audience that were considered theologically naïve (this touches on innovation in the outcomes arena as well, since the people being served shifted from informed Christian to Spiritual Seeker). Coffee and donuts, easy parking, and friendly faces were, in the mid-1970s, downright revolutionary at most churches.

L'Abri, the Swiss spiritual retreat center that flourished in that same era, was known for the experience it delivered. It did not matter what doubts you harbored about your faith. When you came to L'Abri, you were welcomed by a community that embraced your journey.

As a missionary, I learned that hospitality is the "killer app" for the kingdom. To have somebody in your home, eating food you prepared, conversing freely around a table is powerful. Westerners have largely lost the art of simple hospitality, replacing it with "entertaining." I yearn for innovation in hospitality. What would it look like for every believer to offer their homes, even for one night a week, to anybody who would like to come? This could tip the balance of power in the culture.

There is a cultural expectation in the West that an institution, be it a church or ministry organization, will deliver service via the Internet and, more and more, in a mobile friendly way. Giving history, for example, must be online, easily accessed, searchable, and downloadable. Because of the pace of change in these expectations, high service levels are not particularly innovative any longer. They are assumed. This means that it takes even more effort and creativity to craft an experience that is innovative.

The experience of your staff is also important. Websites like Glassdoor allow any employee to anonymously rate their experience working for you. This becomes a part of your public persona. Recently, a friend was looking for a new church. I was surprised when he told me that he ruled out a church after checking on Glassdoor, a website where employees leave reviews about employers. His view was that a church with negative staff reviews is not a church he would attend.

What kind of experience do people have when they come into contact with your ministry?

Identity

Jesus said that it is the love between His followers that was the mark of a disciple (John 13:35). That is incredible branding. Imagine for a moment what it would look like if people in our culture held the view that we are a loving community. In place of this, we are perceived as political, self-serving, and out of touch with the larger culture. To be fair, this was predicted. Yet, our branding as people of God could use some serious re-branding. The identity of your ministry in the broader community is important and offers opportunities for innovation.

Branding and identity, as I use them here, are closely related but different. Branding is the message you control and craft about your organization. Identity is the way you are perceived. Branding contributes to identity. First impressions matter, but identity is also set by the fulfillment of the promises your brand makes.

The Association of Gospel Rescue Missions had a problem. Their leader, John Ashmen, knew that when people heard "rescue mission," it brought up images of "Soap, Soup, and Salvation."[5] The traditional view of what their many member organizations did was not what they were, in fact, doing. They are involved in job skills training, dental and medical care, transportation, housing procurement, counseling, and many other services. Their services were much more extensive, holistic, and redemptive. Yet, their public brand did not reflect this reality.

In 2017, John and his board started a process of rethinking their identity. Any association that has members who are highly committed to the existing brand and identity needs to start by listening to its members. They also undertook an extensive education program about the importance of branding. They highlighted the positive contributions of rescue missions through their founding in the UK, to the New World, and up to today. They celebrated where they had come from. Then they highlighted the many ways rescue missions had "grown up" to become full-service ministries, focused on restoring the people they served. They had outgrown their brand.

Over the course of the next few months they involved the community on a process of finding a new name and highlighting the new identity. As they researched, they developed a list of eight activities that restated the stages of life transformation while embracing the fact that spiritual transformation could occur at any one of these stages.

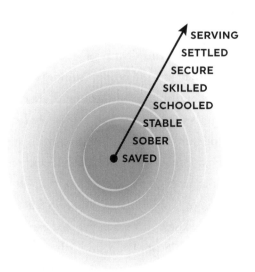

SERVING
SETTLED
SECURE
SKILLED
SCHOOLED
STABLE
SOBER
SAVED

CITYGATE NETWORK'S TRANSFORMATIONAL MODEL

In an unveiling of the brand, Citygate Network, they dropped dated language. Perhaps more importantly, they introduced a new, more appropriate reality about who they were. They did not reinvent themselves. Rather, they discovered who they were in a culturally contextualized way. By rebranding, new partners emerged that would not have thought to work with them before.

A job skills training center leader heard about Citygate Network at a conference. She introduced herself to John and as they spoke, she realized that what she did was what Citygate Network's members were also doing. She decided to join. A low-income medical services facility run by volunteer doctors would never have considered membership in Citygate Network. Yet, by becoming members they can more easily partner with the rescue mission in their city. The people they both serve are better off when they cooperate. By rebranding, this new partnership is far more likely to happen.

It is important to note the branding did not drive their reinvention. Their reinvention drove their rebranding. The new identity opened doors otherwise closed to them. It helped them delineate their services as an association, driving growth and ultimately deeper partnerships.

Another example of innovation on identity is the "I Am Second" campaign. Unlike an organizational or church rebranding effort, "I Am Second" attempts to rebrand the traditional Christian testimony. It does this by combining high quality video stories of people from different walks of life. They feature both celebrity testimonies alongside the stories of regular people. To "live second" means to put God first, yourself second. In a culture that is increasingly dominated by short attention spans, videos and celebrities are a powerful way to communicate.

Issues of branding, how to do it, what should be communicated in a brand, and other topics are a study in themselves. For our purposes, consider that branding influences your identity. It has innovation opportunities embedded within it. Uniquely communicating your mission is incredibly hard work but pays dividends in mission fulfillment.

How do your stakeholders perceive your ministry?

Relevance

Related to identity is the issue of cultural relevance. The best example of this is Jesus' teaching, which I call "retro-revolutionary". I first heard of this concept from N. T. Wright who wrote that Jesus taught on themes that were culturally familiar to His audience (the "retro"), while simultaneously being prophetically challenging to the culture (the "revolutionary").[6] A Jew listening to Jesus teach would immediately understand and appreciate Jesus' message as Jewish. It came from the soil of Jewish culture and resonated as authentic and contextualized. Yet, at the same time, Jesus also taught things that were so counter to Judaism that He was crucified for it. Bridging the gap between culturally contextualized messages and those that are countercultural is a gateway to innovation.

Culture is a mix of historical movement painted on an ever-changing generational canvas. This moving target, in which this year's "hip" ministry becomes next year's cynically critiqued has-been, requires ministry leaders to constantly be on the lookout for innovative ways to connect with people.

Cultural relevance touches on several, very diverse issues, all ripe for innovation. In addition to the generational considerations in ministry, you can innovate on contextualization (adjusting to the context), developing a prophetic voice for a ministry (opposing the culture), using new communication tools (remember that the media one uses affect the meaning of the message), innovating on forms and formats, and tackling current cultural issues like abortion, racism, income wage gaps, and so on.

Steiger International is a ministry with a focus on relevance. In 1983, David and Jodi Pierce began a Bible study on a barge known as Steiger 14 behind the Central Train Station in Amsterdam. The people they were reaching were the punk rockers, anarchists, drug addicts, and those who were walking away from mainstream society. David knew that these people cared a lot about music. It was the early days of the Euro-punk scene so he founded a band, *No Longer Music*. The group grew as the band played in bars, rock festivals, and anywhere they could get an audience.

David Pierce, with his two-foot-long dreadlocks, continues to tour with the band, finding audiences in just about every urban center in the world. Since their founding, the world has changed, making Steiger International *more* relevant now than before. With the advent of the Internet, a global youth culture has emerged. From Azerbaijan to Zambia you can find young people with tattoos, piercings, and a shared worldview, quite distinct from the majority cultures in which they live. Steiger missionaries work in places you might not think headbangers hang out, like the countries of the Middle East. Their missionary training schools, traveling teams, and long-term strategy emphasize how the church can and should speak in ways that people can understand.

There is another angle on contextualization that most ministries never consider. Contextualization is about framing the message to fit the context. Ministries can also do the opposite. They can influence the context to make it better fit the message.

In 1986, Steve (the President of Pioneers USA) and Arlene Richardson moved to Southeast Asia to work among the "Kantoli,"[7] a large Muslim people group. When they asked if there were any Christians among the people in this culture, the response was that to be Kantoli was to be Muslim. There was no other way. A person who is Kantoli cannot be Christian. This made evangelism rather difficult. They decided that they needed to change the worldview so that Jesus was at least an option.

A team was developed to create media that highlighted the lives of Kantoli who were Christ-followers. They developed a television show, printed materials, and a cultural center. Each of these highlighted indigenous Christians. Because there were few resources in their Kantoli language, these resources were novel in a society dominated by the trade language. Word spread and the worldview was changed. Today, if you ask a Kantoli if there are any Christians in their people group, they not only tell you that, yes, there are, they also know where to point you to.

This reverse-contextualization has created a new condition in which the gospel has a chance to be heard.

Is your ministry relevant to its context?

Organization

This next area of potential innovation is more about the internal workings of your ministry. How you organize the ministry should be among the easiest things to change. Yet, because we have become accustomed to the way that we work, it is easy to neglect this type of innovation. Most of us, for instance, consider the sources of revenue that undergird our work to be secondary to vision. Yet, funding affects most areas of ministry, as do structures and methodologies.

Economic Engine

The economic engine that drives a ministry has significant ramifications for all other aspects of its work. How a ministry is funded touches all relationships, both those inside and outside the ministry. Innovation in this area carries high stakes both in risk and potential gain.

For churches, the economic engine seems straightforward. Regular attenders contribute and the church stays in operation because of their generosity. Of course, anybody who has been on the losing end of a donor battle in a church knows that giving in a congregation is not evenly distributed. A few people give the most, and when push comes to shove, they have outsized influence. A pastor with independent funding is considered by many to be dangerous. Why? Because paychecks often translate into accountability.

The Open Network supported by LifeChurch.tv offers free services to any church that needs them. "Free," of course, means that LifeChurch. tv, not you, is paying for them. Because they offer the services for free, they have an audience that others do not. Free services as a business model usually means that the burden of the economic engine is shifted to somebody else. Google charges most users nothing for an incredible array of services. Of course, they sell you and your use of those services to others. When looking at free models, consider where the burden is placed and why. In the case of LifeChurch.tv, they realized that if they were building out these services for themselves, why not go the extra mile and offer them to others? In return, their church has been able to influence thousands of other congregations.

Innovation around finances can change the nature of any ministry. Ministries that charge money for their services are influenced by their economic engine as well. Our ministry charges membership dues. As the CEO, I must always have this in the back of my mind. I need to consider how it influences our work. In the past few years, I have watched other networks develop around specific issues like church planting, reaching the unreached, and so forth. These networks fall into two groups. Those that are free and those that charge membership dues. The two groups behave differently from one another, the amount of ownership participants have is different, and the expectation for service is different.

The Business as Mission movement seeks to upend the support-raising structures that have dominated missionary financing for 250 years. A large part of the "price" for support-raising is time. A support-raised missionary has, in comparison, vastly more time to spend on ministry activities than somebody working full-time in a secular job. One argument is that the full-time business employee has more credibility in the culture they are seeking to reach. In this case, the economic engine has a distinct benefit for the employee.

Many ministries contact me about rethinking their economic engines. The COVID-19 pandemic revealed weakness in how ministries are funded. There is a growing concern that giving patterns among Millennials are changing, regulatory issues have increased the cost of doing ministry, and the expectations of major donors is changing. This is an area ripe for innovation. Churches are not exempt from these changes and I expect there to be changes to church funding in the decade ahead.

Medical missionaries are among the most impactful of all that are sent. You do not have to take my word for that. In 2016, two Jewish philanthropists, Rabbi Erica Gerson and Mark Gerson, created a grant to be awarded to Christian medical missionaries. L'Chaim Prize for Outstanding Christian Medical Missionary Service provides a half million dollars a year to doctors providing direct medial service.

I have personally witnessed the heroic sacrifice of missionary doctors working in extreme conditions. One hospital I visited in South Sudan was under intermittent attack by the Sudan Air Force. Despite the danger, a missionary doctor labored tirelessly to train new doctors. He did this as the only trained medical professional in a region with some millions of people. Unfortunately, medical missionaries face a challenge. Upon graduation, they face years of payments against student loans. This disqualifies many for service in traditional missionary agencies. Even if they were appointed, the fundraising amount is prohibitive and the alternate (to stay home and serve in a Western hospital) is highly lucrative.

MedSend has seen this problem and innovated an entire organization around a solution. They partner with mission agencies to "strategically fund qualified healthcare professionals to serve the physical and spiritual needs of people around the world."[8] They raise the money necessary to pay the student debt of actively serving medical missionaries. In doing so, these doctors can focus more time healing and less of it raising money. This is innovating on the economic engine, removing financial barriers and blessing others.

How do you fund your ministry?

Structure

As a ministry grows so does complexity. This complexity requires organization that stifles agility, focus, and urgency around the mission. Business leaders call this the paradox of growth. While many leaders seek growth, many bigger ministries fondly remember the days when they were smaller. With size, alignment becomes more difficult, specialization creates silos, and members of the ministry cannot see the big picture.

In the business world, both quality and speed matters. Getting to market first, having just-in-time inventory, and being able to make big changes fast equals survival. Having quality offerings that delight people, create loyalty, and drive the bottom line create revenue. Should we who lead ministries have the same values?

People get uncomfortable when speed is discussed in ministry circles. Particularly as it relates to people-centric ministry like church planting, discipleship, and evangelism, speed has a bad name. Yet, our ministry slogans are filled with "speedy" language. We say things like, "Within our generation," or "By 2030 we will . . ." and "Hasten Christ's return by . . ." Is there an equivalent to "just-in-time inventory" for ministries?

James Kelly, a young tech enthusiast from Toronto, Canada, and the founder of FaithTech, organizes hackathons. In one of these gatherings, the group was shocked by some data that presented. Suicide rates, particularly among white males, were on the rise. The group began to research this and soon learned that one of the top Internet searches was "How do I kill myself?" The results showed very specific methods for how one might end their life.

Kelly and the group saw an opportunity. They brainstormed solutions, and something innovative emerged. One person asked, "What if we owned the domain name howtokillyourself.org and made it the top result for that search?" They assembled a few web developers, a communications specialist, and networked with Christian groups that provide suicide assistance online and via phone calls. When somebody clicks on that link, instead of seeing "7 Easy Ways to Kill Yourself," the banner says, "You Are Not Alone." There are helpful videos, links, and a way to instantly talk with somebody about your situation. These innovators created this website over a weekend. When is the most critical moment to deliver our "just-in-time inventory" of loving care to somebody contemplating suicide?

This simple solution took very little structure to create. There were already ministries providing suicide assistance. What Kelly's hackathon team did was to organize a better way to connect those suffering from suicidal thoughts with those who could help.

Structure, the way that we organize and deliver products, processes, and services, affects both speed and quality. The role of innovative structures has been debated in the church for hundreds of years. Catholic orders like the Jesuits and the Benedictines were specially designed structures to perform tasks that the Catholic Church itself was either not doing or wanted done in a different way. The monastics had a unique structure, and the church created the diocese around the city/states of feudal Europe.

Structure often becomes embedded into our mental frameworks and affects much more than structure. My son has been a part of a house church, and one day we were talking about different issues churches encounter (from men's and women's roles to authority to modes of baptism, etc.). The reality is that his church doesn't even experience some of the issues that split larger congregations because its structure sidesteps these issues. It highlights the ways that structure influences a ministry philosophy.

Within evangelicalism, we also have "sodalities and modalities." A sodality represents the missionary team, Paul, Barnabas and company, being sent out from the modality, the local church at Antioch. The modern missionary agency of today is like the sodality of the first century. In fact, much of the missional movement is driven by reducing the difference between these two concepts. They argue that the church itself should have, at its core, the same sort of missionary fervor of the sodality. The challenge is that the freedom to innovate structurally within the boundaries of a local church can be difficult. Many of the organizations that are a part of Missio Nexus were started in local churches but outgrew the structure and were launched on their own.

Structural changes in the eccliosystem can have long-term consequences. The Sunday school movement, for example, changed not only the way church was conducted for 250 years, but how literacy, simple math, and Bible literacy spread in England. Sunday school happened on Sunday because child laborers worked the rest of the days, often for twelve hours. Early Sunday schools also held the promise of receiving free paper and pencils, which were valuable commodities at the time. Christian leaders saw the transformation and the idea spread, Ultimately, millions were influenced by Sunday schools. It was not until secular education was introduced that Sunday schools were turned into Bible-only affairs.

It is important to observe that structural change may or may not be linked to organizations, nonprofits, nongovernmental organizations, and other contemporary models of working together. Often, the structure within our own ministries need new, innovative ideas.

Consider this real-life example of structural challenge within a single ministry. Many missionary agencies have decentralized their leadership structures so that decisions are made closer to the field action. As their staff has grown, they may have added non-Westerners to this leadership. Imagine that a fifty-year-old Arab man is the leader of a region in the Middle East. First Baptist Church has sent out a young, millennial Bible college graduate to work in the region. This will be her first cross-cultural experience. When she arrives, she finds it very difficult to relate to the leader. He refuses to spend any one-on-one time with her, does not treat her as she believes a team member should be treated, and has asked her to make him coffee on numerous occasions, which she finds very offensive. From his point of view, she dresses provocatively, disrespects him in a group by interrupting him, and spends too much time on her phone when she is with others. He wishes she would sit with the women during the team meetings or in the other room with the children.

She calls home to First Baptist and explains her frustration to the missions pastor. He in turn calls the mission agency and demands to speak to her supervisor. The agency has a church relationship team. They take the call and pass the information on to the field leader in an email, detailing the situation as accurately as possible, though it now has passed through two third parties in the retelling. The field leader is astonished by what he reads. He has been publicly critiqued behind his back, shaming him. He asks the young missionary to leave and she does. Upon arriving home, she begins publishing her story on a blog. When the organization asks her to stop, she harshly criticizes the agency for being so out of touch. First Baptist will never again partner with that agency.

As you read this example, you should see how values in structure have affected the way this team was brought to crisis. These values are reflected in how they empower field leadership, place non-Westerners in leadership over Westerners, and default to open communication about disagreements. These are all considered "best of" approaches in international ministry. Yet, there are opportunities in how the structure could be innovated upon to prevent similar incidences in the future. It might take the form of additional training, parallel leadership structures, changes in how missionaries are placed onto field teams, field-based intervention, or all these simultaneously.

> Structural innovation requires that we question assumptions. Like the walls of a house, some are load-bearing and some are not.

Structural upheaval has started in broad swaths of the eccliosystem. As a part of a board, I sometimes sit with Bible college presidents and hear their concerns. Much of what they face has to do with structural change, having built infrastructure for growth but now face diminishing student bodies due to both changes in our culture and in our demographics. House church, traditional church, multisite churches, online churches, megachurches, and combinations of these are structural answers to how we in the kingdom carry out our obedience to be the body of Christ.

Structural innovation requires that we question assumptions. Like the walls of a house, some are load-bearing and some are not. Careful examination before makeovers are made can avoid disaster and open the door to beautiful renovations.

The mental frameworks of structure are often ripe for innovation, which cuts across our categories. Are you a nonprofit, a for-profit, or a "for-Prophet"? An entrepreneur in Asia, Sue Plumb Takamoto, is all three. She created a ministry enterprise called Nozomi Project that also cuts across all of these categories.

Sue had been praying for guidance on how she might gather women together in community. One day, while cleaning up the debris from the tsunami that devastated northern Japan, she noticed broken pieces of pottery, cups, and other fragments. Could these discarded fragments be redeemed? There is beauty in brokenness, she thought, and an idea formed. She created a social enterprise (a business that evaluates its success based on how it improves people's lives versus how much money it makes) that designs and sells jewelry made from these fragments. This social enterprise creates ongoing employment, a chance for women to gather, and beauty. It is a means of meeting and relating to people in a culturally appropriate way. As relationships develop, Sue shares her life, and thus, her faith.

In a recent interview[9] I had with Sue, she noted that as Nozomi Project developed, she had no master plan in mind. Instead, she asked God to reveal to her the "next best step." Now, looking back, she sees God's hand in how things have developed. She told me about the value of building a team. The right people providentially joined the effort at the right time. The multicultural contributions of the diverse Nozomi Project team are a part of what makes the artwork compelling and appealing.

Today, she is exploring new ministry options in Cambodia to vulnerable women, taking people from the team in Japan with her. It is powerful to impact these female tsunami survivors through Nozomi Project. It is even more impactful to see these same women empowered to help other vulnerable women across cultural divides. Featured on

TEDx as an innovator, Sue's story is a category-busting example of impact.

How could your structure better support your mission and vision?

Methodology

In 1998, I encountered a new methodology of church planting for the first time. Church planting movements, in which church planters focus on multiplication rather than simply planting one church, has rocked the global church. David Garrison's book *Church Planting Movements* introduced me to the concepts, which, frankly, I flatly rejected at the time. Since then I have seen how church planting movement methodology has changed the nature of church planting around the world.

When we consider places that are resistant to the gospel, we might troubleshoot and ask ourselves why people are not responding to the message. Garrison did the opposite. He studied places where the church was rapidly expanding and tried to see if there were any similarities between them. He developed a short list and suggested that missionaries should consider aiming toward these elements. Since that time, tens of thousands have been trained in these ideas. Like any other innovation, there are detractors and critics. Yet, the impact of Garrison's model has been widespread globally.

This table summarizes the ways that church planting movement practitioners differentiate their ministry from traditional church planters:

	TRADITIONAL MODEL OF CHURCH PLANTING	CHURCH PLANTING MOVEMENT (CPM) MODEL
DISCIPLESHIP	Discipleship happens in the context of the church. Healthy churches produce healthy disciples.	The church happens in the context of discipleship. Healthy disciples produce healthy churches.
PEDAGOGY	Training is paramount – the argument is that somebody needs to "rightly handle the Word of God."	Learning/Learners are paramount – the argument here is that the "Holy Spirit is able to teach anybody."
CHURCH PLANTER ROLE	The church planter is incarnational and participative. They teach, disciple, and lead.	The church planter is catalytic and incidental. They organize, shepherd, and coach.
MESSAGE DELIVERY	The message delivery is didactic and directive.	The message delivery is Socratic and self-discovered.
LEARNING STYLE	The emphasis is on deduction (Understand a general principle then apply it specifically to the text. The criticism is that it relies on systems of theology).	Emphasis is on induction (Understand a specific text then apply it to your life. The criticism is that it is too subjective).
CHURCH FORM	Favors "higher" or more formalized church government. The church is more stable, organized, and potentially more institutionalized.	Favors "lower" or less formalized church government. The church is discontinuous, less structured, and potentially more transient.
GROWTH	Growth is slower, steady, and deep. Numeric growth will follow depth.	Growth is faster, sporadic, and wide. Numeric growth will follow discipleship.

Each one of these is an alternative to a long-standing way of doing ministry. How do these philosophies translate into methodology? Traditional church planting methods emphasize the role of the preacher while devaluing firsthand discovery. Thus, the church planter encourages people to read the Bible themselves, organizing discovery Bible studies. In many cases, the church planter coaches the seekers in a simple study method in which the Scripture is read, discussed, applied and then the participants are asked to tell others about what they learned. Rather than sharing a simple gospel message using an illustration like the Four Spiritual Laws, the Bible texts are selected to highlight the story of redemption. The group is never encouraged to sit and listen to a preacher feed them the text. When people respond to the gospel, they already have the tools for starting a new group. This leads to multiplication and the cycle repeats itself.

Detractors have vociferously opposed the unseating of the church planter as the primary teacher and preacher. After three hundred years of the pastor and missionary being the center of church planting methodology, this should be expected. Their main contention is that the New Testament commands preaching, not self-discovery. Often these critiques are emotionally charged. "This will create heresy!" is one such charge, despite the amount of heresy projected weekly from the pulpits of traditional churches. I am not aware of any study that indicates greater heresy among churches planted in this way. There are issues with any method, and this one is no different. Yet, it has fundamentally changed the way church planting is happening throughout the world.

The Bible provides great flexibility in methodology. I like to teach aspiring ministry leaders to be wary of inflexibility with methodology. I warn them that "when your methodology becomes your theology, your ecclesiology becomes a pathology." Church history is filled with methods we find nowhere in Scripture as a command. Bible translation, the use of seminaries, chronological Bible teaching, making use of media, are methodological. Nowhere in the New Testament do we see the church forms we take for granted in contemporary society. No New Testament church is described as holding title to a building, having a band or choir, or having youth groups. These are all methods. How best to utilize this freedom in method to further the kingdom?

What methodology might be employed to better reach your goals?

COMBINING INNOVATION TARGETS

These nine areas for potential innovation should not be considered in silos. Changes to the economic engine will no doubt create changes in other areas of your ministry. Collaboration will have consequences for your ability to control how somebody experiences your ministry. Serving a new set of stakeholders will rattle existing stakeholders.

In *Ten Types of Innovation,* the authors write,

> Having analyzed and used the Ten Types for more than 15 years, we can now confidently generalize: you must look beyond products in order to innovate repeatedly and reliably. By combining multiple types of innovation, you will be more assured of bigger and more sustainable success.[10]

As you investigate possible innovation targets within your ministry, map them according to the types with a goal to seeing innovation happen across more than one area.

Operation Mobilization is employing this approach in their missionary agency. Operation Mobilization has a long history of recruiting and deploying of missionaries. As the leadership has watched changes in the global environment, they believe that the future calls for a different missionary structure.

They have developed Scatter Global in response. Unlike the traditional business as a mission model that emphasizes business startups and entrepreneurs, Scatter Global focuses on providing employment opportunities for Christians who want to use their vocational skills overseas.

Advantages of this model include lower deployment costs, a culturally acceptable identity, and an avenue for fulfilling one's career aspirations and calling. Scatter Global is driven by the belief that the traditional missionary sending model is not going to work in our future.

In my correspondence with Scatter Global,[11] I used the term "marketplace missionaries." They gently corrected me. They suggested I replace this with "intentional Jesus-followers in the marketplace." A key area of their innovation is disrupting the idea that a special class of Christian exists; in this case, missionaries. They seek to activate everyday followers of Jesus to live their lives on mission for God in the marketplaces of the world. This is for everyone. Their premise is that "missionary," along with terms like "calling," "ministry," and similar terms, carries historical baggage. Rather than redefine them, a whole new way of thinking is necessary.

Scatter Global is seeking to innovate across different areas of the innovation taxonomy. They are innovating the financial model of mission. They are innovating structurally. They are innovating through collaboration (Scatter Global is an alliance of missionary sending agencies). They believe that traditional missionaries' identity harms their witness and are innovating identity as well.

This is a significant shift for them to make and time will tell if it produces better outcomes than the traditional sending model. Over the past one hundred years, the global church has experienced incredible growth while the Western church has struggled. At least a portion of this success globally is due to traditional missionaries. However, we live in a world of staggering change and radical departures from traditional models may, in fact, be in our near future.

One final word on developing targets for innovation. Cast your net broadly for ideas. The chances are much better that ministry innovation will come from organizations outside of the ministry sphere. My sense is that we in ministry leadership are struggling to innovate. Look past your own tribe and cross-pollinate your innovation with businesses, nonprofits working in other sectors (like hospital systems or NGOs that are not faith-based), educational institutions, networks, and so on. Attend secular conferences on innovation, look for trends in similar service sectors, and ask corporations if you can visit their innovation labs. There is much more to be learned "out there" than in our traditional ministry sphere. Why not redeem the best ideas for the kingdom?

Summary

This chapter presented a taxonomy of innovation that you can use to ideate about potential innovation targets. These are categorized as outcomes (stakeholders, collaboration, and evaluation), service (experience, branding, and relevance), and organization (economic engine, structure, and methodology). Identifying new opportunities is challenging because they are flavored by the way we understand our ministry today.

APPLICATION & DISCUSSION

Questions to Ponder

1. What are the big assumptions about your ministry that keep you from seeing opportunities?

2. What is your ministry's economic engine, and is it powerful enough to propel your mission to fulfillment?

3. Compare the current ministry strategy with the innovation taxonomy. Where do current approaches fall on the taxonomy?

TEAM EXERCISE & DISCUSSION

Homework:

Have each team member use the innovation taxonomy to list three areas they think are ripe for innovation.

Facilitated Discussion:

1. Ask each team member to share their list areas that are ripe for innovation and why. Write these on a whiteboard and look for consistent answers.

2. As you survey the team's provided innovation targets, can you identify any that are able to be combined or do any of them naturally complement one another? Discuss whether two or more of the strategies need to be considered together.

3. Try to select one potential innovation target and agree upon a follow-up meeting to further define it.

8

INNOVATIVE LEADERSHIP

You manage things; you lead people.[1]
GRACE MURRAY HOPPER

*Therefore, stay awake, for you do not know on what day your Lord is coming.
But know this, that if the master of the house had known in what part of the
night the thief was coming, he would have stayed awake and would not have let
his house be broken into. Therefore you also must be ready, for the Son of Man
is coming at an hour you do not expect.*
MATTHEW 24:42–44

Consider an endeavor that stretches back in time, hundreds, if not thousands of years. It produces a well-known commodity, something that many people enjoy and have been for a long time. A cadre of experts, professionals, academics, and mature leaders propel this venture into an uncertain future. Trained by those who have gone before, there is a prescribed and well-understood way of doing things. Passed down through the generations, one might think that the "standard operating procedure" would be up for scrutiny. Little innovation has occurred through the centuries.

There was a time when great change happened in a relatively short span of time. This created some wonderful change. One might think that resurrecting this spirit of change would be a goal because it was so helpful the first time around. Yet, things remain largely the same despite threats and attacks on this decentralized and distributed effort. There have been conferences held to address the rising problems, papers have been written and there is much hand-wringing about obvious problems. Despite their best efforts, experts have been unable to identify and prescribe a solution to the issues at hand. Tradition and default thinking perpetuate old ways of doing things.

You know what I am describing, right? The church? No, not the church. This is the modern beekeeping industry.

Bees used to be kept in straw baskets or baskets carved out of logs. Harvesting the honey was a labor intensive, sticky mess. Not to mention painful at times. When honey was harvested, the combs were destroyed, and the bees essentially started over because the hive was decimated. Bees often decided to move house completely. Beekeepers had to find new swarms. Honey was expensive and hard to come by.

In 1885, there was a beekeeping reformation. Just as the Protestant Reformation was led by the clergy, so was the beekeeping reformation. The Reverend Lorenzo Lorraine Langstroth, a congregational pastor, developed a hive that would change the world. By spacing the frames inside a wooden box, bees were led to create nice rows of honeycomb. The concept of using frames had been around for some time. The Langstroth hive added something important to the mix. The frames could be spaced in such a way as to lead the bees to making honey in neat, orderly rows on the frames. This is called "bee space" and turned the frame system into a disruptive innovation. It made possible the harvesting of honey without destroying the comb.

The Langstroth hive was much better than the former system. The frame is removed, the "caps" of the honeycomb cells are cut off. The honey drops out of the comb when spun in a centrifuge. The frame is put back in the box with the comb still intact. The bees refill the comb and the cycle repeats itself. Today, a plastic starter comb is often placed in the frames. The bees put wax on top of the starter comb, giving them a head start in building their colony. The bees can spend more of their time making honey and we can spend more of our time eating it.

It is not hyperbole to say that Langstroth disrupted the beekeeping industry. It goes much further than that, however. Bees have made possible the modern agricultural miracle that we know today. Without bees there would be nowhere near the food production that we enjoy. Not only do we get honey from bees, but we get better crops.

That is why a concerned world cares about "colony collapse disorder" in which bee populations are diminishing today. We do not know why, but it has been happening for some years. Some attribute it to pesticides. Others point to the varroa mite, a parasite that attaches itself to bees. Climate change, shrinking biodiversity, and pollution are also considered contributors. While there is optimism that colony collapse disorder is slowing, this crisis is ongoing.

Agricultural experts are making a global call for more beekeepers. The number of hives worldwide has been leveling off and it is expected that there will soon be fewer hives and thus, fewer bees.

In 2015, the world was introduced to the first significant invention in beekeeping since the Langstroth hive. A father and son duo from Australia invented a new system for collecting honey. Stu grew up around his father's beekeeping. He wondered how this process could be made faster, cleaner, and less disruptive to the bees. Having the roof of your house removed and some giant reaching in to snatch away the rooms (and your hard work) cannot be pleasant.

For ten years, they tested new ideas in their workshop. Their eureka moment happened when they devised a system for cracking the plastic starter combs. The comb is opened and closed with a handle. When opened, the honey flows. When closed the bees fill it with honey. The Flow Hive makes beekeeping much more accessible. Rather than the messy process of extracting the honey from frames, one simply inserts a handle into the hive and turns it. Golden honey pours out of the hive into a jar, ready to be enjoyed. Turn the handle back and the bees get to work.

The Andersons launched a crowdfunding campaign on Indiegogo. They set a goal of $70,000 to raise the money to create the plastic injection molds to make the new frames. Within fifteen minutes of posting their project, over $250,000 was pledged. Six weeks later they had raised $16.4 million dollars representing over 14,500 investors. Flow Hive remains among the most successful crowdfunding campaigns in history.[2]

You might be thinking, "Beekeepers must be delighted!" You would be wrong.

Rather than rejoicing at this technology breakthrough, many traditional beekeepers have been protesting the introduction of the Flow Hive. To be fair, there are valid reasons to question any new disruptive technology and the Flow Hive is no exception. Chief among them are the price and the use of plastic. If one reads the comments posted in online forums and websites by traditional beekeepers much more emotional reactions surface. Irrational, traditional, and just plain hostile.

Among the strongest protests involve the claim that the Flow Hive will create emotional detachment from the bees. That sounds terrible, I am sure you agree, because bees are so cuddly, right? The other critique is that people who use the Flow Hive will ignore other aspects of beekeeping. Beekeepers regularly check the hive for parasites, to make sure the queen is healthy, and make sure that the hive has enough stores for that time of the year. None of these activities are impacted by the Flow Hive. The Andersons, of course, never advocated ignoring bees between tapping the hive. I cannot help but wonder if Langstroth put up with similar protests about his invention in 1885.

If you innovate, prepare for push-back. People love what they know. Innovative leaders are targets.

LEADERS STAND IN THE INNOVATION GAP

In 1962, the year I was born, Everett Rogers wrote a book titled, *Diffusion of Innovations.*[3] He explained how innovation is spread, why it spreads, and what factors impact that process. This book has stood the test of time and is now in its fifth edition. Leaders would be wise to take Rogers's theory into account as they embark on their innovation quest.

Rogers wrote that there are four elements through which an innovation or idea can spread. These are the innovation itself (people seeing the idea and adopting it), media and other communication channels, the passing of time, and social mechanisms, which can spread the innovation. If you have heard the term "critical mass," then you know about Rogers's theory already. He theorized that at a certain point in time an innovation spreads to the point where it cannot be stopped. Not many innovations make it to this point.

The adoption curve is how innovation spreads. Rogers stated that in any population there are a small number of innovators (just a few percentage points). These people are the ones who generate the innovation and spread it to early adopters (more, but still a minority). If the innovation continues to grow among the early adopters then the early majority begins to utilize the innovation, then the late majority, and finally the laggards come along.

What do innovative leaders do in pushing their followers through the various stages of diffusion? They become the bridge, standing in the gap between the early innovators and the late majority. Leaders fail at this by paying too much attention to the status quo (sustaining) or by pressing too hard on innovation and leaving the flock behind.

In the back of a church in northern Ontario is an antique projector. Believe it or not, the projecting of hymns onto the church wall predates the widespread use of hymnals. Hymnals were expensive and the projector was a cheaper way to distribute the music to the worshippers. The pastor of the church told me the story surrounding the introduction of hymnals to the congregation in the early part of the 1900s. The congregation had been using the projection system when a committee decided that they should modernize by purchasing hymnals. The cost of the hymnals caused quite a stir in the community. The hymnals were returned to the publisher, and the church used the projection system well into the 1950s, until the plates containing the songs were no longer being produced. Since the plates were made of glass and some had been lost, the move to hymnals was forced (I have wondered, since that visit back in the early 2000s, if that same church has now gone back to the use of projectors, which is now more widespread than hymnals).

What happened in this story of failed innovation? Is this the story of a leader who lost their nerve about the decision that had been made? Perhaps not enough time had been spent on setting the stage for the new technology. Maybe the innovation itself is inadequate and did not meet the need. Usually, innovation fails for multiple reasons. How does leadership affect innovation success?

Innovators and early adopters need no assistance in seeking out a preferred future. They are the tinkerers, the testers, and those with the latest gadgets. When presented with a new idea, they are programmed to consider the idea and are open to adopting it. That is only about 15 percent of the total population, though. Should a leader focus their message on the 15 percent or on the other 85 percent as they seek to diffuse their innovation?

Contrary to what you might think, the research suggests that well less than 15 percent is enough to influence the rest of the group. Reminiscent of the Pareto Principle (otherwise known as the 80/20 rule), much change in history has started from a small group of activists. When Christ ascended, His followers were few. Within a few centuries they had permeated most of the known world.

Innovative leaders do not focus on the laggards, or even the early and late majority. Instead, they empower those who live in the first two spaces on Rogers's chart, the innovators and early adopters. Malcolm Gladwell, in his book *The Tipping Point: How Little Things Can Make a Big Difference*, wrote about the influence of three important groups of people.[4] Connectors are people with large social networks, who know everybody, and who like to make introductions. Salesman are the persuaders; they not only tell others about ideas but encourage their adoption. The last group are the mavens. Mavens read widely, watch online videos, discuss new ideas with others, and are information hoarders. They are the people you turn to when you need additional information about any topic.

Within your ministry you have Connectors, Salesmen, and Mavens. Identify them and direct your communication in their direction. They will diffuse your ideas using their special gifting. Others naturally turn to them for direction, advice, and information. I am sorry, pastors, but preaching will only get you so far. Use the power of the social network God has given you to deepen your influence.

Leaders Create an Innovation Culture

Through the past few decades, several leadership theories have emerged. Transformational leadership describes a leader whose primary approach is to create personal transformation among followers. Trait theory focuses on natural gifting, traits, that people have that make them adept leaders. In Leader/Member Exchange Theory,[5] leaders wield influence and there is a give and take between them and followers. Servant leadership has been called the most Christian of leadership paradigms, highlighted in the life and ministry of Jesus.

Each one of these has value and leaders utilize almost all of them at different points in their ministry. There is one more, though, that has had more influence in the past two decades than the others. Culture theory claims that the primary role of the leader is to set the culture of an organization. Once set on a particular course, the culture creates the desired outcome. Books like *Good to Great* and *Built to Last* followed business guru Peter Drucker's influence in both the business and ministry world. As Drucker is quoted as saying, "Culture eats strategy for breakfast."

Leading innovative projects, without diffusing a culture of innovation, is better than no innovation at all. What is a culture of innovation? It is a ministry in which everybody innovates personally and corporately. A ministry with an innovation culture sees improvements in all they do, all the time. When I spoke with Rob Wassel from Seeds, he said that when they started the lab, they assumed they would be assisting others with innovative projects. What they quickly learned, however, was that culture was far more important.

The culture of your ministry has an incredible influence on how innovative it will be. How each person sees their role, how relationships extend or inhibit creativity, whether failure is embraced or punished, how approachable leaders are, and many other "soft" attributes of ministries affect culture. Intentionality in creating innovative culture is a prime directive for any leader. If you fail to lead in this area, innovation will be challenging in your ministry.

> A culture of innovation is a ministry in which everybody innovates personally and corporately.

In hundreds of interactions I have had with ministry leaders, I have observed a sharp contrast between founders and the leaders that follow them. This contrast may be one reason why ministries tend to become less innovative as they age. Founders tend to see themselves as breaking with tradition and doing something new. Follow-on leaders, in contrast, typically see themselves as the stewards of an inherited culture. The protection of that culture is a higher priority, often unspoken, than breaking with the past.

Leaders Make Space for Innovation

Innovation authors have suggested several models for making space for innovation within existing institutions and organizations. I have found that they usually have something important in common. Leaders separate innovation from operations when the desired changes are substantial. I call these "parallel strategies" because they all run innovation tracks parallel to their current operations. This does not mean that current operations do not need innovation. When the change from the status quo is substantial, that is when parallelism becomes necessary.

Among aviation fans, there is one airplane that stands out above all others, the SR-71 Blackbird. Its origins can be traced back to 1943. The Germans were well ahead of the allies in developing jet airplanes. The US military commissioned Lockheed Aircraft Corporation to build an airplane that could rival the Germans. Because of the secretive nature of the project, the development team was siloed from the rest of the company. Engineers were not allowed to talk about the project outside of work, the team was placed in a secret location, and there were not the usual government procurement practices that slowed down engineers. There was no contract, no official bidding process, and no interference from politicians. They built the first airplane in 143 days, seven days ahead of the planned time line.

Kelly Johnson, the leader of the effort, had pioneered the use of siloed teams creating the P-38 Lightning. His view was that the role of a leader in a creative project was to protect the team from anything that got in the way of the creative process. Accountants measuring costs, administrators preparing progress reports, marketers concerned about selling, and middle managers fighting turf wars were all walled off and kept out of the project. He did this in the name of absolute secrecy but would later write that this approach protected his team from meddling. It freed them to be the engineers and designers they were. They called this a "Skunk Works" project, taken from an obscure reference in a Li'l Abner comic strip.

The Lockheed Skunk Works also designed and delivered the U-2 spy plane. Upon delivery of the airplane, Kelly warned the team that it would have a limited lifespan if missions were run over Russia. Thus, a new plane was ordered, the A-12, the predecessor of the SR-71 Blackbird.

The innovations in the SR-71 are many. It flew at over three times the speed of sound at altitudes that enemy missiles and aircraft could not reach. It evaded enemy attack by accelerating. It literally outran whatever the enemy shot at it. It used a titanium airframe, a unique shape, and a special paint to avoid detection by radar. Its loose-fitting skin and airframe grew as it warmed up, reducing drag. Because of these loose-fitting materials, an SR-71 leaked fuel when parked on the ground. But it was not built to be parked on the ground. There were also new life support systems for the pilots who were often flying at the edge of space. None of these innovations would have gotten by the pencil pushers at Lockheed's headquarters. Great freedoms were given to the team to innovate. The standard Lockheed Aircraft design and production facilities continued to operate, oblivious to the SR-71. They ran in parallel.

Skunk Works projects are possible in your ministry. The key is to shield them from the larger organization's natural tendency to neuter out-of-place ideas. This might include you, if you are the leader of the ministry. Select the innovators that have been yearning for freedom, empower them with the necessary resources, and step back. Do not try to control what they are doing.

A second type of innovation parallelism is written about in the book *Dual Transformation*.[6] The authors suggest that there are two necessary transformations that must take place to prepare for future disruption. The first transformation researches the existing status of a business (in our case, ministry) to better understand how disruption might occur. Innovation around the existing model can make it more effective and resilient. The motivation for this is to use the existing model to pay for the second transformation both financially and by buying more time as the second transformation unfolds.

This second transformation is the search for where the future lays. The authors suggest that leaders find "areas of constraint in the market." In a ministry context we might say to look at needs that are currently underserved. This is like a blue ocean approach in which you seek new opportunities where you believe the future is headed.

The electric car industry highlights a contemporary example of dual transformation. While Elon Musk has created an entirely new car, legacy carmakers face a different set of problems. They must reposition themselves for an electric future. They are doing so by setting goals for where they believe the future lies while strengthening resilience in the current lineup. Ford, for example, has dropped all but one car model (the Mustang) so that they can focus on the more profitable SUV and truck segment of the market. This is remarkable. Had somebody suggested a few years ago that Ford would only be selling one model of car, they would not have been credible. Yet, Ford has made this decision to survive the disruption in the auto industry. This is their first transformation. In the second transformation they are preparing for a fossil-fuel-free future by creating electric vehicles. Their strength in manufacturing and distribution is being leveraged for this eventual reality.

The final approach that highlights parallel strategies for innovation is the "Three-Box Solution," detailed in a book of the same name.[7] This model states that leaders must manage three different "boxes" at the same time to successfully innovate. Box 1 represents the current business. Box 3 is the development of something entirely new, anticipating disruption, and preparing for it. Box 2 is, for me personally, the hardest one. It is the ending of unproductive Box 1 activities. These are things you are doing in your church or organization that have become irrelevant, yet you continue to do because it is what you know. If these are not ended, they suck resources from the other two Boxes and make transformation difficult.

In each of these approaches (Skunk Works, Dual Transformation, and the Three-Box Solution) there are common lessons to be learned. The primary operation of the organization becomes resistant to innovation per the innovator's dilemma. Because of this, innovation efforts must be protected from the operational functions of your ministry. Organizations make space for innovation by creating parallel strategies.

This suggests that change management and innovation are different. Change management is about moving an organization toward a preferred future. Parallelism is less optimistic about the status quo. Instead of making change, it suggests that a break from the past frees up innovation. This is more disruptive than simply asking people to join a "change curve." Parallelism encourages internal revolution. If the innovation is successful, the ministry may move to the new paradigm, which then becomes the new incumbent strategy, in need of innovation.

Leaders Encourage Failure

Andy Keener leads an innovation team at Wycliffe Bible Translators USA. He told me that when they take on innovation problems, one goal is to fail in the right direction. "This year, our goal is to make brand new mistakes."[8] For Andy, innovation means trying out new things, and many of those things will not work as hoped. That is acceptable, as long as they are learning, and the direction is toward solving problems.

Andy explained that one reason why people do not innovate is that we seek perfection. Sometimes, partial solutions are better than those that will never actually come to fruition. He told me about an internal team that asked for some assistance with innovation. They were seeking to broaden the reach of a key program that promotes Bible translation to Wycliffe stakeholders. The team presented a plan that cost hundreds of thousands of dollars. He responded with, "I will give you a budget of $1,500 and I want to see some solid ideas toward the goal in thirty days." He checked in on them two weeks later and there was no progress. They brought up the big plan again, which he rebuffed. As the days ticked down, he asked again if they had made progress. Finally, a team member said, "Let's try this . . ." and they started on a small-scale solution within the parameters given. Soon, a prototype had been put together, and to the team's amazement, it was a helpful step in the right direction. Better yet, the cost to test the idea was far less than the original proposal. When I last spoke with Andy, that prototype was being prepared for use in the real world.

The culture of your ministry has a big impact on how open your people are to failure. Leaders must learn to embrace not only success, but also readily welcome failure. Your staff watches your reaction to failed projects. If disappointment is communicated, expect less innovation in the future. Conversely, if you express curiosity about the nature of the failure and are open to a debrief followed by a new iteration, that will grow openness to failure.

The fear of failure is natural. We reward success. It is on leaders to create a culture in which failure is embraced and not punished.

Leaders Empower Entrepreneurs

Entrepreneurs need special assistance from ministry leaders. Those with the most disruptive ideas will need the most help. Because they are entrepreneurs, they will often forge ahead, without much care or thought for the collateral damage they are creating. Yet, these are the people who have the potential to deliver disruptive innovation. Leadership is often about balancing the self-affirming culture of the organization against the wild ideas of an entrepreneur. A failure to do so may result in your ministry missing out.

The story of the founding of Frontiers is documented in Greg Livingstone's book *You Got Libya*. Greg has the spirit of an entrepreneur. He was tasked with helping his organization, North Africa Mission, recruit and deploy new staff.

One of the drivers behind North Africa Mission, which made it distinct among missionary agencies, was its focus on Arabs. Many missions have much broader ministry goals than just one language group. But Arabs comprise a large swath of countries and cultures. The heart of Islam is in the Arab world. Thus, one can understand why at least one agency might consider having that singular focus. Greg was successfully recruiting new workers when he had an idea. "What if, instead of recruiting missionaries, we coach them on how to recruit a team and pastor them to hang together." The team leaders that recruited could not leave for their field until at least two people signed a memorandum of understanding about the goals of the team and how they would work together.

That sounds like a simple enough idea but consider why the larger organizations might not like this very much. In most organizations, current leaders choose who will be the next leaders. If you are overseeing the ministry in Morocco, after all, you might have an interest in choosing the team leaders in Morocco. Greg was suggesting that the hierarchy be bypassed. In fact, he was bypassing several rules, many of which had good reason for existing. His new scheme would encourage the appointment of greenhorn missionaries, people with no field experience, *as leaders*. Within the leadership ranks, the plan was questioned but, with some persistence, Greg was given the go-ahead to run a few teams this way as long as they did not create trouble that other leaders would have to sort out. After a time, they would evaluate. Soon, Greg was running into more resistance, and it was politely suggested that he take his innovation elsewhere.

Thus, Frontiers was born. Today, it is the only major mission solely focused on reaching all Muslim people groups for Christ. North Africa Mission has folded into another, larger agency. The field staff continue to faithfully serve among Arab people. Would they have done it differently had they known that Greg's foresight in recruiting team leaders would work out so well? It is hard to say, but there is an important lesson in the founding of Frontiers. You can talk about the core values, the mission's statement, the reasons for the rules all you want. Entrepreneurs are going to entrepreneur. They lead you, not the other way around. If you decide to "get off the bus" of the status quo, there might be consequences. Some of those consequences could be very positive.

For many years, people have discussed the power of positive thinking. Let me tell you that the power of negative thinking is also a powerful force. If you have ever worked on a team in which there was an idea-killer, you understand the power of negative thinking.

Negative thinking is not all bad, particularly in the early stages of developing new ideas. In fact, this is where conflict, the right kind of conflict should be gardened. I like the word "gardened" because it implies the work necessary to get something to grow. You must first do the hard work of breaking up the ground, then carefully planting seeds, and then weeding, fertilizing, trimming, and pruning. Managing conflict is a primary task in the innovation process. Making sure that team members can appropriately engage in constructive conflict is key.

High performing teams go through stages of development. The stages are forming (in which the team is pulled together), storming (a time for conflict and role identification), norming (when the team emerges from internal conflict), and performing (when the team focuses on the task they were given).[9] To Tuckman's four stages I would add a fifth. Teams also reform. Whenever a team member is added or removed, the team must again storm and norm.

My experience is that very few teams reach the performing stage. If you think back over your own involvement with teams, you might be able to come up with only one, or perhaps two, instances of a high-performance team. This is true of most people, even though we have been on many different teams. Why is this? It is because most teams get bogged down in the storming that is necessary before they can build the trust necessary to work together unselfishly.

Take those same concepts about teams and think about the innovation curve. Only the first two groups, innovators and early adopters, warmly welcome innovation. The other 80 percent are suspicious, more so in the later stages of the curve. Thus, most teams have built-in friction against new ideas. A leader understands that innovators are seldom going to be in the majority. They protect these innovators from the negative pressure that is almost inevitable.

Leaders Create Urgency

In their book *The Founder's Mentality*, Zook and Allen give a list of ways that organizations head toward sustaining and stagnating. One that fits many ministries is "Death of the Nobler Mission."[10] By this they suggest that the original mission was noble. The status quo has replaced that noble mission and the organization itself becomes the mission. Leadership teams caught in this situation must recognize the danger they are in and rediscover their original purpose or adopt a new one. In business settings, money makes this a pressing issue. Too often in ministry, economic engines that drive the ministry continue to operate, enabling the ministry to carry on for years and decades without a pressing mission that forces innovation. Strategies for recovering the "nobler mission" range from study of the original purposes, to crafting a whole new purpose.

Ezra comes to mind as a leader who fought for a noble vision. Imagine having your entire nation deported to the land of your oppressors. Ninety years later, Ezra comes along, gets the blessing of Artaxerxes to rebuild the temple, and prods a group of exiles to take on this mission with him. The bigger story includes a shift from conquering and pillaging to vassal states, but Ezra is intent on seeing the Jewish people return to Israel. When they arrive, they find that the remaining Jews had lost the nobler vision. They had interbred with the pagan nations around them. Ezra leads a renewal, rediscovering the Scriptures and, in an act of vision casting, has them read to the people. This is leadership that seeks to rediscover the mission that they once had.

If you are in a ministry that has an original purpose that is no longer valid, then you have freedom to really innovate. An example might be missionary organizations that worked in frontier situations. They were the first ones in, planted the church, and now there is a thriving group of fellowships in that region.

For innovation to happen, the nobler mission must be paired with urgency.

Your purpose must shift to something besides frontier missionary work. Partnership with the newly planted churches in sending missionaries and theological education for growing movements have been two ways that missionaries have responded to this sort of success. What happens when they do not make this shift? They create unhealthy dependency in the churches they plant by performing ministry better conducted by national leaders.

For innovation to happen, the nobler mission must be paired with urgency. A mission that is both important and urgent is compelling. These two traits dictate the level of energy a ministry is willing to spend to achieve its mission. It dictates how far it will go in creative problem-solving and making changes that are hard work. The pace of your team is influenced by its embrace of urgency.

If you find yourself leading a ministry that is stagnating or struggling to sustain itself, creating urgency about the mission is a good first step. If you struggle to see the mission as urgent, reconsider how important that mission is. Another possible issue could be you. The leaders with the biggest challenge in communicating urgency are usually those with substantial experience. They have often paid the price of hard work in their former leadership days. They have created something (often, something great). They are willing to innovate on what already exists, but they resist fundamental transformation. It is too easy to retreat into justifications for the status quo.

Summary

Innovation is dependent on leadership. Leaders guide people through the changes that innovation brings into their lives. Developing an innovative ministry culture is far better than having an innovative project. Developing an innovation culture pays dividends in all areas of ministry. People that are highly innovative depend on leaders to shield them from forces in the ministry that discourage innovation. By creating a powerful mission and sense of urgency, a leader influences the willingness of a ministry to create innovation.

APPLICATION & DISCUSSION

Questions to Ponder

1. What is an innovative product, service, or process that you have observed gain acceptance over time? Describe how it progressed through the stages of acceptance noted above.

2. Evaluating the culture of your current ministry, do you think it encourages or discourages innovation?

3. How would your current ministry react if you proposed a Skunk Works project? What sort of projects might be considered?

4. Can you think of people in your ministry that are naturally entrepreneurial? What can you do to encourage them?

5. How important is your mission? Do you think that people sense urgency when they hear it?

TEAM EXERCISE & DISCUSSION

Homework:

Have each member of your team chart where they believe the team currently sits on the team scale of forming, storming, norming, performing, and reforming.

Discussion:

1. Ask each team member to explain their chart and the reasons they plotted the team where it currently sits among the five stages.

2. Ask the team to discuss why the charts are similar (or different). Key decisions or the failure to make decisions, successful projects, level of trust on the team, or other issues could be contributors.

3. Have the members of the team explain what steps could be taken to either become a high-performing team or to continue being a high-performing team.

9

YOU, THE INNOVATOR

The instrument through which you see God is your whole self. And if a man's self is not kept clean and bright, his glimpse of God will be blurred.[1]
-C.S. Lewis, *Mere Christianity*

Whoever loves discipline loves knowledge, but he who hates reproof is stupid.
Proverbs 12:1

Some years ago, I was the speaker at a missions conference in the farmlands outside of Wichita, Kansas. I stayed with a farmer who had a huge spread and many cattle. I told the farmer about my recent trip to India. I was in a cab just outside of New Delhi when a cow, a "sacred" cow, stepped out into the road. The driver swerved, narrowly missing the oblivious bovine. The driver began shouting in Hindi. My companion, a missionary who had lived for years in India, translated that the driver was scared. Had he hit the cow, the crowd around us would have pulled us out of the vehicle and beaten us. The farmer shook his head in amazement. The week before his crew had loaded a few hundred head to be slaughtered.

Looking at me intently, he asked me a very important question. "Do you think people can change?" He was thinking about the masses in India, and the size of the task that a missionary faced, and the tremendous hold a worldview can have on us. We talked about that into the evening. He did not think people changed. They were who they were. I took the position I hold today. If people cannot change, then the gospel itself is up for grabs.

I hope that by this point of the book you have understood that ministries, companies, and just about any team of people can cultivate and grow innovation. This goes for individuals as well. You can grow your innovation quotient.

The theory behind the diffusion of innovation suggests that only a small number of us are natural innovators. Whether this is a nature versus nurture issue, is debatable. In this chapter, we are going to look at six attributes of innovators, and you can judge for yourself just how innovative you are. Then we will turn to a few attitudes you can adopt to grow as an innovator.

Even if we are not all on the level of William Carey, we are all members of teams in need of innovation. Our personal contribution in this space is important even if it is not our specific gifting. As we have seen, innovation is also about discipline and there are tools that we can employ in pursuit of both personal innovation, innovation within our ministries, and innovation across the eccliosystem.

SIX INNOVATION TRAITS

There is an online assessment at my website, https://theinnovationcrisis .com. You can use the tool to determine how innovative you are in each of the following areas: risk-taking, curiosity, initiative, creativity, collaboration, and flexibility.

Risk-Taking

Risk taking is anything that you do that may fail or involves danger. Everybody has a different tolerance level for risk. Some enjoy the rush that comes with risk-taking; others abhor it. To be innovative means that some level of risk-taking must occur. Ministries with more to risk are more risk averse. Finding the appropriate balance between "duty of care" and risk-taking is a challenge in our safety-oriented world.

Risk has personal facets, as well as corporate facets. As a leader, you may be most concerned about the latter. For Christians, risk is inherent to our identity and way of life. In our day and age, it is risky to say that without Christ, people are condemned. Yet, that is part of the message our churches are tasked with making. Ministry means that you take risks to share the kingdom with others. As you consider whether you are personally risk-oriented, keep in mind that Christians are called to a life of risk.

Our family has had a taste of ministry risk. In 1992, we moved to the Balkans, where ethnic hostilities had erupted into three or four different wars. Then, some four years later, we moved into the city of Sarajevo just after the Dayton Peace accords were signed.

Over one million mortar rounds had landed in this city over a three-and-a-half-year siege. Virtually no building was left untouched by the bullets, shrapnel, and bombs that fell on the city. The first landmark you encountered upon descending from the main road into the valley was the old newspaper building. Standing at the intersection of the highway and the main artery that cut through Sarajevo, it was shot through and half demolished. Behind it was Dobrinja, where the faces of entire apartment complexes, some fifteen to twenty stories tall, had been shot off and you could look directly into the rooms of the apartments. Sarajevo was served by a tram system, an urban train that ran the length of the city. Alongside this railway was the main road. If you were somebody who watched the news back in the 1990s, this road was the infamous sniper alley. People died all along this route and you could not help but consider this as you drove toward downtown.

Many people in Sarajevo died when they were forced out into the open to collect water, shot by snipers or hit by random mortar fire. We saw cables that had been strung across city streets and then draped with blankets. This kept the snipers from having a clear view down the street and no doubt saved many lives.

There were no functioning hotels in 1996 except the Holiday Inn, which was filled with NATA and United Nations personnel. Thus, on our first night in Sarajevo, we found a local woman with an apartment who let us stay with her. She lived in a high-rise apartment building. When you looked out over the city, you saw a blue gray haze. It was the garbage being burned from almost four years of no garbage collection. That night my wife and I, with our six-week-old daughter between us, slept to the occasional sound of gunfire in the distance.

During our first months in Sarajevo, we heard landmines going off every few days. Most were tripped by dogs rummaging through the debris, but not all. In the park behind our house, neighbors warned us that our children were not to walk anywhere but on the pavement. It would be a year or two before those landmines were cleared.

As strange as this might sound, *none of this felt risky to us.* We heard from others about how risky it was, but we did not internalize that risk. We spoke the local language, had good friends in the culture that were quick to warn us of potential dangers, and had already been in the region for some time. More important than these factors, though, was the sense of overwhelming purpose we had. We had started our missionary journey almost eight years before. Each step of the way, from disappointments to victories, had led us to Sarajevo. There was no doubt in our mind that we were supposed to be there at that time in history. It was God-ordained in our hearts and minds.

We often see risk as a calculation. How much benefit do I gain by accepting the chance of a loss? This is one aspect of risk. Another aspect, though, is related to one's sense of calling. I am not suggesting here that everything will turn out in the positive column if we risk in faith. That is a simplistic view of faith. In fact, in the great faith "hall of fame" listed in Hebrews, plenty of people are mentioned for their suffering and martyrdom. The point is that the benefit that is gained (obedience to one's calling) is greater than the potential risk.

As you think about your tolerance for risk, the extent to which you feel called to the project at hand comes to bear. As a leader in a ministry role, as a member of a team seeking to be innovative, or even in consideration of a personal challenge requiring risk, ask yourself how certain are you that innovation should be sought?

Sometimes, of course, we find ourselves being innovative in ways we did not consider. Martin Luther is an example of a leader who did not set out to be innovative. He did, however, seek change in a system that was in dire need of change. Your convictions about what needs to happen make risk-taking secondary to the possible benefits.

Curiosity

Curiosity may kill cats, but it also gives birth to innovation. Curiosity is the desire to know something. Innovators are curious learners. Children are naturally curious. If you have ever met a three-year-old in the "why?" stage of life, you know just how they can be. It is too bad that we discourage this until they ask only the socially appropriate amount of questions.

Francesco Gino, writing for the *Harvard Business Review*, states that there five benefits that come from cultivating curiosity. It combats confirmation bias (coming to conclusions that confirm preconceived notions), helps employees be more innovative in both creative and non-creative jobs, reduces conflict, creates open communication, and yields better team performance. The author cites studies supporting each of these areas.[2]

Sadly, the same article states that managers discourage curiosity: In a survey of some 3,000 employees across a wide range of firms and industries, Gino found that just one-quarter reported feeling curious on the job regularly, and 70% said they faced barriers to asking more questions at work. Gino found that leaders discourage curiosity for two main reasons: First, they believe that if they let employees explore new ideas and approaches, they'll have a managerial nightmare on their hands. Second, their single-minded pursuit of efficiency leaves little room for experimentation.[3]

Curiosity also drives learning. One of my favorite passages of Scripture is embedded in the final verses of 2 Timothy. Verse 13 is not very inspirational until you think about it. Paul writes, "When you come, bring the cloak that I left with Carpus at Troas, also the books, and above all the parchments." This is an old man, with many years of ministry experience, including direct contact with Jesus, and think about what he asks for. He is cold, evidently, so he wants the cloak that he left to Carpus. That is understandable. But what is remarkable are the next two items. Bring the books and bring the parchment. As he approaches his last years, Paul is still reading and learning. He is an example of a lifelong learner.

Initiative

I have attempted to make the point repeatedly in this book that sacrificing the status quo is a requirement for innovation. Initiative is related to bias to action. Included in it is the willingness to forego one opportunity for another. As we saw when we studied the innovator's dilemma, past success almost guarantees future failure. Somebody who takes initiative sees a new opportunity and makes the leap, leaving behind what was there before. It is hard for ministries to lay aside the familiar. The same can be true of people.

A new acronym entered the vernacular in the past few years, FOMO: fear of missing out. People are often driven to do something not because they really want to do it, but because they do not want an opportunity to pass them by. One way I measure if I should do something is using the "Heck Yeah Rule." Somebody recently asked me to join their board. As I mulled it over, I realized that I did not really want to spend my time this way. There was no "Heck, yeah, I want to be on that board!" Not all opportunities should be evaluated this way, of course, but it is a good measuring habit. It helps me to avoid taking on things out of a sense of obligation.

Initiative is related to reading weak signals. Professor Vijay Govindarajan describes these as "early evidence of emerging trends from which it is possible to deduce important changes in demography, technology, customer tastes and needs, and economic, environmental, regulatory, and political forces."[4] In ministry, understanding the early signs of change will make the leap to something new more like a jump. These signals are considered weak because it requires something of a supernatural sense to discover them.

Weak signals in ministry take many forms. Perhaps zoning laws in your municipality are creating fewer single-family homes. Your congregation is filled with young families, just about ready to buy a new house, which entails a move to an outer ring suburb. Seeing this before it happens, making changes now, well before it is necessary, is part of taking the initiative. While the shift occurs, your church thrives because it has shifted outreach to the new demographic before it happened. Changes in giving patterns, generational shifts, and immigration all contain markers of your future. Initiative led by discernment produces innovation.

Creativity

Creativity is the ability to generate new concepts, mix existing concepts into something new, and challenge conventions. When we create, we are mimicking our Creator. If you are reading this book, you are probably well acquainted with the glories of God's creative power.

As I wrote this book and looked for examples of innovation, one thing emerged that I should have expected but did not. When I asked others for examples of creativity among churches, almost all the examples were focused on the arts. I appreciate the arts very much. I play a couple of musical instruments. Creativity and the arts are, of course, inextricably linked. Culture is influenced by the arts. Yet, the creative arts are just a subset of the innovation needed today. It is easy to spot creative people in the arts. It is harder to spot "organizational artists" although they may influence more than we realize.

There are so many innovative ministry needs today. These are things like mission structures, collaborative church networks, strategies to serve the underserved, financial models that create generosity, new Bible education methodologies, new media outreach, and the use of apps and mobile devices for ministry. These entities do not just appear, they are created. Connecting people in new and collaborative ways that empower mission fulfilment is art of another form.

Collaboration

When my wife and I were going through missionary training, we did an exercise focused on teamwork. It was called Desert Survival. The facilitator read a story about an airplane crash in which you are the lone survivor. There is a set of objects, including a knife, a plastic tarp, a mirror, salt tablets, and other items that are available to you. In this scenario, you must prioritize which items are most important for your survival and which items are less important. In a room full of people, you will be working with four to five others to develop the list of priorities. As the process unfolds, each person in the group makes their list independent of the others. Then, the group comes together and must agree on an overall list.

The exercise is not about desert survival, of course. Rather, it is about how you work with others to discuss, argue, compromise, and come to agreement on the list. By comparing your original list with the list that the group eventually comes up with, you can find out who is dominant and who is better at making their point and convincing others to go along with their way of thinking. The group carries into it many biases. For example, imagine you are in a group with the following four people. One is a recent seminary graduate, recently married to his high school sweetheart. Another has been working as a secretary in a law office and is twenty-seven years old. She is quiet, bookish, and demure. The third member of your group is a forty-five-year-old pastor. He has successfully planted numerous churches and is quite confident, has a winsome personality, and a warm and welcoming manner. The last person in your group recently left the military, where he was an Army Ranger. He is athletic and confident, but perhaps likes to joke a bit too much.

Given the makeup of the group, who is most likely to be listened to in that group? Let us look at each one in turn. The seminary grad does not have much life experience. We would be cautious to think that he would know much about a plane crash in the desert. The same is true for the secretary. Her personality is quiet, but she most likely will not speak much. The pastor appears to have high emotional intelligence. He would probably do a good job in seeking to pull in everybody and make sure all have a chance to share. He is no expert on desert survival, though. Of course, the Army Ranger is where we would put most of our confidence. Surely, he will know what it will take to survive in the desert.

This was, in fact, like the makeup of the group in which I participated. True to form, the secretary spoke very little during the time that we spent discussing the objects. The seminary grad was a contributor but also aware of his shortcomings. He turned out to be a pretty good listener, and he quickly gave in when challenged about some of his selections. The pastor spent quite a bit of time arguing about one object in particular, the knife. I remember thinking at the time that he was more concerned about attacks from wild animals that he was surviving. The Army Ranger, with a smirk on his face, agreed with the pastor and wondered how many of us knew how to use a knife. Our group spent a great deal of time talking about the knife and how we might use it. I felt an urgency as the time window began to close for the discussion.

Yes, I was the fifth member of the group, a twenty-six-year-old computer consultant from Minneapolis. Like the others, I knew very little about desert survival. But, because I have such a big mouth, exuded a bit too much confidence, and was young and rather brash, I forced my choices on the rest of the group. I elevated the salt tablets as the most important single item. At the objections of one or two others, I forced my will on the group, and we made this the number one item to take.

When the facilitator described each object in its importance, it was suggested that nobody take the salt tablets. They would not help with dehydration and in fact may be harmful. Nobody in our group got the top item correct except the secretary. When stranded in the desert, the primary objective is to be found. The small mirror can be used to signal an airplane flying overhead. It increases the chances of being found many times over and was the most helpful object at our disposal. The secretary had argued for the small mirror.

This little exercise taught me so much about who I am as a person, in how my lack of collaboration skills might lead to bad outcomes for others. It also taught me about built-in biases that I had. I do not recall anybody in our group taking the secretary seriously. On the other hand, we all believed the Army Ranger had much to contribute because of his background. In retrospect, his personal list was no better than most of the answers the rest of us had given.

As we have seen in other chapters, collaboration and innovation are often close partners. The extent to which you can work with others is important. In our group exercise, our failure to truly collaborate, to pull out information from those who we might socially discount, led to a failed outcome. Just as importantly, my personality and its dominance in the group led us down the wrong path. Through the years, this problem has surfaced many times, despite my best attempts to squash it. Am I any better today than I was when I was younger? I think so, but it has taken effort to become a better collaborator.

How much do you value working with others? How much are you willing to compromise as you seek your objectives? How well do you listen when others are offering contrary opinions? These are questions you can think about to improve your ability to collaborate.

Flexibility

Flexibility is how willing you are to adjust to new ideas, people, and experiences.

Many of the attributes here, from collaboration to initiative to risk taking, require flexibility. Psychologists use the term "cognitive flexibility" to describe the ability to think in different ways than their initial programming. Psychologists have conducted tests on children using cards with different attributes. Some are red while others have animals or objects on them. The youngest children sort the cards according to one of these attributes. When presented with an alternate method, most initially reject the alternate, even though there was no training about how to do the sorting the first time.[5]

Our brains are not wired to be completely open; cognition is driven by the fact that we can generalize and make conclusions. But when these mental models replace reality we are in trouble. Innovation will not happen if our thinking process is rigid, the proverbial "box" we are told to avoid.

Confirmation bias is the tendency to project a belief that we already have on new information. Nobody is immune to it, but some are more prone. In contemporary society this problem is getting worse. The Internet allows us to filter out contrary viewpoints and data; confirmation bias is on the rise. Most of us down-vote news feeds we do not like. Over time, we drive ourselves into a narrower and less flexible worldview as we see fewer opposing or different positions.

One can grow in flexibility. Psychologists have tested this by giving children a set of cards with shapes and colors. They can teach a three-year-old to sort by one dimension or the other. By the time they are five, most children can sort by two dimensions. This cognitive flexibility shows that we develop cognitive flexibility over time. Yet, most people would assume that cognitive flexibility decreases with age.

Neil Postman coined the phrase "hardening of the categories." As we mentally organize the world around us, our brain tries to lump similar things together. When confronted with something new, we first attempt to place the new thing into existing categories even if the "fit" is not right. As we grow more confident in our categorization system, it takes precedence over reality. Often, those with the most experience and expertise have the "hardest" categories.

Flexible people avoid letting these categories become their reality. They can shift their thinking when necessary. Resilient cross-cultural missionaries learn to be flexible. Their environment forces them to see the world through very different worldviews.

INNOVATE YOURSELF

You can get better at innovation, and you can also apply innovation principles to your own life. The Shoemaker Rules apply not only to whole ministries, but also to individuals.

See a Problem Worth Solving

As an activist in global Great Commission ministry, one of the joys of my life has been meeting missionaries. They are, as a group, unique in so many ways. I once visited a medical clinic in the remote areas of the Middle East. The clinic was staffed by two doctors, both lovers of Jesus. One was an Israeli and the other a Palestinian. Together, they were heroically treating thousands of mostly Muslim herdsmen. Their little clinic, understaffed and lacking equipment, was nevertheless an outpost of miracles for the surrounding community. At one point in our conversation, I asked them about their backgrounds. Either one could have been highly successful financially but had chosen this life instead. They knew that the problem they were solving, a lack of health care among a large population, far outweighed the joys of owning the latest European sports car. They had seen a problem worth solving.

> **Finding meaning in life often means contributing to the spiritual, physical, and emotional health of *others*.**

Finding meaning in life often means contributing to the spiritual, physical, and emotional health of *others*. We can all innovate ourselves but seeing a problem worth solving typically lies outside of ourselves. Some people develop life mission statements to give clarity to the problem they are solving.

Ride the Wave of Existing Innovation

Riding the wave, in this time of incredible innovation, should be easy for all of us. There are countless tools, hacks, and other means that put personal innovation into our hands.

Bill Burnett is the executive director of the *d.life lab* at Stanford University. The lab uses design thinking to design one's own life. It is a standard course for Stanford graduates that begins by asking the question, "What do you want to be when you grow up?" The innovation ideas talked about in this very book are the ones that Burnett emphasizes with his students. This is riding the wave. It is taking advantage of the environment and innovations already occurring to better ourselves. In fact, by combining a spiritual worldview with the mostly secular approach that design thinking uses, the wave grows exponentially.

Be Biased to Action

Of the five Shoemaker Rules, personal application of "be biased to action" is perhaps the easiest and yet, most difficult. It is easy because, often, the action step has limited consequences, affecting only you. It is hard because it typically involves discipline. Do you want to lose weight, get in shape, or learn a new computer skill? All of these require you to *do something*. Growth in personal innovation similarly means you must act. I have read a fair number of books on the topic of personal growth. I cannot remember a single one that didn't urge action.

In addition to an overwhelming number of books about design thinking, there are certification courses, free material online, and conferences on innovation offered. This methodology in particular has potent personal application.

Empathize, then Strategize

Empathizing is about understanding your stakeholders; in this case, you are the stakeholder. Solutions are derived from our perceptions, which are impacted by our self-awareness. This includes being emotionally self-aware (knowing our own feelings and their impact on others), an accurate self-assessment (knowing our own strengths and limits), and having realistic self-confidence (an accurate sense of worth and capabilities). Maturity in these three areas make objective understanding possible. We can more easily identify when our subjective self is affecting our perception.

Paul warns each of us in Romans 12:3 "not to think of himself more highly than he ought to think, but to think with sober judgment, each according to the measure of faith that God has assigned." One of the concepts that business consultant Jim Collins emphasizes is that leaders must "confront the brutal facts." When it comes to understanding ourselves, we similarly must learn to see ourselves more as God sees us. This is, in fact, the ultimate understanding we can pursue about ourselves.

When we truly understand our own motivations, we can strategize about our life's course in a much more effective way.

Think Big

In 2012, I had the gift of a sabbatical. I had watched how my peers had gone before me, using their sabbaticals for writing, simply getting away from work and ministry, or going to a remote location to think and pray. Three months of uninterrupted time. Among ministry leaders, there is a propensity to plan sabbaticals and meet various objectives. Typically, this happens when burnout is imminent, or a life change is in the works. In my case, the expectation was that I would come back charged up and ready for the next season of ministry. What should I do with this incredible gift?

Setting aside what I did end up doing, think about how that sabbatical framed that three-month window. I had great freedom as long as I kept the big goal of personal renewal in mind. What would happen if we took every three-month chunk of time and treated it this way? We would start to dream bigger about life. Instead of the do-list and the next week of work, our horizon would lift a bit higher and our perspective would be more ambitious.

I cannot say what thinking big might mean for you. I can, however, suggest that you will think bigger if you think more long term than just the next week or month. Set your sights down the road, dream about the person you want to be.

For me, spending time with two of my boys seemed epic. We decided to go on a bicycle ride together. We left New Orleans and rode to Minneapolis over thirty days, using the balance of my time to visit my family in Minnesota, spend time with my other kids, and be with my wife. Looking back, I can think of no better way to have used that precious gift. It was big!

INNOVATING FROM WITHIN

I have spoken on innovation several times to large groups of people. More than once, somebody has approached me after the session to ask, "I am not a leader in my organization. What can I do about innovation?" This is an understandable sentiment as so much of our theory about change is leadership-focused. When one is not in the primary chair, or at least breathing the thin air at the top of the mountain, it is hard to know what can be done.

Be a Whole Person

Everybody is the boss of something. It might be just your cubicle, assuming COVID-19 did not send you to work in a home office. But even in a home office, you are the boss. Consider what innovation principles apply in your domain and put them to work. Others will notice and your future innovation will be welcomed.

Creating influence in the lives of others starts with character. What lies below the water line and out of sight is the most important part of a sailboat. Without a keel and rudder, the boat goes nowhere. Self-leadership, in which we purposefully set a course for ourselves and pursue it, is a lifelong skill that all innovators should develop.

Along with spiritual depth, be an interesting person. In the book, *The CEO Next Door*, the authors write about "identity theft."[6] This happens when your job becomes your identity, replacing the real you with a work-focused you. This happens to many senior leaders. The antidote to this kind of identity theft is to grow as a person outside of your work life. Take on unique hobbies, invest in local projects in your community, and get perspective through deep relationships with others. Often, when I ask ministry leaders what their favorite hobby is, they say reading. I like reading, too, but for most of these leaders they are reading ministry books. Interesting people race motorcycles, play music, savor gourmet food (or learn to cook it), and enjoy a host of other interests. It both reveals and creates curiosity in us when we sample a wide variety of what life has to offer us. Innovative people are often interesting people.

Get Outside Perspective

Just like organization and churches benefit when somebody outside looks in, we as people need to cultivate outside influence in our lives. This can be done formally or informally.

Mentoring is an important part of any leader's development. If you do not have a mentor, consider finding one. Most people do not have mentors because they have not asked somebody to be their mentor. If you have been in your ministry role for more than ten years, it is important that you have two to three mentoring relationships going at any time. I personally mentor others for a nine-month period. I do not use a curriculum but rather talk with the person about their situation, and together we process a book, video series, or other resource. The best time, though, is the nondirective discussion. As the mentor, I am convinced I learn more than they do.

Rob Wassel (Seeds) has organized his own board of directors. There is no legal entity but a group of individuals that Rob pursues on a regular basis to advise and consult with him on his own personal development. After a few years of connecting one on one with these advisors (all substantial leaders in their own fields), they got together for an extended meeting. The people on this advisory board are not in Rob's immediate circle of work friends. In fact, only one is in a ministry role. These advisors bring an outside perspective to Rob's work and personal life.

PRACTICE PERSONAL INNOVATION

Here are a few practical suggestions that you can do to increase your innovation quotient.

Even if you cannot change the direction of your organization, most of us can at least influence our own team. Ask your team lead about innovation and the role it plays in the work. Take time to practice empathy with your team members.

Put yourself in situations where you must exhibit the six attributes. If you are weak on flexibility, take a vacation without planning. If you tend to work alone or in isolation, commit to a collaboration effort. One can literally scan the list and devise small steps toward greater innovation.

Janus was a Greek god, represented by a head with two faces, looking in different directions. Janusian thinking is when you look at the same problem from two different (often opposing) perspectives. At Missio Nexus, we have had to adjust our expectation on income from virtual events in the wake of COVID-19. In a discussion on price setting, one team member asked, "Why do we even charge for these virtual events? Let's focus on in-person events and make the virtual component free. More people will attend and we may see a rise in registration for in-person events." This was not even on the table, but it proved to be the route that we went. The assumptions of our discussion were reframed by Janusian thinking.

A helpful tool for any leader is to do a time line analysis of one's own ministry career. Bobby Clinton's *The Making of a Leader*[7] provides a strategy for understanding how spiritual leaders develop throughout their lifetime. Similar to Adizes' *Organizational Lifecycles* (chapter 2), Clinton reveals the natural trajectory of a leader's development. By mapping our own life experience against his outline, we better understand ourselves and can innovate our own development.

Summary

Each of us uniquely contributes to innovation. Understanding ourselves and our best contribution is important. We can also grow in our ability to innovate. Risk-taking, curiosity, initiative, creativity, collaboration, and flexibility are attributes that help us evaluate how innovative we are. We can use the same Shoemaker Rules individually that we apply to churches and organizations. We can grow our ability to innovate by being interesting, getting outside perspective, and through daily disciplines that contribute to our personal development.

APPLICATION & DISCUSSION

Questions to Ponder

1. Take the online innovation assessment at https:// theinnovationcrisis.org.

2. In what ways are you purposefully practicing lifelong learning and developing your curiosity?

3. Review or create a life mission statement.

4. List your mentors. If you do not have one, create a list of potential mentors and ask them to consider mentoring you.

10

WHAT IF?

Life is not an inevitable decline into dullness;
for some it is an ascent into excellence.[1]
EUGENE PETERSON

"If you can?" said Jesus. "Everything is possible for one who believes."
MARK 9:23 (NIV)

This book started out with a negative argument. I told you that there is a crisis of innovation in ministries and churches. By now you should realize that there is great reason to hope that innovation is within our reach. What if there was an explosion of innovation in the church today? Imagine the effects of innovation on discipleship, community, racial reconciliation, hospitality, and giving!

GIANTS TO BE TACKLED

What would happen if innovative ministries helped people in the church take *discipleship* seriously? What would it look like if each person, everyone sitting in a church service this Sunday, were to eagerly pursue the Lord each day? What if they were to grasp fundamental truths about theology and let these truths change their hearts and souls?

What if a movement of discipleship took hold and each Christian saw their neighbors as Christ sees them?

Discipleship, one of the most basic Christian practices, is ripe for innovation. How is that going to happen?

Consider the effects of Christians taking *community* seriously, of living life with others in ways that we currently are not able to envision. Perhaps this community takes on a new form. It would not copy the secluded monastic life that bypasses culture and isolates. Nor would it chase after the popular culture in a never-ending quest to be relevant. This community would be something different. Conflicts would be gracefully but directly addressed; outsiders would be welcomed but growth would be an incidental outcome rather than a strategic goal. Love would dominate relationships so that each day thousands would be added to its number. What if this community were flavored with a holy, reverent fear and thirst for righteousness?

An innovative, life-giving, culture-influencing, love-embracing community.

What if Sunday morning, instead of being called the most segregated hour of the week, were known as the most integrated? What if the leadership of local churches were the most multicultural, multiracial, and multigenerational leadership demographic in our societies? What if the dreams of Martin Luther King Jr. were manifest in the church? What if our major news outlets eagerly invited Christians to speak on issues of racial justice because they saw us as just and inclusive? Today, that position is held by diversity experts in secular universities and corporations, people who rarely look to Scripture for wisdom.

What if the church, the entire eccliosystem, in humility, was leading the way in racial reconciliation instead of running to catch up?

What would happen in our world if Christians extended hospitality in radical new ways? Perhaps an innovative ministry could expose ordinary Christians to the habits of simply opening their homes to others. This new, massive network of hospitality stations could surpass Airbnb as the biggest provider of way stations for weary pilgrims. Or perhaps it is something as simple as one shared meal, with people from the community, each week.

Imagine the shift in the church that would create.

Think about the benefits of Christian men and women working together in mutual support and respect. While we have been consumed with theological debate about the role of women in the church, the shared *imago Dei* of the two genders has taken a backseat. While the first century church was astonishingly empowering of women, the contemporary church can be seen by culture as harmful to women.

Who is going to innovate new ways to communicate and grow healthy relationships between men and women?

What would it mean to the church if leaders were exponentially better equipped to empower others rather than place themselves at the center of its activity? Who is going to create the ministry model that focuses on deep, life changing application? The current operational model of most churches leads one to conclude that didactic teaching is the most important activity of the church. From sermons to small groups we have decided to let the voice of one person dominate the structure and discourse of our faith. What if that were turned upside-down and every believer was equipped to rightly handle the Word of God?

Who will find the balance between leading and empowerment?

Consider that after two thousand years of effort on the Great Commission about one-third of the world's population will live their entire life without a single Christian relationship. Touching the lives of these people requires radical intervention. While great progress has been made and much has been learned about effective missionary work, few Christians consider long-term cross-cultural ministry.

What if we not only preached financial tithing but also tithed each gathering of Christians such that a missionary movement greater than any other exploded across the world?

Since we mentioned finances, consider the vast amount of money that Christians control. Some estimates have the amount in line with the percentage of believers worldwide, or about 15 percent of global wealth. Just in the United States, donor advised funds hold billions in reserve, money technically given to charity but withheld from ministry uses until it is transferred to a ministry organization. Consider the millions of dollars held in real estate by churches globally. Most statistics that estimate global giving suggest that about 98 percent of Christian wealth is spent on Christians, and a little less than 2 percent is given to any form of ministry.

What if the generosity of Christians could be leveraged to bless the world?

Think of the vast resources owned by members of the global ecclio-system. From dollars to fixed assets the number is staggering. If an innovative ministry created a means to unleash an epidemic of generosity, the world could be changed. As I have traveled globally, I have observed that poverty and joblessness go together. The holistic integration of ministry and business holds great promise, yet the business as mission movement struggles to deliver breakthroughs. Similarly, chartable efforts fall short of expectations. There is often a polemical war between these two much-needed ministry paradigms.

What if these efforts are fused together in some sort of new breakthrough approach that delivers on both?

A Time for Courage

These are just some of the giants waiting for ministry leaders to tackle. These are outward facing issues that can connect with our mission statements. Suggesting they can be conquered is both faith-filled and audacious. It will take courage to aim innovation at these problems.

We also need courage in addressing the internals of our churches and organizations. Stagnating ministries need to pull the emergency lever. With the ever-increasing effects of cumulative change, the end can come swiftly. Leaders experiencing this sort of crisis will often point to external forces that create a final crisis. Things like COVID-19. When a stagnating ministry hits an existential crisis, free fall can set it. The reality is that stagnation has more likely been a slow-growing cancer. The triggering event is just the last stage of an almost irreversible slump toward obsolescence. Zook and Allen's research suggests that about 5 to 7 percent of companies are either in free fall or beginning to fall into it.[2] If this is true for industry, I believe the number must be double or more for ministries. Leading a stagnating ministry takes enormous amounts of courageous leadership to change course.

A triggering event might include a mortgage payment for a church with a building they can no longer afford. It could be a sexual harassment lawsuit revealing a toxic organizational culture. It might be as simple as the inability of a ministry to attract and hire staff because the mission has fallen into irrelevancy. These triggering events are best seen as gifts. They create the conditions for change and courageous leaders embrace them for what they are.

Sustaining ministries have a different set of challenges. I hope that one message you have read in this book is that existing ministry structures and paradigms are often the roadblocks for venturing down unknown, innovative paths. Signs that these roadblocks are going up are many. You might begin to sense that you are good at what you do, but this is competence in the status quo. You might have climbed the organizational ladder and now look down on a familiar domain. Unfortunately, the domain becomes the problem.

Sustaining ministries have time to make the sort of changes that can bring renewal. Even so, building a sense of urgency is paramount to getting stakeholders on board for the sort of change required. Avoid the temptation to tweak the existing systems. Instead, use the time to make wise changes. Adopting a significant change in mission can be done without severe trauma to the people involved. Disruptive change does not have to mean harm to the people involved.

You need courage to make significant, innovative change if you find your ministry stagnating or sustaining.

A Time for Renewal

When I took over leadership at Missio Nexus, the budget was losing about 20 to 25 percent per year. We had reserves, but membership income was declining, the pricing model was not working, and conversations were mostly focused on sustaining what was in place. We were forced to make difficult decisions about our membership model, questioned the validity of each program that we were providing to members, and began to listen to our members about what they wanted from us.

We adopted a new mission statement, created personas around our primary stakeholders, diversified our board, created new pathways for collaboration, and worked to build greater empathy for our primary members. The ship did not right itself overnight, but today we have a growing membership, financial stability, and a renewed sense of purpose. Sustaining ministries can be renewed. I do not think we have arrived or that our future is all roses—far from it. Yet, God has blessed the changes we have made.

In our case, a leadership transition was one reason why the changes were possible. It was not a matter of my leadership being better than that of the previous leader. It was because I came in without any attachments to the current strategy, freeing up perspective. Sometimes, leadership change is a necessary step to help a church or other ministry realize its potential.

> Renewal should be, both personally and in the ministries that we lead, an ongoing process. Innovation is a path to renewal.

Some of you reading this book may need to think about your own willingness to initiate innovation. You may be feeling too tired and discouraged to take on the hard tasks ahead. You may be too confident and unwilling to change course. It takes courage for an existing leader to evaluate their own leadership and make the decision to free up the leadership spot. It takes courage for an elder board or a nonprofit board to seek leadership change if that is what is necessary. These transitions are both risky and filled with opportunity, but for some of you, renewal awaits.

The New Testament is filled with images of renewal. If any man is in Christ, he is a new creation. Be transformed by the renewal of your mind. Our inner man is being renewed day by day. The Holy Spirit regenerates and renews. Be born again. Renewal should be, both personally and in the ministries that we lead, an ongoing process. Innovation is a path to renewal. It is the acceptance that the old no longer serves as it once did and must be replaced with something new.

A Time for Perspective

For those of us that are not feeling this sort of "innovate or die" crisis, innovation is an opportunity. Every project has the potential for innovation. Every job description can embed innovation as a standard trait for a team member. Long held assumptions can be thoughtfully questioned.

The first industry I worked in as a recent college graduate was information technologies. I was part of a team installing the first iterations of personal computers in farm cooperatives across the United States. These computers were equipped with modems to communicate sales information back to our mainframe computer in St. Paul, Minnesota. Most of the sales were for truckloads of fertilizer and agricultural chemicals. At one site, one of the large farm cooperatives in our system, the modem kept failing during transmission. Our help desk people could not fix the problem and it was elevated to our technical team of which I was a part. I flew out to the farm cooperative with a couple of new modems and the task of fixing things before we lost this important customer.

The office was very busy and loud. The administrative staff were crammed into a small office. The storefront was bustling with customers. On the other side of the wall was the radio dispatcher for the fleet of trucks delivering the product to farms in the region, shouting out directions to drivers who could never seem to hear him. I got to work, exchanging the old modem for a new one and then starting the modem transmission, which worked fine. I began running tests and soon realized that the new modem failed but without any sort of consistency. I studied the data, tried a second and then a third modem. We switched out the computer. The problem persisted. What I thought would be a short, one-day visit stretched into three days, and then four.

In a moment of desperate exasperation, I walked into the hallway and looked back into the administrative office's open door at the failing computer system. The parallel room with the radio dispatcher had its door open as well. My eyes caught the dispatcher looking at me and he shook his head with a smirk as he pressed the microphone button to shout another order. The college boy from the city was not doing his job.

And then it hit me.

I started up a long download on the computer and turned the screen toward the hallway. I went back out and turned to watch the dispatcher. After a few minutes, his radio called out, a truck wanting new orders. The dispatcher keyed his microphone and, as I looked back at the monitor, the download failed. I discovered to my amazement that the powerful radio in the next room was knocking the modem offline. We moved the computer doing the downloads into another part of the building. It began to work flawlessly.

I would never have made that discovery had I not changed my perspective. Seeing the problem from a different angle allowed me to see what I could not see. The same is true for many of us in leadership. We need to work in the children's ministry for a few weeks. Or perhaps we should be the ones to handle the front desk calls for a day. Maybe we need to get on an airplane and spend time with the people our staff are serving, just to see things from a new perspective.

Problem reframing, a core innovative skill, is directly tied to gaining a new perspective. What would happen if we as leaders grew in this skill?

Conclusion

I believe we have a crisis of innovation among ministries today. There is no doubt that we find stellar examples that buck this crisis. Yet, there are brutal facts we must face. The Christian worldview is waning in Western society. The enormous cultural and religious shifts around us are making decades of ministry irrelevant. Despite creating the conditions for massive innovation, the COVID-19 epidemic has not produced a wave of innovation. Legacy ministries continue to use many of the same methods and systems developed for a previous generation.

> Each new generation seems more welcoming and embracing of innovation. We have tools, systems, and new methodologies. Do we have the will to put them to work?

There is hope. There is great hope. We are awash with innovation outside the eccliosystem. The people that sit in our pews, read our fundraising letters, and pray for us have been conditioned to accept innovation. Each new generation seems more welcoming and embracing of innovation. We have tools, systems, and new methodologies. Do we have the will to put them to work?

It starts with ministry leaders like you. Let me encourage you to see a problem worth solving, ride the wave of innovation that is washing over us, take action, listen well to your stakeholders before devising solutions, and stretch your faith by thinking big.

In our day, William Carey would be called a blue-collar worker. He educated himself, saw a need, and acted. He was doubted. He met with many hardships; no doubt due to some of his own personal failings. Here on my desk is a small, framed postage stamp. The text on the stamp is in both Hindi and English, the price in Rupees. The stamp features a hero from India's past. William Carey. How astonishing, considering the reputation of the British colonizers in India, that the Indian postal system would honor Carey in this way. It is a testament to his innovative, courageous life.

My prayer is that you, too, will be a Shoemaker.

GLOSSARY

TERM	DEFINITION
A/B Testing	Testing in which small changes are made between two items. Often used in email campaigns in which subject lines are subtly changed and the results compared.
Affinity Diagram	A graphical representation of ideas in which related concepts are grouped, showing their similarities. Helpful to classify items leading to common understanding of issues or solution sets.
Aggregating	Finding smaller chunks of a resource and adding them together to make them more useful. Amazon aggregates many seller's products into one retail website.
Agile	A project management strategy in which work is grouped into relatively small, incremental projects (called a "sprint"). These are then tested and adapted.

Alignment	When an organization or ministry has agreement about goals and objectives and the various team members are working together toward these common ends.
Analogous Situations	A similar situation in a parallel sector or industry. An analogous situation may have application to one's own situation and is helpful for analysis and problem-solving.
Analytics	Any metrics that are used for evaluation. Most often these are numeric metrics.
Beta Testing	Initial testing of a product or service by those who will be using the service. This is different from internal testing, which is typically conducted by the designers and developers of the product or service.
Bias / Confirmation Bias	When one has a preconceived notion. Confirmation bias is when one looks at results and infers a conclusion based on their bias.
Brainstorming	A session in which ideas are collected. In design thinking, there are rules around how a brainstorming session works.
Breakthrough Innovation	An innovation that creates significant change and disruption.
Business Model Innovation	An innovation that changes the nature of how an organization or ministry conducts its work.
Capacity Utilization	Strategies that seek to expand the use of a resource such that it does not go underutilized.

Card Sorting — A process of categorizing ideas, typically written on cards (or their digital counterparts), with a goal of better understanding a design problem.

Collaborative Design — When multiple stakeholders are brought into the design process.

Crowdsourcing — When a larger problem is broken down into smaller problems that are more easily solved by individuals. Funding, for example, is often crowdsourced as people are more able to give smaller amounts, which can add up to a significant amount.

Dashboarding — When metrics are pulled together to create a simple view of an organization, ministry, or process.

Design Thinking — An innovation methodology that emphasizes empathy, definition, ideation, prototyping, and testing.

Diffusion of Innovations — A theory that explains how ideas are spread. Popularized by a book of the same title written by Everett Rogers.

Disruption Innovation — An innovation that creates massive change in an industry or sector.

Empathy — The process of understanding the end users of a product or service.

Entry Points / On Ramps — The ways that end users become customers or participants. For example, a newcomers orientation class is an entry point.

Exit Points	The ways that end users cease to be customers or participants.
Field Study	Research conducted in real-life situations.
First Mover Advantage	Describes the benefits that are given to the first organization or ministry to offer a service or a product.
Focus Groups	A research methodology in which a group of people provide feedback.
Gap Analysis	A study of where an organization or ministry currently is, where it wants to go, and what will be necessary to get there.
Groupthink	A phenomenon in which social pressure creates group decisions that individuals would not make if there was no group influencing them.
Hackathon	When a group of developers (most often software developers but not limited to this) gather for a concentrated time of problem-solving.
Human-Centered Design	The philosophy behind design thinking, which emphasizes the way people interact with products and services.
Ideate	To creatively come up with new ideas for consideration.
Incremental Innovation	Innovation that occurs through small steps over time.
Innovation Culture	An organizational or ministry culture that welcomes new ideas and their development.
Innovation Team	A team with a specific focus to bring innovation into a project, team, or problem.

Innovator's Dilemma	When an organization or ministry is designed to deliver an innovative product or service only to find that the solution is no longer viable, requiring new innovation. The concept was popularized by Clayton Christensen in a book of the same title.
Iterate	To repeat a process, such as the development of product or service, making improvements along the way.
Journey Mapping	A design thinking exercise in which the end user's experience with a product or service is envisioned and mapped out.
Mass Collaboration	Large scale efforts to organize people and resources to cooperate on addressing an issue.
Matchmaking	Connecting two or more people based on their needs and wants.
Minimum Viable Product	This describes a product or service that meets very basic requirements. In design thinking, a minimum viable product or service is often favored over a fully developed product because it can test the usability and designers can learn about enhancements.
Open Innovation	This is an innovation methodology in which stakeholders are broadly invited into the design process. Typically, open innovation is the opposite of secret development or development that is owned by a single organization or ministry.
Persona	A description of a stakeholder. This is used to inform the designers about the product or service they are creating.

Platform	A set of tools, typically technology, which enables users to complete an array of related tasks.
Process Innovation	A design methodology that reworks processes so that they better serve the people they were designed to serve.
Prototype	A model of a proposed solution. Prototypes may be physical or conceptual.
Reframing	Restating a problem in a way that opens new avenues for how it is understood and what solution sets might be appropriate.
Role Playing	A design thinking exercise in which people act like stakeholders to assist designers as they develop empathy around a problem.
Scale	A technology platform.
Scenarios	Describe interactions your stakeholders have with your ministry.
Service Design	A subset of design thinking, which focuses on services instead of products.
Service Moments	Crucial times in a service, such as making a decision, that need to be designed well.
Slicing	When a resource is divided up and shared among many users.
Stakeholders	Anybody who influences or is influenced by a ministry.
Storyboard	A methodology in which cards are used to tell a stakeholder story.
Touchpoints	Any interaction stakeholders have with your ministry.

Trust A crucial component of sharing economy products and services.

Use Case The reason that a product or service exists.

User Journey A methodology that traces the way a stakeholder experiences your product or service.

Vanity Metrics Metrics that you use to satisfy internal goals. Often counterproductive to understanding.

Viral When a product or service spreads through social networks, typically at an increasing rate.

Wicked Problem A very difficult to solve problem with a specific set of attributes.

Wireframing To design a product or service through simple drawings, typically used in the development of mobile apps.

APPENDIX:
INNOVATION QUOTIENT

I have created a short test to assess how innovative you might be. This is not a scientifically validated test, but as more people take it, the pool against which you are assessed becomes larger, helping you to see where you stack against others. You can find this test at:

https://theinnovationcrisis.com

ACKNOWLEDGMENTS

When Duane Sherman of Moody Publishers asked me about writing a book, the topic at hand was "movements." As I watched how movement theory and theology had disseminated throughout the church globally, I also observed the resistance to it. I have also seen firsthand the inability of ministry leaders to grasp new ideas and translate them into their own context. Duane understood that the topic of movements was a foil for how I understood the importance of innovation. He got behind the idea with gusto and was certainly responsible for this project.

The book points out the lack of innovation in ministry today. Yet, examples were needed to illustrate how it does happen. I must thank each person I interviewed for this book. They are the heroes of our day. I am sure that I missed many opportunities but am glad for Duane for pushing me in this area. The book is better because of his gentle but direct notes, asking for examples when I was concerned about finding any.

Innovation in ministry has been on my mind for a long time. Writing this book was, at times, cathartic and a little like getting counseling. The more I wrote, the better I felt that I was "on topic." This past Sunday I ran into Steve Richardson, Pioneer's US President, as we left church. We spoke for a few minutes and, as I walked out to my car, I realized that much of my thinking about innovation came out of my time at Pioneers. I will always have deep respect for Pioneers and Steve in particular. It is no accident that *The Seeds Global Innovation Lab*, ably led by Rob Wassel, who offered me advice along the way, was birthed from Pioneers USA.

My life partner, Annette, was very patient as I upped my focus and time spent on this project. She proofed text for me, let me bounce ideas off her, and warned me when I was too critical or negative. My colleague Michael VanHuis was always open to listening to my rants and provided great input to me. Amanda Cleary Eastep from Moody Publishers has been a great editor to work with on this project. Wendy Wilson, who provided an endorsement, was an early reader. She noted the lack of women innovators in the book, much to my shame. I wrote to Carolyn Custis James for ideas, and she responded, "You are lucky to have Wendy," and she is right about that. Amanda gave me the time to research and find excellent examples that were included in this text. The work done in the final few weeks was critical to making *The Innovation Crisis* what it is.

I apologize to the many family members, friends, and colleagues who have had to listen to my ramblings about innovation and this book. I also deeply thank you for your insights, corrections, and suggestions. 2020 was a hard year to write a book. But it also created a ministry environment in which there was great openness to innovation. So, thanks, 2020. Most of us are glad you are gone, but we hope to take advantage of you for decades to come.

NOTES

Chapter 1: A Crisis of Innovation

1. Timothy George, *Faithful Witness, The Life and Mission of William Carey* (Worchester, PA: Christian History Institute, 1998), 32.

2. Rob Reiner, et al, *A Few God Men*, 1992.

3. Rodney Stark, *The Triumph of Christianity: How the Jesus Movement Became the World's Largest Religion* (New York: HarperCollins, 2011), 114.

4. Albert R. Jonsen, *A Short History of Medical Ethics* (Oxford, UK: Oxford University Press, 2000).

5. Sarah Pulliam Baily, "Southern Baptists See Historic Drop in Membership - The Washington Post," *The Washington Post*, June 4, 2020. https://www .washingtonpost.com/religion/2020/06/04/southern-baptists-see-historic-drop-membership.

6. "In U.S., Decline of Christianity Continues at Rapid Pace | Pew Research Center," n.d., https://www.pewforum.org/2019/10/17/in-u-s-decline-of-christianity-continues-at-rapid-pace.

7. The Joshua Project, www.legacyjoshuaproject.net.

8. George, *Faithful Witness*, 23.

9. Basil Miller, *William Carey, Cobbler to Missionary* (Grand Rapids, MI: Zondervan, 1952), 32.

10. George, *Faithful Witness,* 32.

11. The phrase, "The despair of tidy minds," was first used by a historian to describe the former Yugoslavia, where our family lived following the Balkan wars. Trevor Beeson, *Discretion and Valour* (Glasgow: Collins-Fontana, 1974), 255.

12. William Carey, *An Enquiry into the Obligations of Christians to Use Means for the Conversion of the Heathens in which the Religious State of the Different Nations of the World, the Success of Former Undertakings, and the Practicability of Further Undertakings, Are Considered*, Public Domain, Section 5, 1792.

13. Transhumanism is a movement seeking to extend man's human and mental abilities using science and technology.

14. Walt Kelly, *Pogo: We Have Met the Enemy and He Is Us* (New York: Simon and Schuster, 1972).

15. Hedda Hopper with James Brough, "Marilyn—A Child of Tragedy," *Chicago Tribune*, February 26, 1963.

16. Samuel Foes, *The Calf-Path, Whiffs from Wild Meadows*, Public Domain, 1895.

Chapter 2: See a Problem Worth Solving

1. G. K. Chesterton, *The Complete Father Brown Stories, The Scandal of Father Brown* (London: Ebury Publishing, 2013), 727.

2. J. Q. Wilson, *Political Organizations*, vol. 46 (Princeton, NJ: Princeton University Press, 1995), 30.

3. Clayton M. Christensen, *The Innovator's Dilemma: When New Technologies Cause Great Firms to Fail (Management of Innovation and Change)* (Boston, MA: Harvard Business, 2016).

4. Chris Zook and James Allen, *The Founder's Mentality: How to Overcome the Predictable Crises of Growth* (Boston, MA: Harvard Business, 2016), 51.

5. Peggy E. Newell, ed., *North American Mission Handbook: US and Canadian Protestant Ministries Overseas 2017–2019* (Pasadena, CA: William Carey Publishers, 2017).

6. Charles Thomas Studd, *The Laugh of Faith* (pamphlet), https://archive.org/details/laughoffaith00stud, 17.

7. Adizes Institute, *I Want to Remember, He Wants to Forget*, Documentary Film, 2011.

8. Ichak Adizes, *Corporate Lifecycles,* the Adizes Institute, 1990.

9. Jim Collins, *Built to Last: Successful Habits of Visionary Companies* (Boston, MA: Harper Business, 2001), 107.

10. W. Chan Kim, *Blue Ocean Strategy: How to Create Uncontested Market Space and Make the Competition Irrelevant* (Boston, MA: Harvard Business, 2014).

Chapter 3: Ride the Wave of Existing Innovation

1. Gustave Aimard, *Les Francs-Tireurs,* 1861, 68.

2. The Joshua Project, *Bible Translation and Language Status.*

3. To find out more about Refugees Welcome International, visit their website https://refugees-welcome.net.

4. Arthur Zuckerman, "55 Online Dating Statistics: 2019/2020 Market Share, Dangers and Benefits," CompareCamp, May 12, 2020, https://comparecamp.com/online-dating-statistics/#:~:text=55%25%20of%20US%20online%20dating,or%20apps%20have%20been%20positive.

5. Robin Chase, *Peers, Inc: How People and Platforms Are Inventing the Collaborative Economy and Reinventing Capitalism* (New York: Public Affairs, 2015), 37.

6. Sangeet Choudary, Geoffrey Parker, and Marshall Van Alstyne, *Platform Scale: How an Emerging Business Model Helps Startups Build Large Empires with Minimum Investment* (New York: W. W. Norton and Company, 2015), Kindle location 233.

Chapter 4: Be Biased to Action

1. Winston Churchill, *Churchill by Himself: The Definitive Collection of Quotations,* Richard Langworth, ed. (New York: Public Affairs, 2008), 160.

2. J. B. Harvey, "The Abilene Paradox: The Management of Agreement," *Organizational Dynamics,* 3, no. 1, 1972, 63–80.

3. Phone interview with Brian Mosley, August 19, 2020.

4. Chris Anderson, "The End of Theory: The Data Deluge Makes the Scientific Method Obsolete," *Wired,* June 23, 2000, https://www.wired.com/2008/06/pb-theory.

5. Stefan Thomke, *Experimentation Works: The Surprising Power of Business Experiments* (Boston, MA: Harvard Business, 2020), 97.

Chapter 5: Empathize, then Strategize

1. Henri Nouwen, *Out of Solitude: Three Meditations on the Christian Life* (Notre Dame, IN: Ave Maria Press, 2004), 38.

2. Bob Eberle, *Scamper: Creative Games and Activities for Imagination Development* (Waco, TX: Prufrock Press, 2008), 3.

3. Steve Corbett and Brian Fikkert, *When Helping Hurts: How to Alleviate Poverty without Hurting the Poor . . . and Yourself* (Chicago: Moody, 2014).

4. Phone interview with Brian Fikkert, Septempber 11, 2020.

5. Phone interview with Keith Sparzak, September 15, 2020.

Chapter 6: Think Big

1. E. Jeffrey Conklin and William Weil, "Wicked Problems: Naming the Pain in Organizations," (white papers), Touchstone Tools and Resources, n.d., http://www.accelinnova.com/docs/wickedproblems.pdf.

2. Ibid.

3. Gallup polls report that 45 percent of American adults smoked in 1954, 40 percent in 1963, 42 percent in 1971, and 43 percent in 1973. Rick Blizzard, "U. S. Smoking Habits Have Come a Long Way, Baby," Gallup, October 19, 2004, http://www.galluppoll.com.

4. Niall McCarthy, "Poll: U.S. Smoking Rate Falls to Historic Low, [Infographic]," *Forbes*, July 6, 2018, https://www.forbes.com/sites/niallmccarthy/2018/07/26/poll-u-s-smoking-rate-falls-to-historic-low-infographic/#100134263351.

5. Leroy E. Burney, "Lung Cancer and Excessive Cigarette Smoking," *CA: A Cancer Journal for Clinicians* 8, no. 2, 1958.

6. Allan M. Brandt, *The Cigarette Century: The Rise, Fall, and Deadly Persistence of the Product That Defined America* (New York: Basic Books, 2007), 4.

7. Truth Tobacco Industry Documents, n.d. https://www.industrydocumentslibrary.ucsf.edu/tobacco.

8. *Smoking and Health Proposal,* Tobacco Institute, 1969, 9.

9. Brandt, *The Cigarette Century*, 53.

10. Ibid., 51.

11. "Consumption," The Tobacco Atlas, 2018. Note: Some might contend that vaping has decreased smoking rates. That is true, but only in the past two to three years. The decline in smoking rates had already been underway from some years before vaping became a smoking alternative.

12. Robert D. Woodberry, "The Missionary Roots of Liberal Democracy," *American Political Science Review* 106, no. 2, 2012.

13. Phone interview with York Moore, November 23, 2020.

14. Phone interview with Jon Hietbrink, August 20, 2020.

15. https://everycampus.com/where-to-launch/state-lists/.

16. Email exchange with Carolyn Custis James, April 2020.

17. The ministry I lead, Missio Nexus, is blessed to be served by *The Women's Development Track* as a partner ministry. Led by Wendy Wilson, it is an example of many other movements and organizations which have been influenced by the Synergy Women's Network.

18. Judith B. White and Ellen J. Langer, "Horizontal Hostility: Relations between Similar Minority Groups," *Journal of Social Issues*, 1999.

19. Adam Grant, *Originals: How Non-Conformists Move the World* (London: Penguin Books, 2017).

20. Mark Snowden, ed., "Orality in America 2," Mission America Coalition, 2016, 6.

21. Phone interview with John Fletcher, September 11, 2020.

Chapter 7: Identifying Innovation Targets

1. Peter Drucker and Warren Bennis, as quoted in Stephen R. Covey, *Seven Habits of Highly Effective People* (New York: Free Press, 1989), 101.

2. Jim Collins, *Good to Great and the Social Sectors: A Monograph to Accompany Good to Great* (New York: Random House, 2006), 1.

3. Larry Keeley, Helen Walters, Ryan Pikkel, and Brian Quinn, *Ten Types of Innovation: The Discipline of Building Breakthroughs*, 1st ed. (Hoboken, NJ: Wiley, 2013).

4. Frontiers (home page), https://www.frontiers.org.

5. Phone interview with John Ashmen, August 18, 2020.

6. N. T. Wright, *Jesus and the Victory of God* (Minneapolis, MN: Fortress Press, 1996), 131–33.

7. Kantoli is a pseudonym used for security reasons.

8. "About," MedSend, https://medsend.org/about.

9. Phone interview with Sue Plumb Takamoto, April 7, 2021.

10. Keeley, Walters, Pikkel, Quinn, *Ten Types of Innovation*, 106–107.

11. Phone call with Scatter Global leaders, November 19, 2020.

Chapter 8: Innovative Leadership

1. Grace Hopper, as quoted in *The Wit and Wisdom of Grace Hopper* by Philip Schieber, OCLC Newsletter, No. 167 March/April 1987.

2. Flow Hive website (About Us), https://www.honeyflow.com/pages/about-us.

3. Everett M. Rogers, *Diffusion of Innovations,* 3rd ed. (New York: Free Press of Glencoe, 1983).

4. Malcolm Gladwell, *The Tipping Point: How Little Things Can Make a Big Difference* (New York: Little, Brown, 2006).

5. George Graen and Mary Uhl-Bien, "The Relationship-Based Approach to Leadership: Development of LMX Theory of Leadership over 25 Years: Applying a Multi-Level, Multi-Domain Perspective," *Leadership Quarterly* 6, no. 2 (1995): 219–47.

6. Scott D. Anthony, Clark G. Gilbert, and Mark W. Johnson, *Dual Transformation: How to Reposition Today's Business While Creating the Future* (Boston, MA: Harvard Business, 2017).

7. Vijay Govindarajan, *The Three-Box Solution: A Strategy for Leading Innovation* (Boston, MA: Harvard Business, 2016).

8. Phone call with Andy Keener, November 3, 2020.

9. Bruce Tuckman, "Developmental Sequence in Small Groups," *Psychological Bulletin* 63, no. 6 (1965), https://doi.org/10.1037/h0022100.

10. Chris Zook and James Allen, *The Founder's Mentality: How to Overcome the Predictable Crises of Growth* (Boston, MA: Harvard Business, 2016), 73.

Chapter 9: You, the Innovator

1. C. S. Lewis, *Mere Christianity* (1952; New York: HarperCollins, 2001), 164.

2. Francesco Gino, *Why Curiosity Matters* (Boston, MA: Harvard Business Review, 2018), https://hbr.org/2018/09/curiosity#the-business-case-for-curiosity.

3. Ibid.

4. Vijay Govindarajan, "Planned Opportunism," *Harvard Business Review,* 2016, https://hbr.org/2016/05/planned-opportunism.

5. The Understood Team, "Trouble with Flexible Thinking: Why Some Kids Only See Things One Way," n.d., https://www.understood.org, Accessed September 6, 2020.

6. Elena L. Botelho and Kim R. Powell, *The CEO Next Door* (New York: Currency, 2018), 273.

7. Bobby Clinton, *The Making of a Leader: Recognizing the Lessons and Stages of Leadership Development* (Colorado Springs, CO: NavPress, 1988).

Chapter 10: What If?

1. Eugene Peterson, *Run with the Horses: The Quest for Life at Its Best* (Downers Grove, IL: InterVarsity Press, 2009), 25.

2. Zook and Allen, *The Founder's Mentality: How to Overcome the Predictable Crises of Growth* (Boston, MA: Harvard Business, 2016), 55.

WHAT IF, INSTEAD OF REACTING TO CHANGE, YOU COULD GET AHEAD OF IT?

HOW TO ALLEVIATE POVERTY WITHOUT HURTING THE POOR . . . AND YOURSELF

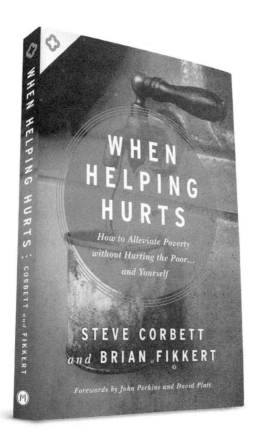

When Helping Hurts is a practical tool to help your ministry or team make a real long-term difference in the plight of the poor or suffering. This book provides clear, foundational principles of relief work and relevant applications that keep you from strategies that do more harm than good.

978-0-8024-0998-0 | also available as an eBook